D1336816

WITHDRAWN

Advance Praise for *The People of the Eye*

"A valuable contribution to Deaf Studies and other fields, *The People of the Eye* will certainly improve our understanding of humanity."
—Yerker Andersson, President Emeritus, World Federation of the Deaf

"A wonderful contribution that certainly makes a convincing case for Deaf ethnicity."
—Dennis Cokely, Director, American Sign Language Program; Director, World Languages Center, and Professor and Chair, Department of Languages, Literatures and Cultures, Northeastern University

"Outright fascinating."
—Richard Eckert, Assistant Professor, Department of Sociology, University of Wisconsin—Richland

"Elegant prose, meticulous research, and well-aimed quotes make a convincing case for ethnicity. I especially enjoyed the spirited debate in the 'Yes, But' section, which had me on the edge of my seat. The historical portrait of early Deaf American life, which the authors painted so vividly, is sure to inform and inspire many generations to come."
—Anna Mindess, Interpreter Educator, and author of *Reading Between the Signs: Intercultural Communication for Sign Language Interpreters*

"The genealogical work in this book is groundbreaking. It goes beyond elite-driven histories and shows a dense web of interconnections among grassroots Deaf people. This book fundamentally alters our understanding of the origins of the American Deaf community."
—Joseph Murray, Assistant Professor, Department of Deaf Studies, Gallaudet University

The People of the Eye

Series Editors
Marc Marschark
Patricia Elizabeth Spencer

A Lens on Deaf Identities
Irene W. Leigh

The World of Deaf Infants: A Longitudinal Study
Kathryn P. Meadow-Orlans, Patricia Elizabeth Spencer, and
Lynn Sanford Koester

*Sign Language Interpreting and Interpreter Education: Directions for
Research and Practice*
Edited by Marc Marschark, Rico Peterson, and
Elizabeth A. Winston

Advances in the Sign Language Development of Deaf Children
Edited by Brenda Schick, Marc Marschark, and Patricia
Elizabeth Spencer

*Advances in the Spoken Language Development of Deaf and
Hard-of-Hearing Children*
Edited by Patricia Elizabeth Spencer and Marc Marschark

The Gestural Origin of Language
David F. Armstrong and Sherman E. Wilcox

Deaf Cognition: Foundations and Outcomes
Edited by Marc Marschark and Peter C. Hauser

The People of the Eye: Deaf Ethnicity and Ancestry
Harlan Lane, Richard C. Pillard, and Ulf Hedberg

The People of the Eye

Deaf Ethnicity and Ancestry

Harlan Lane
Richard C. Pillard
Ulf Hedberg

OXFORD
UNIVERSITY PRESS
2011

OXFORD
UNIVERSITY PRESS

Oxford University Press, Inc., publishes works that further
Oxford University's objective of excellence
in research, scholarship, and education.

Oxford   New York

Auckland   Cape Town   Dar es Salaam   Hong Kong   Karachi
Kuala Lumpur   Madrid   Melbourne   Mexico City   Nairobi
New Delhi   Shanghai   Taipei   Toronto

With offices in
Argentina   Austria   Brazil   Chile   Czech Republic   France   Greece
Guatemala   Hungary   Italy   Japan   Poland   Portugal   Singapore
South Korea   Switzerland   Thailand   Turkey   Ukraine   Vietnam

Copyright © 2011 by Oxford University Press, Inc.

Published by Oxford University Press, Inc.
198 Madison Avenue, New York, New York 10016
www.oup.com

Library of Congress Cataloging-in-Publication Data
The people of the eye: deaf ethnicity and ancestry/Harlan Lane,
Richard Pillard, Ulf Hedberg.
p. cm.
Includes index.
ISBN 978-0-19-975929-3
1. Deaf—United States—History. 2. Deafness—Social aspects—United States.
3. Heredity.
4. Ethnic groups. I. Lane, Harlan L. II. Pillard, Richard C. III. Hedberg, Ulf.
HV2530.P36 2011
305.8′0920973—dc22   2010025247

9 8 7 6 5 4 3 2 1
Printed in the United States of America
on acid-free paper

On the nature of the Deaf:

"The deaf are ... first, last, and all the time the people of the eye."
> —George Veditz (President, National Association of the Deaf, 1861–1937). *Ninth Convention of the National Association of the Deaf and Third World's Congress of the Deaf*, 1910. Philadelphia: Philocophus Press, 1912. p. 30.

On sign language and the Deaf:

"The topic that concerns you, gentlemen, rather than an ordinary medical issue is, above all, a lofty question of humanity and civilization which requires deep reflection, not only by doctors but by teachers, philosophers and scholars."
> —Ferdinand Berthier (French Deaf leader and educator, 1803–1886). *Observations sur la mimique considérée dans ses rapports avec l'enseignement des sourds-muets. A M. le Président et à Messieurs les Membres de l'Académie Impériale de Médecine.* Paris: Martinet, 1853. (transl. H. Lane)

Contents

List of Illustrations

Acknowledgments

We thank the following people who assisted us in gathering, analyzing or displaying our findings: Ms. Ellen Adams, Ms. Carole Browne, Ms. Isabelle Chopin, Ms. Mercè Crosas, Ms. Flossie Dere, Col. Wayne Frank, Mr. Jason Freitas, Ms. Mary French, Ms. Emily Gilchrist, Dr. Sue Hotto, Ms. Katarzyna Kaczynski, Ms. Eunice Ladd, Ms. Kay Lam, Ms. Shannon Locke, Mr. Jean-Louis Martinez, Ms. Jillian Motyl, Mr. Edward Murkland, Ms. Kelly Milligan, Mr. Michael Olson, Ms. Harriette Otteson, Ms. Cheryl Patten, Ms. Nancy Porter, Dr. Judy Shepard-Kegl, Mr. Tommy Strunk, Mr. Gary Wait, Ms. Sherry Walrath, Mr. Christian Wayser, Dr. Bencie Woll, Dr. James Woodward, Dr. Del Wynne.

We are indebted to the following colleagues who made many valuable suggestions concerning the manuscript: Dr. Yerker Andersson, Dr. Kathleen Arnos, Dr. Doug Baynton, Dr. Dennis Cokely, Mr. Russell Dover, Dr. Carol Erting, Dr. François Grosjean, Dr. Tom Humphries, Dr. Robert E. Johnson, Dr. Paddy Ladd, Dr. Harry Lang, Ms. Ella Lentz, Dr. Ceil Lucas, Dr. Harry Markowicz, Ms. Anna Mindess, Dr. James Morris, Dr. Joseph Murray, Dr. Carol Padden, Mr. Frank Philip, Ms. Joan Poole-Nash, Dr. Rachel Rosenstock, Mr. Gerald Shea, Dr. Theresa Smith, Dr. Ted Supalla.

In addition to the preceding colleagues, we had fruitful discussions of Deaf ethnicity with: Dr. MJ Bienvenu, Mr. Aaron Brace, Dr. Jere Daniell, Dr. Richard Eckert, Dr. Nora Groce, Dr. John Hinnant, Mr. Bill Moody, Ms. Sharon Neumann-Solow, Dr. Vincent Parillo, Mr. Brian Riley, and Dr. James Woodward.

We acknowledge gratefully the following organizations: the Gallaudet University Archives, the Harvard-MIT Data Center of the Institute for Quantitative Social Science, the History Factory, the Maine Historical Society, the Maine State Archives, the Maine State Library, the New England Historic Genealogical Society, Northeastern University Inter-Library Loan service, the Volta Bureau. The Office of the Provost, Northeastern University, provided partial support for this research and for Dr. Lane's sabbatical year. He acknowledges with appreciation the support of his scholarly work by his chair and dean.

Introduction

The United States has many ethnic groups—it is a hallmark of our culture. This book asks if we have failed to recognize one: Americans whose primary language is American Sign Language (ASL).* No one knows how many such people there are but estimates generally range from half a million to 1 million members in the United States.[1] For the present purpose, we need to distinguish Deaf ASL signers from the much larger and more heterogeneous group of more than 10 million hearing-impaired Americans who communicate primarily in English or another oral language.[2] Most of the people in this larger group had conventional schooling and became deaf after acculturation to hearing society—many of them late in life. Accordingly, they do not see themselves as members of a sign-language minority nor do they participate in its organizations, profess its values, or follow its customs; rather, they consider themselves hearing people with a hearing disability. Something similar is true in all nations: there is a group of visual people[3] who use a natural visual-manual language (ASL in the United States) and who are often not distinguished from the larger group of people who view themselves as hearing impaired and who use a spoken language in its oral or written form.[4] We warmly endorse calls for greater recognition and study of both groups.[5] This book is about the Deaf signers of ASL, for if any class of deaf people constitutes an ethnic group, surely it is the signed language minority. In choosing to address this minority, we also benefit from considerable research about its language, culture, history, and social structure.

This book, then, is about the linguistic minority in North America whose language is American Sign Language and whose members have a culture they call, in that language, the Deaf-World. Who is in the Deaf-World? Deaf ASL signers are.[6] It is often said and repeated that very few Deaf children are born into the Deaf-World, since as few as 4 percent have Deaf parents.[7] In fact, however, most ASL signers have inherited their membership in the Deaf-World; rather few are Deaf due to disease or trauma. We explore this in Chapter 1; suffice it to say here that Deaf ASL signers are most often the fruit of ancestral transmission from the beginnings of our society and even before; thus, they are indeed "born into" the Deaf-World. As soon as one recognizes the

---

* We follow current scholarly practice in the English-speaking world distinguishing deaf, in varying degrees unable to hear, from Deaf referring to a language and cultural minority. The subscript symbol ᴅ indicates a Deaf person.

Studies Today (Orem, Utah: Utah Valley State College, 2005), 17–35; C. Padden and T. Humphries, *Deaf in America: Voices from a Culture* (Cambridge, Mass.: Harvard University Press, 1988); "For they are first, last, and all the time the people of the eye." George Veditz, "The President's Message," Ninth Convention Of The National Association and the Third World's Congress of the Deaf, August 6–13, 1910 (Philadelphia, Pa.: Philocophus Press, 1912), quotation from p. 30.

4   This contrast is often expressed in the scholarly literature by the use of capital-D Deaf for those who use a sign language primarily and small-d deaf for members of the larger group who do not, following a convention first proposed by James Woodward in 1972. J. Woodward, *How You Gonna Get to Heaven If You Can't Talk to Jesus? On Depathologizing Deafness* (Silver Spring, Md.: TJ Publishers, 1982).

5   J. Fernandes and S. Myers, "Deaf Studies: Barriers and Pathways," *Journal of Deaf Studies and Deaf Education* 15 (2010), 17–29. S Myers and J. Fernandes, "Deaf Studies: A Critique of the Predominant U.S. Theoretical Direction," *Journal of Deaf Studies and Deaf Education* 15 (2010), 30–49.

6   C. Padden, "From The Cultural To The Bicultural: The Modern Deaf Community," in I. Parasnis, ed., *Cultural and Language Diversity: Reflections on the Deaf Experience* (Cambridge, Mass.: Cambridge University Press, 1996), 79–98. See also: C. Padden, "The Culture of Deaf People," in C. Baker and R. Battison, eds., *Sign Language and the Deaf Community, Essays in Honor of William Stokoe* (Silver Spring, Md.: National Association of the Deaf, 1980), 89–103.

7   R. E. Mitchell and M. Karchmer, "Chasing the Mythical Ten Percent: Parental Hearing Status of Deaf and Hard of Hearing Students in the United States," *Sign Language Studies* 4 (2004): 138–163.

8   For a study of Deaf ethnicity using survey data, see R. Eckert, *Deafnicity: A Study of Strategic and Adaptive Responses to Audism by Members of the Deaf American Community of Culture.* (Ph.D. diss., University of Michigan, 2005); R. Eckert, "Toward a Theory of Deaf Ethnos: Deafnicity ≈ D/deaf (Hómaemon • Homóglosson • Homóthreskon)," *Journal of Deaf Studies and Deaf Education* 15 (2010): 317–333.

9   The concept of Deaf ethnicity was first explored in the United States in articles and chapters by (alphabetically): C. Erting, "Language Policy and Deaf Ethnicity in the United States," *Sign Language Studies* 19 (1978): 139–152; C. Erting, "Deafness, Communication And Social Identity: An Anthropological Analysis of Interaction among Parents, Teachers, and Deaf Children in a Pre-School" (Ph.D. diss., American University, 1982); C. Padden and H. Markowicz, "Crossing Cultural Group Boundaries into the Deaf Community" (paper delivered at the Conference on Culture and Communication, Temple University, Philadelphia, 1975.); T. Humphries, "An Introduction to the Culture of Deaf People in the United States: Content Notes and Reference Material for Teachers," *Sign Language Studies* 72 (1991) 209–240; R. E. Johnson and C. Erting, "Sign, Solidarity, and Socialization" (paper presented at a meeting of the American Anthropological Association, Cincinnati, Ohio, 1979); R. E. Johnson and C. Erting. "Linguistic Socialization in the Context of Emergent Deaf Ethnicity" in C. Erting and R. Meisegeier, eds., working paper No. 1: *Deaf Children and the Socialization Process*

(Washington, D.C.: Gallaudet College Sociology Department, 1982); R. E. Johnson and C. Erting, "Linguistic Socialization in the Context of Emergent Deaf Ethnicity," in K. Kernan, ed., *Wenner-Gren Working Papers in Anthropology* (New York: Wenner-Gren, 1984); R. E. Johnson and C. Erting, "Ethnicity and Socialization in a Classroom for Deaf Children" in C. Lucas, ed., *The Sociolinguistics of the Deaf Community* (New York: Academic Press, 1989), 41–84; H. Markowicz and J. Woodward, "Language and the Maintenance of Ethnic Boundaries in the Deaf Community" (paper presented at the Conference on Culture and Communication, Philadelphia, 1975); H. Markowicz, "La Langue des Signes et l'Éducation des Sourds: Une Perspective Sociolinguistique" (Mémoire de Diplôme d'Etudes Approfondies, U.E.R. de Linguistique, Université de Paris V, 1989–1990); H. Markowicz and J. Woodward, "Language and the Maintenance of Ethnic Boundaries in the Deaf Community," *Communication and Cognition* 2 (1978): 29–37; H. Markowicz, "La Communauté des Sourds en tant que Minorité Linguistique," *Coup d'œil* 1980 (suppl.): 1–12; B. Mottez and H. Markowicz, *Intégration ou Droit à la Différence, les Conséquences d'un Choix Politique sur la Structuration et le Mode d'Existence d'un Groupe Minoritaire, les Sourds* (Paris: Centre d'Etude des Mouvements Sociaux); Padden, "Culture Of Deaf People"; Padden and Humphries, *Deaf in America.*; C. Padden and H. Markowicz, "Cultural Conflicts between Hearing and Deaf Communities," in F. B. Crammatte and A. B. Crammatte, eds., *VII World Congress of the World Federation of the Deaf.* (Silver Spring, Md.: National Association of the Deaf, 1976), 407–411; J. Woodward and H. Markowicz, "Some Handy New Ideas on Pidgins and Creoles: Pidgin Sign Languages" (paper presented at the International Conference on Pidgins and Creoles, Honolulu, 1975); J. Woodward, "How You Gonna Get to Heaven if You Can't Talk with Jesus: The Educational Establishment vs. the Deaf Community" (paper presented at the International Meeting of the Society for Applied Anthropology, Amsterdam, 1975); J. Woodward, "How You Gonna Get to Heaven if You Can't Talk With Jesus: The Educational Establishment vs. the Deaf Community," In J. Woodward, ed., *How You Gonna Get to Heaven if You Can't Talk With Jesus: On Depathologizing Deafness* (Silver Spring, Md.: T.J. Publishers, 1982), 11–19.
By date:
1975: Padden and Markowicz, "Crossing Cultural Group Boundaries"; Markowicz and Woodward, "Language and Ethnic Boundaries"; Woodward and Markowicz, "Handy New Ideas"; Woodward, "How You Gonna Get to Heaven." 1976: Padden and Markowicz, "Cultural Conflicts"; 1978: Erting, "Language Policy"; 1978: Markowicz and Woodward, "Ethnic Boundaries"; 1979: Johnson and Erting, "Sign, Solidarity"; 1979: Mottez and Markowicz, *Intégration*; 1980: Baker and Battison, *"Sign Language"*; 1980: Markowicz, "Communauté des Sourds"; 1982: Erting, "Deafness, Communication"; 1982: Woodward, "Educational Establishment"; 1982: Johnson and Erting, "Linguistic Socialization"; 1984: Johnson and Erting, "Linguistic Socialization" *Wenner-Gren.* 1988: Padden and Humphries, *Deaf in America;* 1989: Johnson and Erting, "Ethnicity and Socialization"; 1989: Markowicz, "La Langue des Signes"; 1991: Humphries "Culture of Deaf People."

Part I

Ethnicity and the Deaf-World

Ethnic communities predate the start of written history and they are to be found virtually everywhere today.[1] The smallest are bands or clans, the largest can encompass one or more countries. Every person is a member of some culturally distinctive group and in that sense we are all ethnic, although majorities frequently reserve the term for minorities whom they disparage.[2] There is nothing inherently bad, however, about our ethnic affiliations. On the contrary, ethnic ties are deeply meaningful and strongly felt, rooted in psychology.[3] The strength of emotion evoked by ethnicity is reminiscent of that evoked by family ties, and may be based on them; as the aphorism goes, "Ethnicity is family writ large." Like family, ethnicity is woven into the fabric of everyday life and involves shared obligations and traditions. However, ethnicity surpasses family in its scope: it evokes a rich history of one's kind and a historic fate across generations; it entails stereotypes of "us" and "them." It involves distinct values, customs, and myths. These cultural traits are embedded in language and in behavior. In brief, shared culture is the cohesive force in an ethnic group and one that differentiates it from other such groups.[4]

This cultural perspective on ethnicity only alludes to something important: ethnic groups commonly encounter one another in shared settings and they construct rules to govern those encounters, rules that reinforce cultural differences, maintain boundaries, and sustain ethnic identity. Such externally oriented properties of ethnic groups demand our attention along with the cohesive forces. This distinction between internal cohesion and external boundaries can guide our inquiry into whether the concept of ethnic group applies to the Deaf-World. In the following two chapters, we examine the properties of ethnic groups and compare them to the properties of the ASL minority. We take up first the "internal" cultural properties and put off to Chapter 2 a discussion of "external properties"—ethnic boundaries and their maintenance.

Most of the families cited in this book have pedigrees at the following website: http://dvn.iq.harvard.edu/dvn/dv/DEA.* To see if a given individual appears in one or more of the pedigrees there, consult the Every Name Index in Appendix D at the back of this book. The pedigrees presented here in Figures 2 through 17 also appear at the website with much supplementary detail that could not be reproduced legibly in book format.
*[http://hdl.handle.net/1902.1/12117]

1

Cultural Cohesive Forces

LANGUAGE

Language is a means of communication but it is also the purveyor of culture, including traditions, rituals, norms, values, and the language arts. Language, handed down across the generations, provides continuity with the past. It is a symbol of ethnicity and identity, and a force for social cohesion. There is no more authentic expression of an ethnic group than its language. To disparage that language disparages the people who speak it and praising their language praises them. When an ethnic group demands more equitable treatment for their language (for example, its use in the media and in schools), they are also seeking more equitable treatment for their group and their culture.[1] ASL signers hold very dear the communicative, cultural and emblematic functions of their language.

The language of the ethnic group also provides its name. An ethnic name is a label with which to refer to the group but it is much more than that. Group members feel it captures their very essence and evokes memories of their shared past. Thus it has resonance within the ethnic group and little or none outside. Some Native American tribes retained their tribal names until fully conquered by the Europeans, while others retain them to the present day. The group we have so far designated by its language, the ASL minority, does indeed have a name for their collective by which they refer to themselves in their manual-visual language. We will refer to this language minority by that name, adopting the English translation of their compound sign, DEAF-WORLD.[2] Individual members of the group, when referring to themselves (not their collective), use the ASL sign DEAF.

Competence in American Sign Language is at the core of Deaf identity in the United States.[3] Can a human language really use vision to perceive grammatical messages and body movements to produce them? Yes indeed, and that is one of the most important discoveries in linguistics and neuroscience of the last century: language is a capacity of the brain; if one channel is blocked, language will be expressed in another.[4] The words of ASL are signs; like the words of oral languages, they are constructed from a small set of building blocks; not consonants and vowels, to be sure, but movements, handshapes and orientations, and bodily locations. In ASL, the basic signs undergo regular changes to convey part of speech, derivation, compounding, and more. As do

3

spoken languages, ASL has rules for agreement—for example, using space to convey subject and object or source and goal. It has rules for modifying the movement of signs to convey adverbial ideas, such as repeated, habitual, and continuous actions. It has a rich system of pronouns that can be incorporated into the verb. The basic word order in ASL sentences is Subject-Verb-Object, but there are rules that change the basic order—for example, the topic of the sentence may move to the beginning of the sentence. In ASL, body shifts and facial expressions convey sentence structure and discourse structure.

As linguist Ben Bahan$_D$ points out, the eyes play a role in sending as well as receiving messages in ASL.[5] Eye movements may occur on a single word to convey a meaning, or they may mark noun phrases and verb phrases, or a glance may refer to an actor previously located in space. Eye movements play a role in storytelling and in taking turns in conversation. The ASL signer's eyes may leave the audience briefly to accomplish some of these functions but they soon return to verify that the audience is following the visual narration. It may not be surprising then that there is extensive research evidence showing that fluent ASL signers have heightened perception in the visual periphery, heightened abilities in spatial processing, and enhanced capacity for interpreting rapidly presented visual information.[6] Deaf people are indeed, "The People of the Eye."

As do virtually all languages, ASL has regional dialects, registers that range from intimate to highly formal, and art forms like narrative and humor, discussed below. There is no universal sign language; ASL, for example, is unrelated to British Sign Language. Signed languages such as ASL are full-fledged languages structurally independent from the spoken languages with which they coexist. Generally speaking, the later ASL is learned the less its mastery.[7] If ASL is not a person's primary language, that is likely to be evident very quickly (as with any language). It may be revealed as soon as the newcomer is introduced to a Deaf person. Such introductions tend to follow a pattern. The person making the introduction (let's say, the hostess) positions herself at the vertex of a triangle, turns partly toward Alex and introduces Bill to him. Using the manual alphabet, with a handshape for each letter, she fingerspells Bill's first and last names, and then gives Bill's name sign. (A *name sign* either refers to a salient feature—for example, a big nose or a scar—or incorporates the fingerspelled first letter of the person's first or last name.) The hostess states where Bill is from (the location often refers to that of the Deaf school) and may well mention Bill's work and contacts in the Deaf-World; if Bill is hearing, she mentions that, too. In corresponding fashion, she then introduces Alex to Bill.[8] Finding shared friends and acquaintances in this way is important to Deaf people, linguist Carol Padden$_D$ explains. It is a way of maintaining ties with the dispersed members of the Deaf-World and hence a way of enhancing group cohesion. If newcomers do not know the custom—or if they make errors in grammar, pronunciation, or social appropriateness, then they are revealed.[9] According to Padden_D, membership in the ASL minority entails, in part, using the language and showing respect for it. Also expected are adherence to social ties, and a fondness for storytelling. As ASL is an unwritten language, face-to-face use of the language is the main way to transmit the culture.[10]

Sociolinguist Barbara Kannapell_D, has written of ASL: "It is our language in every sense of the word. We create it, we keep it alive, and it keeps us and our traditions alive."[11] And further, "To reject ASL is to reject the Deaf person."[12] We recognize such evident pride in one's language and the wish to protect it. In France, to take one example, the French Academy (and legislature) have labored for centuries to protect the purity of French from the inroads of other languages. Speakers of several minority languages in France—Breton, Alsatian, and Arabic among them—battle for acceptance of their language and distinct ethnic identity. Closer to home, Native Americans have long struggled for the protection of their languages, and identities; in 1990 Congress enacted a law encouraging the use of Native American languages in the instruction of Native American children.[13]

Language is, then, symbolic of the ethnic group and a powerful force in sustaining ethnicity, but it also has an important pragmatic role in allowing everyday communication. We are all most comfortable, most clear, and most expressive in our primary language. "What makes Deaf people feel at ease when communicating with each other?" Kannapell_D asks rhetorically. And she answers: "Deaf people can understand each other 100 percent of the time [in ASL], whereas outside of the Deaf community they get fragmentary information or one-way communication." She goes on to explain that ASL comes easily and naturally to most Deaf people and allows Deaf people to share meanings, that is, "common experiences, cultural beliefs, and values."[14]

A further feature of many minority languages is their struggle for survival. The national language has prestige, it is used in government and other formal situations, while the minority language is used primarily within the ethnic group.[15] In such a situation, the minority language takes on some of the properties of the prestige language, borrowing vocabulary and syntax. The prestige language may even replace the vernacular in all contexts, including ethnic life (home, community, worship)—as it has done with many immigrant groups in the United States. To accomplish this subjugation and replacement of the minority language, the dominant ethnic group can require its own language by law, use it and no other in the schools, punish children who use the "vernacular," and reward minority leaders who promote the majority language. In a different resolution of the struggle between the prestige and vernacular languages, both are maintained but speakers of the nondominant language are led to believe that theirs is a substandard dialect of the dominant language, a vernacular that should not be employed for serious purposes such as education and government. Language policy in Spain provided examples of both strategies until recently.

Sociolinguist Heinz Kloss, an international authority on minority languages, contrasted the cases of Basque and Catalan:

> So the Spanish government, in trying to establish and maintain the monopoly of Castilian Spanish, must try to blot out the Basque language completely, for there is no possibility that the Basques will ever lose consciousness of the fact that their language is unrelated to Spanish. The position of Catalan is quite different, because both Catalan and Spanish are Romance Languages. There is a chance that speakers of Catalan can be induced to consider their mother tongue as a vernacular, with Castilian as its natural standard language.[16]

When Catalonia became an autonomous region, its leaders felt a sacred duty to restore wide use of their language, which many of its speakers had considered a substandard dialect of Spanish.[17]

ASL has similarly been targeted, in different eras, for recasting as a variety of English or for outright replacement by English. The American initiative that started in the nineteenth century was modeled on one in France in the eighteenth century. It all began when the abbé de l'Epée founded in Paris what was to be the first enduring school for the Deaf. With the aid of his pupils, Epée chose or invented signs for all the word endings in French, and for all the articles, prepositions and auxiliary verbs, and so on. This vocabulary was signed in the order of the original French, so that there was a means of expressing virtually any French sentence. This Signed French was disseminated by Epée's disciples who created schools for the Deaf throughout Europe and the United States. When Epée died in 1789, the new French republic nationalized his school.

Laurent Clerc[D], an eminent student and then teacher at the French national school came to the United States in 1816 to co-found the first enduring school for the Deaf in America. He brought Signed French with him and adapted it to English.[18] However, attempts to bastardize the language of the French Deaf-World (LSF—*la Langue des Signes Française*) with spoken French and, later, to bastardize ASL with spoken English were largely abandoned by the mid-nineteenth century; they violated too many principles of visual language to be intelligible and were rejected by many Deaf teachers and Deaf leaders who preferred their minority language to Signed French or Signed English.[19] Even the simplest sentence in Signed French took on enormous complexity. One example, a line from Racine, "To the smallest of the birds, He gives their crumbs," required forty-eight signs; *gives* alone required five signs: those for verb, present, third person, singular, and "give." To the Deaf pupil, the string of signs in Signed French lacked unity, was full of distractions, was far too long for a single unit of meaning and, in the end, was unintelligible.

The efforts to recast LSF to conform to French and to recast ASL to conform to English failed: pupils used their own sign language most of the time. Despite that failure, this policy had resurgence in the United States in the nineteenth and twentieth centuries with two consequences. First, a new variety of ASL developed among the Deaf, a variety used by the college-educated elite, which incorporated English word order and parts of English grammar. This new hybrid became the prestige language while "grassroots" Deaf continued to use the unrevised ASL.[20] Second, inside the classroom, many teachers used Signed English or, most often and more simply, they spoke English while accompanying some of the spoken words with uninflected signs from ASL—that is, without the modifications of signs to convey subject and object, part of speech, derivation, agreement, manner, and so on.

So much for recasting ASL as a variety of English. When it comes to outright replacement of the minority language, the schools are an important venue. ASL joins many other minority languages as a target of replacement policies imposed in the schools.[21] For example, during the period between the two world wars, successor states to the Ottoman, Habsburg, and Russian empires vigorously pursued language replacement using the schools. Likewise, the schools were the locus for imposing spoken French on Deaf students in France and spoken English on Deaf students in the United States. The first systematic efforts in the United States to replace ASL with English occurred in late nineteenth century, at a time when many Anglo-Americans feared that the proliferation of ethnic groups and languages might overwhelm their existing institutions; the drive was on for restricted immigration of non-Anglos and for assimilation of those already in the country. In the United States, hearing and Deaf professors who taught in the residential schools using ASL resisted replacement at first, advocating bilingual goals, but ultimately the language of the Deaf classroom became spoken English and its mastery the central purpose of Deaf schooling.

The late nineteenth century was also a period of ethnic intolerance in Italy, which was undergoing national unification (the *Risorgimento*). In Milan, hearing educators of the Deaf convened an International Congress on the Education of the Deaf to which Deaf teachers were not invited; of the 164 delegates only five were Deaf. The carefully orchestrated congress voted to replace all sign languages with spoken ones, and consequently all Deaf teachers with hearing ones. Sign languages were not to be tolerated under any circumstance. Older students were quarantined in some schools in the hope that younger students would not learn sign language from them.

Sign language replacement had a wealthy, prestigious, and mono-maniacal advocate in Alexander Graham Bell. In an address to the National Education Association, Bell maintained, like some of today's English-only advocates, that the very future of the nation required eradicating minority languages.[22] Bell wrote: "It is important for the preservation of our national existence that people of this country should speak one tongue."[23] By 1920, four-fifths of all Deaf students were taught spoken English using spoken English itself, which they could not hear, while the rest of their education fell by the wayside.[24]

The Deaf-World at this time so feared for the demise of its sign language that it commissioned a series of films by eminent Deaf orators in order to preserve a record of the language.[25] And so matters largely stood until the ethnic revival of the 1960s and 1970s in America, when a tidal wave of ethnic reaffirmation led to a resurgence of minority languages, including ASL. So much for replacing ASL with English. (We tell about the ethnic revival and the Deaf-World in the section on History below.)

All of the different functions of language—expressing individual and cultural identity, purveying cultural norms and values, linking the present and the past—sustain an ethnic group's love of its native language as the central symbol of its identity and fuel the minority's resistance to replacement of its language by more powerful others.

BONDING TO ONE'S KIND

Members of ethnic groups commonly have strong emotional ties to their kind.[26] Loyalty to their ethnic group may even at times lead them to act against their own personal interests. What are the wellsprings of such commitment, which is exceeded only by family loyalty? Sigmund Freud told a Zionist society in 1926: "What bound me to Jewry was . . . neither faith nor national pride [but] many obscure emotional forces, which were the more powerful the less they could be expressed in words . . . [and also] a clear consciousness of inner identity. . ."[27] Social psychologist Henri Tajfel has shown that the perception of belonging to a group creates solidarity with that group and devaluing of other groups—in a word *ethnocentrism*. His explanation: our self-image is comprised of a personal identity and many social identities—as many as the groups to which we belong. We aim to achieve and maintain a positive self-image, so we are loyal to the groups of which we are a member; we are disposed to think well of them and less well of others.[28] There is no in-group without an out-group, so it has been suggested that ethnic loyalty requires an opposing group.[29] Some writers have contended that ethnocentrism is all the greater nowadays as men and women seek meaningful affiliations to cope with the homogenization and bureaucratization of society and the breakup of traditional authority.[30]

Americans in the Deaf-World do indeed feel a strong identification with that world and show great loyalty to it. There are numerous reasons for such solidarity. No doubt the feeling of belonging is reinforced by the shared experience of being Deaf in a world dominated by hearing people. Moreover, the Deaf-World is a surrogate family; it offers many ASL signers (those with hearing parents) what they often could not find at home: a positive identity, a language model to emulate, easy communication, and lives they can imagine leading. Sign language is the vehicle for much of Deaf people's knowledge of life and the world; no wonder they are bonded to the language and the Deaf-World. That bonding may lead Deaf people to protectively withhold from hearing people information about Deaf language and culture. Kannapell[D] writes:

> ASL is the only thing we have that belongs to Deaf people completely. It is the only thing that has grown out of the Deaf group. Maybe we are afraid to share our language with hearing people. Maybe our group identity will disappear once hearing people know ASL. Also, will hearing people dominate Deaf people more than before if they learn ASL?[31]

Finding it contrary to ethnic solidarity, many ethnic groups have reservations about individual achievement.[32] Deaf stories frequently propound loyalty and the elite are cautioned that when they excel in hearing society they must not forget their roots in the Deaf-World. Success in the hearing world should be achieved using ASL technologies and interpreters and should preserve social ties among Deaf people. It should not be achieved by favoring oral language over sign or by isolating oneself among hearing people.[33] Deaf people who try to pass as hearing are disparaged: Where is their Deaf pride?

In a further expression of the value placed on solidarity, Deaf people commonly believe, as do members of many ethnic groups, that one should marry within one's minority. Historically, Deaf marry Deaf approximately nine times out of ten, and when they marry a hearing person, it is often one with Deaf parents or relatives and thus familiar with the Deaf-World and its language.[34] The Deaf-World collectively values Deaf children highly and takes an almost parental interest in the welfare of Deaf children unrelated to them. Deaf adults in rural areas, for example, will drive great distances to see Deaf children when invited, especially if the children might otherwise lack such contact. Interpreting and intercultural communication expert Anna Mindess makes the case that American Deaf culture is among the many world cultures that are collectivist—so-called because individuals formulate and pursue their goals in terms of their collective.[35]

CULTURAL RULES AND VALUES

The patrimony that one generation of an ethnic group passes to the next includes language, which we have discussed above, and cultural rules and values to which we turn now.[36] Sign-language minorities, like ethnic minorities worldwide, encounter prejudice and discrimination in the host society. Ethnic communities, threatened by marginalization, find reaffirmation of their values and way of life in their cultures. Perhaps for these reasons cultural loyalty is the bedrock value of the Deaf-World.

Pride in one's cultural heritage and efforts to maintain and enhance traditions not only add meaning to ethnic members' daily lives, and contribute to defining their identity, but also aid in combating stigma.[37] Central to that patrimony are the unique values of the ethnic group, starting with the value of being a member of the group. Members of the Deaf-World — like members of most ethnic groups we daresay—are generally quite content about their identity and have no wish to change it, although they are aware of the inconveniences or worse of membership in a minority and in particular their minority.

Values, like the value of being Deaf, underlie cultural rules of behavior. The rules of a culture and the rules of its language have this in common: In both cases, it is difficult for us, as members of the culture and speakers of its language, to state the rules in a systematic way, yet we are quite promptly aware when a rule has been broken. Thus we clearly know the rules in some sense—we have cultural competence as well as linguistic competence. And just as all languages must have rules for certain basic functions, such as identifying in the sentence who did what to whom, so, too, all cultures must have rules for such universal functions as relating to the group, gaining status, making decisions that affect the group and so forth. Cultural rules are not always honored any more than linguistic rules are. Such rules tell what you must know as a member of a particular cultural and linguistic group, but what one actually does or says depends on a host of intervening factors, including other rules that have priority. When we make claims about Deaf culture in the following, we are making claims about the underlying rules, about cultural knowledge. Although members' behavior will tend to honor the rules, there can be many exceptions depending on the situation and the people involved. Moreover, culture is not static but variable; Deaf culture changes as social forces change, among them language and education policy. In this discussion of Deaf culture, we are focused on the last half century but Parts II and later report on early American Deaf people.

The reader should not expect too much that is exotic in Deaf-World rules and values.[38] As with recognized ethnic minorities, the Deaf-World absorbs some of the dominant ethnicity that surrounds it.

Moreover, as sociolinguist Joshua Fishman points out, cultural proper- ties at earlier stages of social development tend to fall away with increasing acceptance, leaving a smaller set of behaviors, values, and beliefs to define ethnicity.[39]

There are of course many more rules in Deaf culture and many more provisos about their operation than we list here. We have sought to provide enough information for the reader to assess the similarities and differences of Deaf culture with those of recognized ethnic groups. As with many ethnic groups, the Deaf-World has received only modest attention from sociologists and cultural anthropologists. The rules we are about to state are best viewed as hypotheses, subject to revision, about the cultural grammar that all native members of the culture have internalized.[40]

Managing language

Most English-speaking Americans take their language and culture for granted, but ASL signers do not. Rather, in this regard, they are similar to the French, who reify their language and culture and take measures to preserve their cultural patrimony. Members of the Deaf-World create organizations, events, and archives to foster the transmission of Deaf language and culture and they resist inroads by other languages and cultures. There are rules in Deaf culture for when and with whom to use ASL and when to use English-marked varieties of the language.[41] In everyday conversations among Deaf people, signing that is heavily influenced by English is disparaged (unless used to rhetorical effect). Invented signing systems, which originated with educators and not the Deaf-World, are also disparaged. Deaf people may speak English when communicating with hearing people but in Deaf culture, using an oral language is not considered appropriate.[42] Language use is governed by politeness rules, such as those for taking turns in a conversation, for speaking frankly and for speaking tactfully, for sharing information, for greeting, and for leaving.[43]

Gaining status

Heroes in ASL folktales and stories serve as models and are admirable because they help Deaf people. Likewise, the ideal Deaf person in America today serves on Deaf committees, acts as chairperson for Deaf events, hosts social affairs, contributes to the local Deaf-World pool of resources by devoting labor and time, and may help other Deaf people secure employment.[44] Affirming one's individual achievement breaks the rule of cultural solidarity. Horatio Alger stories that recount indi- vidual triumphs over obstacles are unlike Deaf success stories. The model Deaf person presents his or her achievements as those of the local Deaf community, and is respected for crediting the contributions of other members.

Naming rituals

The giving and receiving of a name is an important event in Deaf culture. The following are the norms, from which individual cases may depart. Deaf children from hearing homes frequently arrive at school without a name in sign language. As their mastery of ASL and their acculturation proceeds, they receive a name, and that sign becomes their name for all except administrative purposes. The giving of a name sign is a rite of passage into the Deaf-World. Frequently the honor of conferring a name falls to a Deaf authority figure or a Deaf peer with Deaf parents. Hearing people who learn ASL and mingle with the Deaf will be given a name sign as well. Deaf parents will often choose for all their children a name sign at a single location where signs in ASL occur—for example, on the chin. The handshape they place there is the fingerspelled first letter of the child's first name. What if the names of two or more of their children start with the same letter? Then handshape is held constant and the location changes. In conversation, name signs are used only to refer to a third person who is not present.[45]

Decision-making

Consensus is the rule, not individual initiative. Deaf people characteristically caucus to decide a course of action and the interests of the Deaf-World are paramount. There may be diverse views, and votes are often taken but disagreements are normally resolved first. Making a decision for the group without its full participation breaks the rule. In making a decision, testimony from other Deaf people—especially eye-witness testimony—carries great weight, scientific findings less so.

Managing social relations—introductions

When two Deaf people meet, they position themselves in relation to Deaf culture. As we saw earlier, they say at the outset what schools they attended, what Deaf relatives and friends they share. Everyone in the Deaf-World is connected to every one else, if only by mutual friends, so the trick is to find the connection. Deaf peers and friends hug on meeting and on separating. It seems to us that they hug more often and hug a wider range of people than do their hearing counterparts. Remaining aloof, failing to hug, giving priority to individuating information (such as profession) rather than cultural information all break the rules for introductions. Although Americans are rather informal compared, say, with the French or Japanese, Deaf Americans seem even more informal. Lifelong friendships in Deaf culture are the norm.

Pooling resources

When a Deaf person incurs a debt to another Deaf person, what is received and paid back is generally not money but work or a commitment of time. Although there is this one-on-one reciprocity in Deaf culture, there is also group reciprocity. A Deaf person donates information, favors, or work to one or more Deaf people or activities and then, when he or she is in need, Deaf people—not necessarily the same ones who benefited directly—will reciprocate. Thus A will help B move and C will fix A's car. Deaf people have a sense, without record keeping, of who has contributed a lot and who too little. Paddy Ladd$_D$ describes this reciprocity in U.K. Deaf clubs, and calls it "Deaf-gelt."[46] Anthropologist Theresa Smith calls it "indirectly reciprocal," and Deaf educator, Marie Philip$_D$, calls it "reciprocity."[47]

Constructing discourse

Ethnographers study the discourse of ethnic groups to learn their rhetorical strategies (such as narration, cause-effect analysis, argumentation) to shed light on the beliefs and worldview that underlie them. For this précis of ASL discourse we draw heavily on Theresa Smith's work. ASL discourse is narrative. The core perspective is personal, that of a participant rather than an observer. ASL discourse favors providing context. It normally goes from specifics, which provide context, to the general conclusion; from the beginning to the end in narrating a series of events, since prior events contextualize later ones. ASL discourse is holistic and focuses on relationships between people. Texts reflect and move through various settings and perspectives but the focus of Deaf discourse is broad, the meaning is in the larger whole. Smith contrasts ASL discourse with mainstream American English discourse on some two dozen traits.

In quoting other people, the narrator frequently assumes their roles in the story: sophisticated reasoning requires the ability to take the perspective of others. In doing this, the narrator exploits the possibilities of using space in ASL. We saw a Deaf comedian tell the story of an overweight customer, a flirtatious waitress, and an uncooperative hamburger at a McDonald's. First the narrator took the role, and hence the position and demeanor, of the customer placing an order, then those of the waitress writing it down, those of the cook preparing it, those of the waitress delivering it, and those of the customer again, now getting ready to devour an oversize hamburger. Then the narrator shifts his torso toward the hamburger's position (rotating, leaning down, and looking up at the customer) and pleads for mercy. A rapid return puts him in the role of the startled but implacably hungry customer. In the ensuing dialog between burger ("Don't eat me!") and customer, the narrator needs only to shift eye-gaze up or down and turn his head slightly to indicate who is talking, the hamburger or the customer. The Deaf audience has to observe where in space the narrator has placed the signs for waitress, customer, and hamburger; it must keep a mental image of the scene in order to interpret who is speaking to whom. The audience also has to transform spatial relations with each successive shift in narrative roles, all the while processing the grammar and meanings of the sentences. The Deaf narrator is like a movie director, shifting perspectives, moving in and out. This is true in virtually all stories, not just in entertainment.

Teaching in Deaf discourse is primarily conducted by modeling or telling stories, rather than by explanation or direction. To argue a point, Deaf people commonly relate their personal experiences as a specific illustration. These experiences are more convincing than abstract evidence because their narration includes the needed context and has the authenticity arising from a firsthand observer. Such storytelling also affirms shared experience and bonding. Minimizing the importance of personal testimony breaks the rule. English-based rhetorical structures break the rules. (Some storytelling genres are sketched below under language arts.)

Managing information

We all seek information daily as it relates to our lives, our work, our health, and so on but many minority language users, including those who sign ASL, encounter a major barrier in that search: much of the information they seek is inaccessible or hard to access because delivered in a language not their own. This fact may underlie the high value in the Deaf-World placed on obtaining and sharing information.[48] Of course, not everything is shared, but averaging over diverse situations, we may say that the cultural norm is to pass information along to other members. In some ways the "grapevine" serves like the media in a people that has had limited access to the English-based media. Direct, clear communication that exploits the capacities of a visual language for graphic detail is highly valued. Candor is required, even if not always honored. The themes calling for candor—the boundaries between public and private—differ in the Deaf-World from mainstream American culture. Marriage and divorce, personal wealth, bathroom practices, sickness and death, sexual behavior—none of these topics is taboo for Deaf people. In the same vein, Deaf people are normally expected to share what is happening in their private lives, though of course they can evade answering a question, for example, by changing the topic. Hinting and vague talk in an effort to be polite are often inappropriate and even offensive. Direct negative comments on the other person's appearance are generally allowed–they just show you care. Rudeness that breaks the rules includes: withholding information from those who, according to the culture, have a right to know; refusing to watch someone signing to you; holding someone's hands to stop him or her from signing; holding a spoken conversation when there are Deaf people present.

A value that appears to underlie all these traits of Deaf culture is allegiance to the group. Many Deaf writers use the metaphor of family to convey this: We are all in the same family, they say. Allegiance is expressed in the prizing of one's membership in the Deaf-World, in marrying a Deaf person, in gaining status by enhancing the group and acknowledging its contributions, in disparaging Deaf beggars and others who are seen as bringing discredit to the Deaf, in defining oneself in relation to the culture, in the priority given to evidence that arises from experience as a member of the culture, in the treasuring of the language of the Deaf, and in efforts by Deaf people to promote the dissemination of culturally salient information.[49] Indeed, these expressions of allegiance can be seen as family values raised to a social level.

SOCIAL INSTITUTIONS

In addition to a cultural grammar, every culture has a set of social institutions. Over time, some ethnic institutions die out while others arise and flourish, and so it is with the Deaf-World. It was in the residential schools where Deaf children have for centuries acquired language, a cultural identity, and the values, mores and knowledge passed down from one generation of the Deaf to the next. Enrollments in the residential schools have been dwindling for several decades now owing to the influence of the mainstreaming movement in special education. However, there are some robust residential schools that are attracting growing numbers of pupils, especially from Deaf-World families.

The Deaf clubs are another bastion of Deaf culture. They have played important roles in the lives of the Deaf.[50] Their numbers have been dwindling as other social practices take their place. Many large cities had Deaf clubs with hundreds of members that were the main site of acculturation for young people who had graduated from a school or program for Deaf children; a few Deaf clubs survive.[51] At the clubs, there were dances, raffles, banquets, costume parties, skits, beauty contests, lectures, gambling nights, and anniversaries along with the customary elections, celebrations, business meetings, distributions of awards recognizing service to the club and to the local Deaf-World. Deaf clubs often had athletic teams that competed under the mantle of the American Athletic Association of the Deaf. (That organization was replaced in 1997 by the USA Deaf Sports Federation and its twenty-four affiliates.)[52] The Federation fosters and regulates competition among Deaf athletes and provides social occasions for members and their friends.

Nowadays, Deaf people gather in many venues in addition to athletic events, among them bars, interpreted religious services, senior citizens' clubs, ethnic associations of the Deaf and state, national and international conventions. Leisure and recreational associations have taken over some of the functions of the Deaf clubs, providing opportunities for Deaf people to socialize. Professional organizations bring together Deaf linguists, historians, sign-language teachers, psychologists, rehabilitation counselors, and Deaf teachers of Deaf children, among others.[53] Why are Deaf clubs dwindling? Padden_D explains that these professional and advocacy associations made Deaf clubs obsolete as the clubs were created initially to provide Deaf trades workers with a place to socialize at the end of the day.[54] The advent of captioned television programs and DVDs are also often cited as likely contributing causes.

More social institutions: there are Deaf-run social service agencies, Deaf theater companies, Deaf literary clubs (the literature is that of ASL or of English), and Deaf television programs—conducted by and primarily for Deaf people. (See language arts, below.) In a study of the French, Hispanic, and Jewish press in the United States, Fishman concluded that ethnic press is a powerful force for maintaining ethnic vitality.[55] For more than a century, the "silent press"—publications by and for Deaf people–has been an important force bonding Deaf people in the United States. Publications have kept scattered Deaf people informed about the lives of their peers, friends from school, and leaders. They inform Deaf people about social and political gatherings, about athletics and opportunities for employment. Since the Deaf have had limited access to the telephone, publications and gatherings have traditionally been the two main ways of staying in touch. Printing was a leading trade taught in the residential schools; numerous schools had their own newspapers that had stories about prominent Deaf people, education, sign language, and current events. Stories were also reprinted from other newspapers and magazines.[56] The first such school newspaper began in 1849; there were fifty by 1900.[57] Other newspapers were established by Deaf publishers who also brought out books, videotapes, and other materials—and continue to do so—exclusively concerning the Deaf-World. Nowadays these media are supplemented by interactive websites, blogs (individual web sites with regular entries) and vlogs (a blog with embedded video).

Most states have state associations of the Deaf with a political agenda and these associations are gathered under the umbrella of the National Association of the Deaf.[58] In many ethnic minorities, there are charismatic leaders who are felt to embody the unique characteristics of the whole ethnic group and are the major actors on the social stage.[59] This is true for Deaf leaders as well. A 1976 study conducted in Washington, D.C., found that the Deaf elite in that sample all had higher education; they had Deaf parents twice as often as the general Deaf population; and more than half had ASL as a first language.[60] ASL was the language of communicative contact among the elite as it was between them and the rank-and-file, otherwise known as "grassroots" Deaf. Theresa Smith explains, "grassroots" means "really Deaf," untouched by hearing values and ideals, hence unsullied; but that can mean unsophisticated. A "grassroots leader," however, is a term of respect and affection.

In recent decades, Deaf professionals with college or more advanced diplomas have come to play a larger role in agencies serving the Deaf. To be viewed positively as a "professional leader," someone who straddles the boundary between the Deaf-World and the mainstream, the Deaf professional must be committed to Deaf values and beliefs but at the same time able to move easily in the mainstream.[61]

All of these social institutions in the Deaf-World—clubs, leisure activities, sports, politics, religion–are associated with distinct organizations with overlapping membership. The aims of those organizations, in addition to their central themes, are to bring Deaf people together so they may see friends, catch up on each other's lives, meet dates and potential spouses, find out who is hiring Deaf people, and share information in general, all by communicating freely in ASL. When the club doors close, when the theater lights dim, when the game is over, Deaf people congregate for many hours in the halls, in the lobby, and finally in the street near a lamppost, prolonging the joy of togetherness.

In Part II we describe how a Deaf elite gave rise to the first organizations of the Deaf in the United States.

THE LANGUAGE ARTS

The language arts of an ethnic group entertain and reinforce ethnic identity and solidarity. Ethnic narratives, plays, and poetry explain who we are—to ourselves and to others. They recount our struggles, victories, and defeats; they tell what separates us from others; they express our values and relate how a member of our ethnic group ought to live. Ethnic groups have central myths that affirm their values and traditions. Frequently, they are embellished dramatic tales of distant origins that are widely accepted as true.[62]

American Sign Language has a rich literary tradition. The storyteller and the story have an important role to play in the bonding of the Deaf and the transmission of the Deaf-World's heritage and accumulated wisdom.[63] Storytelling develops early in schools for Deaf children, where youngsters recount in ASL the idiosyncratic mannerisms of hearing teachers and, in the absence of TV captioning, the plots of cartoons, westerns, and war movies. Some children soon emerge as the ones with the most loyal and sizable audiences. Those children soon identify themselves as storytellers, a fact confirmed by their audiences. Their craft is perfected as they watch Deaf adults tell stories at home, in school, at the Deaf club, or at other cultural events. In later life, the self-identified storyteller volunteers or is paid to tell a story at some event. This later storytelling is sometimes more formal—for example, bearing witness to the acts and character of important Deaf figures or significant events, or relating part of Deaf culture. A skilled storyteller has an excellent command of ASL and of nonverbal communication, makes suitable selections from a repertory of stories, and knows how to monitor audience response and adjust to it.

As in most ethnic groups, the Deaf-World has stories that are archetypal. One genre is the "success story." In brief: The Deaf protagonist grows up in a hearing environment and has never met any Deaf people. He meets a Deaf person who teaches him sign language and the ways of the Deaf-World. He becomes increasingly involved in that world and leaves his past behind. Padden$_D$ points out that these Deaf success stories reinforce the belief that it is good and right to be Deaf, in much the same way as Americans support and propagate the "American Dream."[64]

ASL signers giving a lecture often start with a personal story embodying the main points to be made. For example, in *The Book of Name Signs: Naming in American Sign Language*, Sam Supalla$_D$ tells the story of his own name sign, how he got it, and how it relates to his family's name signs. Then he explains how the story reflects the usage of name signs in ASL.[65] Theresa Smith calls "kernel" stories these personal narratives that serve to introduce an abstract topic.

Another common genre of ASL stories, called "One Deaf" stories, is comprised of cautionary tales, success stories, and tales about a fictional Deaf leader. These stories start with the words "One Deaf" and end with the word "Well," as in "Well, what do you make of that!" inviting the audience to consider not only the feelings of a Deaf person in that situation but also to see the deeper truth. Here is an example:

> One Deaf was working in the mill, cutting cloth. The machine was big, dangerous, and the man had to be careful. Out of the corner of his eye he noticed some movement and he turned to look. One Hearing was walking through the factory. As the Deaf man watched, suddenly the cloth pulled his arm into the machine and it was cut off. Well?!

The hand—the means of communication—is cut off. The moral is clear: hearing people can be dangerous, do not let them distract you.[66]

Another popular genre is the legend of origins. One such story is the founding of Rome, where a wolf suckles Romulus and Remus, twins fathered by the god Mars. A Deaf legend of origins has been retold countless times in America and many other lands—how the abbé de l'Epée came to establish the first schools for the Deaf.

> The abbé de l'Epée had been walking in a dark night. He wanted to stop and rest overnight, but he could not find a place to stay, until in the distance he saw a house with a light on inside. He approached and knocked at the door, but no one answered. The door was open, so he entered the house and found two young women seated by the fire sewing. He spoke to them, but they failed to answer. He walked

closer and spoke to them again, but they still failed to respond. The abbé was perplexed, but seated himself beside them. They looked up at him and did not speak. At that point, their mother entered the room. Did the abbé not know that her daughters were deaf? He did not, but now he understood why they had not responded. As he contemplated the young women, the abbé realized his vocation.[67]

Although the legend is broadly consistent with the abbé's own published account, accuracy is not the point of the story.[68] What is the point? Padden[D] and culture and education scholar Tom Humphries[D] state it well in *Deaf in America: Voices from a Culture*. The legend symbolizes the transition from a world in which Deaf people live in isolation to one in which they participate in a cultural, social, and linguistic group. ASL literature includes history, stories, tall tales, legends, fables, anecdotes, poetry, plays, humor, naming rituals, sign play, and more. Deaf humor is often a response to oppression. Humor invites the audience to identify with the culture from which it arises ("This is our kind of humor"), and to revel in the solidarity of attending, expecting, laughing, and applauding. ASL is an unwritten language, so literature such as storytelling and humor carry much cultural information that, in cultures with written languages, would be passed down in print. At Deaf events there have been traditionally a variety of cultural activities, including performances, storytelling, skits, and comedies.[69]

Deaf theater is of course an expression of Deaf culture. A dramatic story line proceeds through choreography and mime, the artistic use of language, and the recognizable conventions of Deaf theater and culture. For the viewer familiar with ASL and Deaf culture, Deaf theater is a dazzling display indeed. Plays with Deaf actors in the United States probably originated in the mid-nineteenth century in the residential schools, where plays developed about Deaf school life, Deaf history, and Deaf family situations. In these plays, students can give free rein to their talents for acting and the expressive use of ASL. Deaf theater is to be found in the Deaf clubs (especially informal skits and mime shows), at Deaf literary societies, and at the numerous Deaf theater groups, both regional and national. The National Theatre of the Deaf is the oldest, continuously performing professional touring theater company in the country. Its actors went from occasional bookings at Deaf events to full-time performance on the national and international stage. In over ten thousand performances, it has not only served Deaf audiences but has also made a large hearing audience aware of the Deaf and the power and beauty of their signed language.[70] Among regional Deaf theaters with national and international impact, Deaf West Theatre presents several original productions in ASL, as well as ASL adaptations of plays written in English.

THE VISUAL ARTS

In the mid-eighteenth century, Deaf artists played an important role in creating awareness of the abbé de l'Epée's pioneering efforts and those of his successor. For example, one of Epée's Deaf pupils was a painter, another a sculptor, and each presented a Deaf person's vision of "the father of the Deaf." Ever since, Deaf artists have been presenting Deaf culture to the Deaf and the world beyond. Exhibits of Deaf art are often to be found at Deaf congresses and occasionally in galleries and museums. There have also been several international congresses devoted in part to the Deaf arts. There are lithographs, oil paintings, watercolors, acrylics, pen-and-ink drawings, neon sculptures, photography, and animated films. These works capture aspects of the lives of Deaf people. The renunciation of sign language, formally approved at the 1880 Milan congress, is a recurrent theme, as are the experiences of American Deaf schoolchildren brought up under that regime, where only spoken language was allowed. Many canvases celebrate sign language and Deaf culture. The flourishing study of signed languages in the last few decades and the associated empowerment of Deaf people, have fostered a particularly prolific period in the Deaf arts.[71]

HISTORY

Scholars agree: "Without memory there can be no ethnicity."[72] History is so central to ethnicity that the British House of Lords, in a study of ethnic underrepresentation in government, declared that an ethnic group has two core properties: a cultural tradition of its own, and an awareness of a long shared history that it keeps alive and that distinguishes it from other groups.[73] As members of an ethnic group, our history places us on a time line: looking back at past generations, we have a heightened sense of our identity; "the past is a resource used by groups in the collective quest for meaning and community."[74] Looking forward, future generations will know our history, which then grants us a measure of immortality.[75] The striking parallels with the role of kinship—our ancestors are our past, our descendants our future—suggests that claims of history and of kinship are alternative ways of building ethnic solidarity and giving it timelessness. Indeed, sociologist Anthony Smith points out that some ethnic groups have heroes in their history who are tied to the group only by exemplifying shared values and not by genealogy.[76]

The history of an ethnic group, a product of the group's culture, is quite different from a scholarly account. An ethnic history is not judged by how accurate it is but rather by how well it organizes experience in the light of cultural values and by its emotive power.[77] From this perspective, Deaf history and, more broadly, Deaf Studies are important resources in defining and redefining Deaf ethnicity. Cultural claims, icons, and imagery are used by activists in ethnic mobilization. For example, the official meaning of the 1880 Congress of Milan has long been the renunciation of sign language and the affirmation of the mainstream oral language. However, the Deaf-World in the United States as elsewhere has appropriated that event for ethnic mobilization; it became a symbol—not merely of a particular congress stacked against the Deaf and their language, but of the power imbalance between hearing and Deaf people more generally.

The American Deaf-World has a rich history recounted in stories, books, films, and the like. It has its legends, heroes, and important sites. Earlier we recounted the legend of the abbé de l'Epée (how he came to establish the first Deaf schools). Another legend of beginnings concerns the gathering of Deaf people in early America, precipitated by the founding of the first permanent school for the Deaf. The legend begins:

> In the spring of 1814, a young minister named Thomas Hopkins Gallaudet was home in Hartford, Connecticut, recuperating from an illness. One day he observed his younger brother playing with the neighbor's children, including the eight-year-old Alice Cogswell$_D$. She had become deaf at the age of two owing to German measles, and had not heard or spoken since then. Gallaudet went over to her. He showed her his hat and wrote the letters H-A-T on the ground. He pointed from the hat to the written word. Alice$_D$ responded eagerly, seeming to understand that the letters represented the hat.[78]

Alice$_D$'s plight was symbolic of the plight of countless Deaf Americans. Without hearing, she lived apart from hearing people; without sign, she lived apart from Deaf people as well. In the legend of the abbé de l'Epée, Deaf education began when he led two Deaf women to literacy by employing sign language. Now Gallaudet would do likewise in America with Alice$_D$. The legend continues (translated and abridged) as follows:

> Alice$_D$'s father, Mason Fitch Cogswell, was a wealthy surgeon; he raised money to send Gallaudet to Europe to learn methods of educating the Deaf. In Britain, Gallaudet found a monopoly on Deaf education that claimed to use speech exclusively with Deaf pupils and would not allow him to learn its methods. At the Paris school founded by the abbé de l'Epée, where sign language was the rule, Gallaudet was welcomed. He studied with Laurent Clerc$_D$, who was then a teacher at the school. Together Gallaudet and Clerc$_D$ traveled to Hartford, solicited funds in several eastern cities, and opened their school, which over the years would bring together hundreds of Deaf children. The Hartford school spawned dozens more in America, all using its sign language, which was based on Clerc$_D$'s.

And that's how the Deaf-World began in America—in legend. In fact, Deaf people gathered for mutual support and socializing long before the opening of the Hartford School, as we report in Parts II, III, and IV of this volume. We are informed that many schools for the Deaf perform the unabridged legend each December 10, on Gallaudet's birthday.[79] There are many more such legends.[80]

Opened in 1817, the Connecticut Asylum for the Education and Instruction of Deaf and Dumb Persons (later the American Asylum for the Deaf and Dumb) was America's first charitable institution and the first enduring school for its Deaf people. Pupils from the large Deaf population on Martha's Vineyard brought their island sign language to school; those from other families with numerous Deaf members brought their manual communication practices; and those raised in a hearing environment brought the "home sign" that served their communicative needs at home. All those pupils learned Clerc$_D$'s sign language, as did disciples who came from other states, aiming to found schools for the Deaf on their return home. What emerged from the meeting between Clerc$_D$'s French Sign Language and the pupils' diverse sign systems has been called a *contact language*—which we now call, in its contemporary form, American Sign Language.[81] In America, as in France, the mother school soon sent its teachers and graduates all over the country to teach in Deaf schools and to found new ones. As early as 1834, a single sign language was recognized in schools for the Deaf in the United States. By the time of Clerc$_D$'s death in 1869, there were some thirty residential schools in the United States with over 3000 pupils and almost 200 teachers. In that same year, the first school for black Deaf children opened in Raleigh, North Carolina. Nearly half of the teachers in the schools for the Deaf were Deaf themselves. Most Deaf pupils and teachers took Deaf spouses and had Deaf as well as hearing children, and this, too, helped to disseminate ASL. The success of the residential schools led to the creation of high school and then college preparatory classes, which led in turn to the National Deaf-Mute College (now Gallaudet University).

A few years before Clerc$_D$'s death, one of his former pupils, Thomas Brown$_D$ of Henniker, New Hampshire, organized the largest gathering of Deaf people ever assembled. (We will have more to say about Brown$_D$ and his Deaf clan, in Part II.) Two hundred Deaf people, some from as far away as Virginia, and two hundred pupils of the American Asylum, gathered in Hartford in 1850. The announced purpose of the gathering was to express their gratitude to Gallaudet and Clerc$_D$ but later events proved that Brown$_D$ likely had a political agenda going beyond gratitude: he wanted to counteract the scattering of Deaf people by gatherings to improve their lot. Engraved silver pitchers were presented to Gallaudet and Clerc$_D$. The engraving was rich in symbolism from Deaf history: One side of the pitcher shows Gallaudet and Clerc$_D$ leaving

France; the ship is at hand and their future school is visible beyond the waves: The Old World brings enlightenment to the New. On the other side of the pitcher there is a schoolroom. On the front is a bust of Clerc$_D$'s teacher, the abbé Sicard (successor to Epée), and around the neck the arms of the New England states. There were speeches and banquets and resolutions and many participants stayed on through the weekend in order to enjoy a church service interpreted into sign language. The desire of Deaf people to gather and to honor their history by presenting it in engravings indicates a sense of peoplehood that rises above the individual and the family.

The gathering in Hartford led to the creation of the first organization of the Deaf in America. Representatives from each of the New England states gathered for a week at the Brown$_D$ home in Henniker to frame a constitution for the New England Gallaudet Association of Deaf-Mutes (NEGA). This document called for a newspaper by and for Deaf-mutes, the *Gallaudet Guide and Deaf-Mutes' Companion*. One of the earliest periodicals in America printed exclusively for the Deaf, the *Guide* contained news of Deaf meetings, marriages, illnesses and deaths; discussions of issues like the education of Deaf children, and such broader social issues as slavery and religion. In the fall of 1854 "deaf-mutes" from "all parts of the union" met in Hartford for the unveiling of a monument to Gallaudet.[82] On it, bas reliefs showed Gallaudet with the Asylum's first three students and his name in the manual alphabet on the opposite face. The entire monument was the "exclusive product of deaf-mute enterprise."[83] Among the Deaf orators at the event, whose signing was interpreted for the hearing people in the audience, Thomas Brown$_D$ reviewed the history of Deaf education. A draft constitution for the New England Gallaudet Association of Deaf-Mutes was read out and adopted and officers were elected with Thomas Brown$_D$ as president. This was the first formal organization for Deaf people in the United States.

After the second convention of the NEGA in Concord, New Hampshire, and a third in Worcester, Massachusetts, the fourth convention was held in 1860 at the Hartford school, with some three hundred attending. The Reverend Thomas Gallaudet of New York (eldest son of Thomas Hopkins Gallaudet) was recruited to interpret ASL into English for the hearing people who did not know the sign language.[84] Brown$_D$ gave the presidential address and Laurent Clerc$_D$ took the assembly to sites significant in Deaf history, such as the house of Mason Cogswell where Clerc$_D$ first met young Alice$_D$. In the evening there was a banquet with toasts, talks and resolutions. The self-perception of the Deaf as a distinct group was in evidence. The solidarity felt was so great that there were published proposals to secure land from Congress for the formation of a Deaf state in the west.[85] (See Ethnic territory below.) Then, as the graduates of the residential schools found ways to gather with the opportunity to socialize in their own language, there were more large meetings of the Deaf and numerous Deaf clubs were founded. Brown$_D$ took on other roles as a Deaf leader and campaigned for a national organization. His hope was realized when in 1880 the preeminent organization of the Deaf in America, known today as the National Association of the Deaf, was founded.

The road leading from Clerc$_D$'s sign language and its use in the classroom to today's appreciation of ASL veered off course in the late nineteenth century. Industrialization, mass immigration, and the rise of eugenics demanded that all citizens cleave to a narrow identity: white, Protestant, middle class, English-speaking, and able-bodied. Increasingly, schools for the Deaf sought to replace ASL with spoken English, culminating with the implementation of the resolutions of the Milan congress. As we told earlier, Deaf teachers, purveyors of Deaf heritage, were dismissed and older Deaf students quarantined as both groups could easily fall into the sin of signing and were not apt in promoting spoken English. Despite the schools' fanatical efforts to eradicate ASL, Deaf people never abandoned sign language. Indeed, they became a more unified minority in the early twentieth century as a response to attempts at forced language replacement.

The return to a role for sign language in Deaf education was fueled by the American civil rights movement of the 1960s and 1970s, by educational policies that accorded greater status to minority languages, and by the growing scientific evidence in the second half of the twentieth century that ASL is a fully autonomous natural language. In 1965, William Stokoe, Dorothy Casterline$_D$, and Carl Croneberg$_D$ of Gallaudet University, published a *Dictionary of American Sign Language on Linguistic Principles*. As Padden$_D$ and Humphries$_D$ explain in their book *Inside Deaf Culture*, Deaf people were cautious in taking up the idea that their sign language was equal to all other natural languages because hearing people had until then always disparaged their language and sought to replace it with English.[86] Nevertheless, the concept that ASL signers had a language and a culture was validating indeed, especially appealing to the new Deaf middle class seeking to replace the old loss-based understanding of themselves and their language. With the recognition of ASL came the demand from parents, professionals, laymen, and students for instruction in the language; this drew large numbers of Deaf people into teaching ASL.

In 1971, Stokoe brought together a group of linguists to pursue the scientific study of ASL and in 1979 Edward Klima and Ursula Bellugi at the Salk Institute published *The Signs of Language*. The book reported on a decade of their research with Deaf collaborators on the structure and functions of ASL. Their studies went well beyond ASL vocabulary to present elements of the grammar of the language and of its art forms. This novel research focused on the language itself and not on culture, as Humphries$_D$ explains. "Contrary to the general assumption that it was the research on ASL that alerted the world to Deaf people and their culture, it was actually cultural processes within the Deaf community that brought into public view the people behind the language." Deaf scholars and performers began "talking culture"—explaining to Deaf and hearing audiences the new vocabulary and way of thinking about Deaf language and culture.[87] The National Theatre of the Deaf, mentioned earlier, also disseminated the new Deaf discourse through original plays based on Deaf culture.

When Deaf people began to think about themselves and their world in this new way, it invited comparison with the standing of other cultural groups and it raised the Deaf standard of fair treatment. Deaf young people of college age had grown up with this new understanding of the Deaf-World and were determined to work for improved civil rights and access.

In 1988 a collective action by Deaf students and Deaf leaders known as "Deaf President Now" (DPN) led to nationwide protests and greater activism by Deaf people that has endured. The event triggering the protest was the selection of the next president of Gallaudet University. Named in honor of Thomas Hopkins Gallaudet, the university was founded in 1864 in Washington, D.C., by Thomas's son Edward; it is the only liberal arts university for Deaf students in the world. American Deaf people have long claimed the school as their own and its campus as their land, even if its affairs were not conducted as they wished.[88] Among the three candidates to lead the institution, two were Deaf and accomplished administrators, the third did not know ASL or the Deaf-World. Prior to the selection, Deaf leaders in the Washington, D.C., area and from other states, along with Gallaudet alumni, lobbied intensively for the selection of a Deaf candidate, and they laid the groundwork for civil disobedience if it were needed.

When the university board of trustees announced the choice of the non-Deaf candidate, with seeming disregard for the two Deaf candidates for that office, the Deaf-World and its faculty and staff allies reacted with shock, anger, disbelief, and tears. Then they closed down the university and prevented the newly selected president from assuming office. Deaf organizations around the country staged demonstrations of support. A torrent of Deaf people converged on Washington, D.C., to protest. Labor unions and candidates for U.S. president publicly took the students' side. There was wide media coverage of the demand for a Deaf president and donations poured in from individuals and organizations. At the end of a week of protest, there was a march on the capitol; in the vanguard were Deaf leaders carrying a banner borrowed from the Martin Luther King Museum that proclaimed "We Still Have a Dream."

For the protestors, the demand for a Deaf president was clearly a civil rights issue, and they presented it as such to the media. The Gallaudet

Board of Trustees reversed itself and agreed to name a Deaf candidate. In the years since DPN and the Gallaudet Revolution, there has been a marked increase in Deaf activism, including protests for more Deaf teachers and a larger role for Deaf culture in the curriculum of Deaf education programs. There has been an increase of Deaf people lobbying state governments and the movie and television industries, and an increase in the numbers of Deaf people heading education and rehabilitation programs for the Deaf.[89]

The four students who led the Gallaudet uprising were Deaf children of Deaf parents; they were deeply imbued with a sense of Deaf-World, and they were natively fluent in ASL. One of them explained to *USA Today* the significance of the event as it relates to the identity of Deaf people: "Hearing people sometimes call us handicapped. But most—maybe all deaf people—feel that we're more of an ethnic group because we speak a different language. We also have our own culture. . . . There's more of an ethnic difference than a handicap difference between us and hearing people."[90]

The revolt at Gallaudet was a reaffirmation of Deaf culture, and it brought about the first worldwide celebration of that culture, a congress called *The Deaf Way*, held in Washington, D.C., the following year. More than five thousand spokespersons from Deaf communities around the world, including scholars, artists, and political leaders, took part in lectures, exhibits, media events, and performances. On the Gallaudet campus, there was a spectacular display of Deaf arts: mime, dance, storytelling and poetry in sign languages, crafts, sculpture, video, and fine arts. It is clear that Deaf leaders and artists in many nations have a sense of ownership of the Gallaudet Revolution, just as they have a sense of special fellowship with Deaf people in the United States and around the globe. This sketch of the history presents a culture that has been constantly evolving, as culture does with ethnic groups. The ties that bind exist in all ages but the expression of ethnicity varies with time and place. Anthony Smith's *Ethnic Revival* puts it this way: "The soul of each generation . . . emanates from the soul . . . of all the preceding generations, and what endures, namely the strength of the accumulated past, exceeds the wreckage, the strength of the changing present."[91]

ETHNIC TERRITORY

"Ethnic minority groups have an imagined and often mythologized history, culture and homeland that provide important sources of identity."[92] As with the claim of common ancestry, to which it is closely related, the claim of a historic common homeland should not be taken literally. The ancestors of Hispanic Americans did not come from one place, nor did those of Cuban Americans, nor, presumably, those of the "indigenous" peoples who lived in Cuba before the Spanish conquest.

On the contemporary scene, the ethnic group may not currently occupy its claimed homeland; it is the feeling of the connection that is important.[93] Ethnic groups in the United States—Hispanic Americans, for example—are much larger than the ethnic enclaves in which some members live. Members are dispersed throughout the land, and some have returned to the old country or immigrated to other lands. "The ethnic community does not exist in a fixed location but rather as a form of consciousness."[94]

As do many ethnic groups, members of the Deaf-World have an enduring vision of "a land of our own," a vision expressed in folk tales, utopian writings, newsprint, theater, and political discussions.[95] This yearning probably arises because the territory of Deaf-Americans, like that of Asian, African, Hispanic, and Native Americans, has no single homeland. Ethnic heritage sites thus take on great significance as a culturally unifying force. Where are the heritage sites of the People of the Eye? The first are the residential schools. Graduates of the residential schools for the Deaf have a strong sense of place there and Deaf travel is often planned around visits to those schools. It would be a mistake to equate Deaf people's ties to their residential schools, where most acquired language and a positive identity, to hearing people's ties to their schools. The Deaf ties are so strong that many Deaf people choose to live in proximity to their schools after graduation. The search for a place away from the residential school after graduation led to the establishment of Deaf clubs across America, tiny reservations of Deaf culture, as it were, where Deaf people govern, socialize, and communicate fluently in ASL after the workday ends. (As we said earlier, both institutions have been dwindling in the United States).

Historic sites and monuments are evocative of ethnic group memories and ethnic group members visit them. For the Deaf, these include the mother school founded by Gallaudet and Clerc$_D$ in Hartford; their graves in Hartford and the graveyard on Martha's Vineyard, Massachusetts, where there were many Deaf people in the 1800s (more on that later); and the campus of Gallaudet University, with its statue of Thomas H. Gallaudet and Alice Cogswell$_D$. Laurent Clerc$_D$'s birthplace, in the town of La Balme-les-Grottes in France, is a heritage site for the American Deaf, who travel to the village on personal initiative and with arranged tours. The National Association of the Deaf, in association with four other American Deaf organizations, made a formal pilgrimage to La Balme and presented the village with a plaque of recognition and a painting of Clerc$_D$.

Many ethnic groups believe in a transnational communality, another expression of ethnic solidarity. This belief adds to the imagined importance of the group and enriches its sense of tradition. Consider the example of the Jews. Although they share a religion, Jews from different parts of the world do not have a single language or homeland.

Indeed, Diaspora Jews may speak mutually unintelligible languages. Even vernaculars such as Yiddish often do not allow communication among Jews of different lands as such languages borrow heavily from the language of the country where the speakers reside. Fishman observed that language and territory are detached from Jewish ethnicity, since the symbolic homeland of the Jews is Israel, but Jewish Diasporas do not originate there.[96] Indeed, diaspora communities that have lost their homelands and independence can maintain themselves for centuries.[97]

As there are distinct Jewish ethnic minorities in numerous lands, so are there numerous Deaf-Worlds; communities using sign languages are no doubt to be found in every country in the world.[98] Although they all have visual languages, their different sign languages are often not mutually intelligible, as we said earlier. Nevertheless, Deaf people, like the Jews, believe deeply in a transnational communality. Theresa Smith illustrates the point: "Deaf Americans feel a kinship with Deaf Italians in a way that is closer, deeper than they do with hearing Americans."[99] The Deaf belief in transnationalism is founded on language.[100] Laurent Clerc[D] tells what transpired when he visited a school for the Deaf in London:

> As soon as I beheld [the students] my face became animated, I was as agitated as a traveler of sensibility would be on meeting all of a sudden in distant regions a colony of his countrymen. On their side, those deaf and dumb persons fixed their looks on me, and recognized me as one of them. An expression of surprise and pleasure enlivened all their features. I approached them. I made some signs and they answered me by signs. This communication caused a most delicious sensation in each of us. . . .[101]

Sign languages have enough properties in common that early Deaf scholars even claimed sign language to be universal, though that is not true literally.[102] When Deaf people from different countries meet, their exchanges will be in a prominent sign language such as ASL, or in a contact variety, or in pantomime. (There is also International Sign, which has arisen from contact among Deaf participants at international meetings. And there was a proposed international sign vocabulary, analogous to Esperanto, called Gestuno, which is not in use nowadays).[103] In addition to international meetings, communication among Deaf people from different nations takes place using the internet, print publications, and individual travel.[104]

KINSHIP

Practices related to kinship vary widely in ethnic groups around the world. In the West, kinship among the members of an ethnic group is largely based on the blood relations they have in common and some scholars insist that there is no ethnicity without such shared ancestry. In many societies, however, kinship depends on socialization, not on shared ancestry.[105] A few examples of this decoupling of ancestry and kinship may suffice. In Langkawi, a Malaysian archipelago, when a mother feeds her biological children along with unrelated foster children, all these children are seen as kin. They are not allowed to marry one another and all are said to resemble the people who raise them, in the same way that children are said to resemble their birth parents[106] Among the Trobrianders, in New Guinea, "The children of a union are not in any way regarded as kin to their father or to his lineage. They are of the same body as their mother."[107] The Yao peoples in southern China adopt many non-Yao children; these foster children are seen as kin in all respects, including participating as Yao in the many rituals of this ethnic group, such as ancestor worship.[108] Among the Iñupiat of northern Alaska most families include adopted children who are seen as kin since the kinship bonds that really matter are with those who raised you, not with those who gave birth to you.[109] For the Navajo, kinship is defined by helping, protecting, and sharing: When two people are bonded in these ways, they see one another as kin.[110] In such ethnic groups, the claim of common ancestors is inaccurate but "as long as people regard themselves as alike because of a perceived heritage, and as long as others in the society so regard them, they constitute an ethnic group."[111]

Further evidence that kinship need not be based on shared ancestry: there are means for acquiring and for losing it.[112] Entire tribes may acquire kinship to members of other tribes without blood relation. Pashtuns in Pakistan and Afghanistan recognize unrelated tribes as sharing their ethnic identity.[113] Some cultures reinforce the bonding of their members with claims about kinship and ancestry while others achieve the same end by claiming connections to similar cultures in ancient times.[114] In the United States and Europe, most people have many different ethnic groups in their ancestry due to inter-ethnic marriages; the people we consider kin are just a small subset of those with whom we share ancestry.[115]

Thus, ethnic kinship, like ethnic history, is culturally constructed.[116] Some scholars attribute the myth of shared ancestry to the common physical characteristics (such as physiognomy or skin color) of ethnic group members or to their shared customs.[117] We conclude that the claim of kinship is an expression of cohesion between members of the ethnic group—the kind of solidarity owed to one's family but more diffuse.[118] Ethnic groups are indeed like a family: "The members feel knit to one another and so committed to the cultural heritage, which is the family's inheritance."[119] A belief in family-like attachments among group members is nourished by language and religion.[120] But the claim of kinship need not be accurate biologically. Traditions and legends handed down across the generations can serve in place of alleged kinship as a link to the past and the future.[121] African Americans, Hispanic Americans, and countless other ethnic groups transmit language and culture across the generations without real or even imagined shared ancestry.

To summarize these observations on kinship and ethnicity: "The sense of unique descent need not, and in nearly all cases will not, accord with factual history."[122] The kinship myth is an expression of solidarity, of family-like attachments based on shared properties such as physical characteristics and cultural practices. In ethnic groups where there is shared ancestry, what is important is not ancestral descent itself but the shared physical features that arise from it and bind people to one another and to their ancestors, along with shared language and culture. Many ethnic groups have neither real kinship nor a kinship myth; there is no necessary link between kinship and ethnicity. A kinship myth may not arise where ethnic solidarity is reinforced by other means; for example, by language, culture, or religion.[123]

ANCESTRY IN THE DEAF-WORLD

As we have seen, family-like attachments between ethnic group members are often grounded not on the genealogical facts of shared heredity but on language, culture, and physical traits. Properties of the Deaf-World that nourish this diffuse enduring solidarity are the transmission of language and culture down the generations and common physical characteristics (ASL signers are visual people). However, the Deaf-World also provides evidence of shared heredity. In Parts II–IV we present the ancestries of numerous Deaf individuals in the early years of the Deaf-World and we reveal the extensive sharing of ancestors that took place.

How widespread is shared heredity in the Deaf-World? We need to ask about heredity and then about sharing. What is the percent of ASL signers who are Deaf due to heredity compared to all other causes? No study of ASL signers has been conducted to give us these numbers— Deaf due to heredity and Deaf for other reasons—but a rough estimate can be had, if we make some assumptions, from the Gallaudet University Annual Survey of Deaf and Hard of Hearing Children. Nearly half of all the children in the 2007–2008 survey were said to have, in terms of audiology, "severe" or "profound" "hearing loss." These children are the most likely to become ASL signers. In this ASL-prone subset, about one-fourth of the children are Deaf due to disease, injury, or maternal illness. These children do not have Deaf ancestry but many will acquire ASL as their primary language, like their hereditarily-Deaf peers. Another fourth of the subset children were known to be hereditarily

Deaf because they had Deaf parents or Deaf siblings (brothers and sisters). The remaining half were "other," Deaf for reasons unknown. Most of those children, however, were doubtless Deaf due to heredity for three reasons. First, if they had been Deaf due to illness or injury that would likely be known. Second, the survey did not ask about Deaf relatives or ancestors (other than parents and siblings); had it done so, more of the children in the "other" category would be recorded as hereditarily Deaf. Third, the "other" category can contain hereditarily Deaf children who have no Deaf relatives or ancestors whatsoever (as we explain later). Thus we have an estimate of three-fourths of the children in the ASL-prone subset were probably Deaf due to heredity.[124]

A comparable result comes from a follow-up polling of parents whose children were included in the 1988 annual survey, where they were said to have become "profoundly hearing impaired" before age two without an environmental cause.[125] Replies identified whether each parent was hearing, Deaf, or status unknown; this yielded six mating types from which it was statistically estimated that 63 percent of these Deaf children were Deaf for hereditary reasons and the remainder for reasons unknown. Sixty-three percent is probably an underestimate of the importance of heredity since it does not take into account the hereditarily Deaf children with hearing parents but Deaf ancestors or relatives—in some cases even unknown to the family. As one investigator put it, "Limited knowledge of family history is frequently observed."[126] These estimates of two-thirds to three-fourths of the Deaf-World as being hereditarily Deaf are based on contemporary surveys. The figures could well prove quite different for the eighteenth and nineteenth centuries, when childhood illness (but also death from illness) was more common.

When ancestry is taken in its most literal sense in the West—that is, the connection by blood of successive generations—it applies to all hereditarily Deaf people. No matter if the Deaf trait is expressed in every generation of their ancestry or if that expression skips some generations, the genetic heritage is always there in every generation. So most Deaf people in the United States today are hereditarily Deaf, but do they tend to share ancestors? As we will show, the practice of Deaf founding families to unite with others through intermarriage tended to proliferate the Deaf trait, expressed or unexpressed, down through the generations and thus their Deaf descendants had shared ancestry.[127] There is a further reason why two hereditarily Deaf people are likely to have an ancestor in common. Suppose we knew the lineages of everyone back to Adam. We would see that, from time to time, a gene associated with being Deaf will originate here and there by random gene variation. The descendents of these originators will spread out geographically, down through the ages. The shared ancestry of those descendants will be all the more likely because any given gene will tend to spread locally since people tend to choose marriage partners who live nearby.

So even if a particular gene is rare among the Deaf population in general, those who do have it will tend to form "islands" of kin related by common descent. After countless generations, the descent group of Deaf people with any given gene variant must be large indeed. As Parts II and III show, the Deaf descent group originating in the English county of Kent spread out in the United States to include Martha's Vineyard, then Maine, and on to other regions of the country. However, the Deaf-World in the United States is undoubtedly comprised of more than one such descent group with a common ancestor. Thus, "Deaf American" is like "Hispanic American"—an umbrella term that, based on shared language and culture, gathers numerous distinct descent groups, each with its own common ancestor.

And what of Deaf ASL signers who are *not* hereditarily Deaf? Like Pashtun and Yao ethnicity, the Deaf-World includes unrelated members; those members qualify because they have the properties of Deaf people (visual orientation, sign language), acquired in childhood. Thus, there is biological unity, as well as linguistic and cultural unity, among the members of the Deaf-World. And as with the ethnic groups discussed above, these unrelated members of the Deaf-World are seen as full-fledged members.

SOCIALIZATION

During socialization, children internalize ethnic repertories, such as language and cultural beliefs and practices, that are highly resistant to change.[128] Children are often socialized by kin to whom they are not related biologically; we may call it proxy socialization. For example, foster children and orphans, more numerous in many cultures than our own, are not socialized by their biological parents. Moreover, when parents and children move to another land, peers will socialize the children in the language and culture of their new homeland long before the parents have mastered them. We cited earlier several ethnic groups that engage in both proxy and parental socialization.

Deaf socialization is often proxy socialization, conducted by peers and Deaf adults, to whom the Deaf child is not related. It is during the period of socialization to the Deaf-World that Deaf children learn their Deaf identity, acquire sign language and all the cultural contents, rules and values, history and myths that we have examined, and with them a deep attachment to that World.[129] If parents are unable to model Deaf-World language and culture for their Deaf child, proxy socialization begins when the child is able to mingle in the Deaf-World—for example on enrolling at a school or program for the Deaf. Interacting with members of the Deaf-World, the Deaf child finds a positive identity and Deaf role models, whose way of being and activities present possible lives for that child. Deaf children are today predominantly placed in local schools where they are most often isolated from peers and role models and thus denied opportunities for socialization during their formative years.

For the Deaf child of hearing parents, socialization in the parents' ethnicity is hampered by the language barrier. In an English-speaking home, the Deaf child not only fails to understand direct communication frequently but also misses the important part of socialization that is incidental—overheard parental interaction, dinner table conversation, and the like. The Deaf child cannot discover possible lives from his or her hearing parents, and the parents cannot perceive the world from their child's point of view and way of seeing. Nevertheless, Deaf children feel natural attachments to their biological parents and, as limited socialization to mainstream ethnicity progresses, they frequently feel divided allegiances, as do children with multiethnic backgrounds. Deaf families, in which parents and child are fluent in ASL, encounter none of these obstacles. The Deaf children are socialized by kin who are biologically related and language acquisition and socialization take their usual maturational course.[130]

Earlier we said that ethnic groups have not only internal cohesive properties but also externally oriented rules in shared settings, rules that reinforce cultural differences, maintain boundaries, and sustain ethnic identity, to which we turn next.

2

Ethnic Boundaries

Ethnic groups conflict and collaborate in various settings so the rules that govern their encounters, that reinforce cultural differences and maintain boundaries, are important to discover.[1] Such boundaries define membership and nonmembership and contribute to group solidarity and political agendas. We need to observe how ethnic groups construct their identities, drawing on their language and culture and present circumstances, and how they deploy ethnicity in behalf of their goals.[2] From this perspective, ethnicity is not primordial but determined by circumstances. However, this circumstantialist view does not square with ethnic members' deep emotional attachment to the group and its language. Moreover, identity construction is constrained by the "facts on the ground," such as self-ascription, shared language, strategies for boundary maintenance, and physical traits. Thus there is more than rhetoric to ethnicity; every representation of ethnic identity must take account of language, culture, and social structures. There is no obstacle to recognizing that ethnic groups possess a deeply felt sense of ethnic identity and a rich history and culture while also recognizing that they actively construct their ethnicity, which is subject to change.[3]

The contexts in which we find active boundary maintenance in the Deaf-World can be sorted into outside and inside forces.

OUTSIDE FORCES

Outside forces include formal classification, official policies, labor markets, residential space, and daily experience.[4] The formal classification of the Deaf tends to reinforce boundaries. Deaf people are welcome to participate in the majority ethnicity provided they do so as disabled individuals. Accordingly, the U.S. government does not count the number of Americans whose primary language is ASL, nor accord them the recognition, perquisites, and legal protections afforded speakers of other minority languages. Furthermore, interactions with the Deaf based on disability reinforce boundaries because Deaf people commonly find disability an alien construction of their identity.[5]

Official policy to accommodate minority needs is influenced by minority size, so accommodations have come little and late for the Deaf-World and that reinforces existing boundaries. For example, interpreters are not present at most public events so Deaf people cannot

participate. Public information—from news to emergencies—is generally not provided in ASL (although some programs are captioned in
English). The Deaf-World has little say over its future, in part because
it lacks a role in assuring early sign language acquisition by the next
generation of Deaf children. Without that role, no language may be
modeled for the Deaf child.

Late exposure to language and monolingual monocultural education in the dominant ethnicity prevent many Deaf children from achieving fluency in any language. The mainstreaming movement in special
education and the consequent isolation of many Deaf students in
hearing classes hinders academic achievement for many and that, too,
contributes to boundary maintenance.[6]

In the United States, poor education, the language barrier, cultural
values, and job discrimination contributed over the years to placing
many Deaf people in the manual trades (notably shoe repair, uphol-
stery, printing, or factory assembly).[7] This separated them from the
professionals who serve them and from middle- and upper-class
Americans and reinforced boundaries. Today there is a growing Deaf
middle class in the United States—this includes lawyers, educators of
the Deaf, ASL teachers, and rehabilitation counselors—but it is ques-
tionable if that has reduced the boundary separating the Deaf-World
from the dominant ethnicity since these Deaf professionals serve primarily the Deaf.[8] Deaf people tend to settle where there are other Deaf
people—in cities and near schools and universities with Deaf students;
this makes it easier for them to spend time with one another and to
militate for change.

INSIDE FORCES

Inside forces concern what groups bring to the making of identity.[9]
Language, common physical features such as height and skin color,
and cultural mores often play a role in delimiting one ethnic group
from the next. Many members of ethnic minorities rely for the most
part on their minority language. In the United States, such imbalanced
bilingualism is found among ethnic groups such as Old Order Amish,
Russian-speaking Old Believers, and segments of the Hispanic-
American and Asian-American communities—and the Deaf-World.[10]
Other members of ethnic groups show more balanced bilingualism,
employing their minority language and the dominant English language
as appropriate. In the United States, the children of ethnic minority parents or grandparents frequently are assimilated by the mainstream,
leaving ethnicity in American society "culturally thin."[11] This is not
true of the Deaf-World. Most ASL signers' limited fluency in the spoken
language and native or near-native fluency in the minority sign language play a major role in boundary maintenance, (although some are

more balanced bilinguals).[12] Moreover, most members of the Deaf-World do not wish to be assimilated but rather to participate while keeping their sign language and culture, and that, too, contributes to sustaining boundaries.

The importance of sign language in maintaining boundaries between the Deaf-World and mainstream ethnicity is supported by reports concerning the island of Martha's Vineyard, which we cited earlier as a significant site in Deaf cultural history. Although the evidence is incomplete, it appears that a great many families on the island had both Deaf and hearing members, and the sign language was widely used by both. In the absence of a language barrier separating Deaf and hearing, there were also few if any cultural boundaries.[13] We examine the Vineyard culture and its genealogy in Part II.

The most powerful force in boundary maintenance between the Deaf-World and mainstream ethnicity may be mutual incomprehension, as each group has an incommensurate theory of the other's identity. What is the *hearing* theory of Deaf identity? Humphries$_D$ has described its major features as follows (adapted):

Polarity (hear/don't hear, speaking/mute, complete/incomplete)

Pathology (having physical and developmental conditions needing medical or prosthetic intervention, behavior related to condition)

Adaptivity (sign, use of prosthetic interventions, adapting resources, use of special procedures, systems, and technology)

Exoticism (noble, special, think without language, visual world, miracles of adaptation, needing to be taught and brought to life)

These can be compared to views Deaf people have about themselves:

Completeness (self-knowing, having a community, whole)

Otherness (one with Deaf people but immersed among others, at risk)

Descendants (recipients and transmitters of ways of being, language)

Morality (value systems based on group experience that define a good life for themselves and their children; ethical)

Aesthetics (possessing concepts of beauty, abstract creators)[14]

With these different understandings of Deaf identity, there were bound to be profound differences on fundamental issues that create and maintain boundaries. The following are five examples, paraphrased from Humphries$_D$:

Designation of Deaf people (Deaf vs. hearing-impaired);

Competence to control Deaf institutions (privileged/incompetent);

Shaping the lives of Deaf children (bilingual education/cochlear
implants);
Cultural status (ASL recognition/ASL replacement);
Discriminatory practices (job networking/prejudicial job descrip-
tions and hiring).[15]

The practice of marrying within one's ethnic group is another internal
force for boundary maintenance, just as the reverse, marrying out
of one's ethnic group, contributes to assimilation.[16] Endogamous marriage goes hand in hand with group cohesion. As we mentioned, an
estimated nine out of ten Deaf people in the United States marry a Deaf
person.[17]

It is instructive to compare boundary maintenance in the Deaf-World
with that among the Roma (notwithstanding Gypsy poverty).[18] Both
are stigmatized by the dominant ethnicity, and both have limited cross-
boundary contact with that ethnicity. In the case of the Deaf, the stig-
mas concern language and disability. The language of the Deaf has long
been seen as much inferior to speech. Furthermore the Deaf-World is
stigmatized as a disability group and also stigmatized by disability
groups and the mainstream for its denial that it is a disability group.
The desire of many Deaf couples to have a Deaf child is stigmatized,
as is the wish of members of the Deaf-World to remain Deaf and their
scorn for Deaf people who "think Hearing."[19] At the same time, language differences impede communication across boundaries (except in
some restricted situations). Thus, stigmatized identity, distinct values,
and language barriers conspire to limit the interaction that Deaf people
have with the mainstream (as in the case of the Roma). As a result, the
significant boundary involves excluding the mainstream or holding
it at bay.

We have seen that ethnic groups are not just culturally cohesive enti-
ties but also, in many arenas, societies unto themselves, networks of
businesses, organizations and friendships that allow their members to
live out much of their lives within the group. In the box below we list
some of the activities that are predominantly carried out by the Deaf
for the Deaf. In some of these activities, hearing people also provide
limited goods and services.

Those who can resolve life's problems by recourse to existing relationships within their own ethnic group have less reason to cross the
boundary. This is particularly true of the Deaf. The choice of a marriage
partner, carpenter or tax accountant, the selection of a school for one's
children, a career to pursue, an organization to support—all these decisions and countless others can be taken in a way that reinforces the
boundary between the Deaf-World and the dominant ethnicity.
Conversely, members of an ethnic minority may seek in several ways
to cross the boundary with the dominant ethnicity so as to participate

---

Box 2.1 Predominantly by and for the Deaf-World

Alumni associations
Art by and for Deaf audiences
Assistive devices—design, manufacture, and sales
Athletics—Deaf schools, clubs, leagues
Civic associations
Computer user groups; internet vlogs
Conferences, workshops
Consumer goods and services, Deaf-related
Deaf Education, charter, residential and post-secondary schools
Deaf-World culture, research and teaching
Deaf history research, teaching, publishing, archives
Finding employment
Interpreter services for the Deaf
Leisure and social activities
Media—Deaf theater, film, and video
Political activities (state and national)
Publishing—newspapers, magazines, videos, books, internet, etc.
Professional services—counseling, financial, legal, medical
Religious services for the Deaf
Service agencies for the Deaf, Deaf-run
Services: car purchase and repair, child care, trades, etc.
Sign language research and teaching

---

in the wider social system: by attempting to pass as a member of the dominant group; by dividing one's time between the two groups; by adopting values and mores of the dominant group; by becoming bilingual.[20]

Despite the attractions of respecting boundaries maintained by outside and inside forces, the Deaf-World does encounter mainstream ethnicity, both close at hand and at some remove. In those encounters Deaf culture reveals both resilience in the face of an engulfing majority and also adaptiveness in reshaping hearing practices.[21] In close-at-hand encounters with hearing people—for example, in their family and among their schoolmates—Deaf people promote communication by signing, writing, and mime. They make arrangements for interpreters (and educate the interpreters in the first place) for mainstream ethnic events such as church services. When Deaf people enter professions serving the Deaf, such as teaching, social work, or counseling, or again various businesses, Deaf clients have fuller access to those services. In the academic world, Deaf scholars have conducted ethnically aware research and they have also disseminated the fruits of that research to Deaf and hearing people. As we have seen, such encounters with mainstream ethnicity should respect the code of conduct with hearing people. The Deaf person is expected to use a "contact" variety of ASL that incorporates elements of English grammar. When signing with Deaf people, however, the Deaf person should use ASL. Furthermore, the Deaf person should be cautious about revealing too much of ASL and Deaf culture. The Deaf-World rejects so-called oralists, who try to pass as hearing, insist on using spoken language, associate primarily with hearing people, and espouse hearing values.[22] In that rejection the Deaf-World reinforces its boundary with mainstream ethnicity. Deaf people commonly wish to conduct their own affairs and are wary of hearing benevolence. Any claim of sameness, destabilizing the boundary, "is threatening to the Deaf self because most Deaf people are still struggling with, or can remember what it was like, to be totally dominated and defined by others."[23] Consequently Deaf people may be aloof in such encounters or even hostile. For many, that caution with respect to hearing people extends to Codas (Children of deaf adults).[24] In the words of Simon Carmel_D, an anthropologist who conducted an ethnographic study of the Deaf-World, "Deaf people look at hearing people as 'usurpers' of power once they enter the Deaf-World and usually do not trust or support their efforts in this world."[25] Aloofness is reflected in the many Deaf-only activities listed in the box. In a few cases—notably sign language teaching and Deaf publishing—the primary audience is not Deaf. However, only Deaf people have authenticity in matters concerning their language and culture, so other things equal they prefer Deaf to hearing people in those roles. Hearing people who interact with the Deaf, such as special educators and coworkers, make their own contribution to maintaining boundaries through little or no ASL fluency, and through ignorance of Deaf culture, history, and the power imbalance.

Deaf people also participate in the wider society but there are limitations because lack of a shared language is a great barrier. Often the Deaf person's relations with hearing parents, siblings, and relatives, as well as people unrelated to the Deaf-World, must be characterized as remote. Many of these contacts are brief, and writing or gesture suffices, as in grocery shopping. Such "arm's length" interactions with hearing people repeatedly remind Deaf individuals of their daily exclusion from full participation in mainstream life.[26] Some Deaf people may use spoken language in these encounters. For many decades, Deaf people used teletypewriters for the Deaf (TTY) for some of these contacts, but that required special equipment, some knowledge of written English, and a relay operator to contact business and other offices that commonly did not have TTYs. In more critical areas, such as medical and legal services, appointments are booked with interpreters. Deaf people can telecommunicate with hearing and Deaf people using email, instant messaging, cell phone texting, blogs, vlogs, and, if both parties know

ASL, videophones and webcam.[27] The Deaf-World does engage in "outreach" to inform hearing people about its culture and language. In addition to classes for this purpose there are autobiographies, histories, political essays, poetry, folk tales, celebrations, art, plays, and TV productions and more, most available from Deaf publishing houses. However, relatively few Deaf people engage in this outreach with relatively few hearing people.

MULTIETHNICITY

The Amish and the Hassidim are two examples of ethnic groups with multiple ethnicities. According to Fishman, for a group to possess two sets of ethnic identities, the group must engage in the distinctive language and behavior required in each of the two ethnic contexts, with little overlap.[28] The multiethnic group controls the schools where their children are taught English so that they can engage in the other culture within carefully prescribed limits. The offspring of interethnic marriage may also be multiethnic.[29]

Deaf people are commonly both multilingual and multicultural. Some ASL signers have an excellent command of English, some may use the telephone, and most switch between their languages and between cultural behaviors as appropriate. For example, a Deaf Mexican-American might be multilingual in ASL, Mexican Sign Language, Spanish, and English. A description of the French bicultural Deaf-World by a French ethnologist also applies well to the American Deaf-World. French Deaf people meeting hearing people promptly switch to behavior governed by hearing norms, as follows. They shake the hearing person's hand, instead of greeting them with a sign, a hug, or the ceremony of introductions. They introduce themselves simply, and do not refer to their life history (parents, schooling, and the like) as they would with another Deaf person. They do not touch their hearing interlocutor, for example, to get his or her attention, as they would when seeking to address a Deaf person. They keep a greater physical distance between themselves and a hearing interlocutor than they would with a Deaf one. They do not gaze at length on their interlocutor's face as they would if he or she were Deaf, and, when leaving, they shorten their farewells.[30]

The Deaf-World of ASL signers takes on attributes of the larger and encircling majority-language world; most Deaf people come from exclusively oral-language homes, attend school with oral-language schoolmates, communicate with oral-language colleagues, and are bombarded as we all are with messages about mainstream American culture. As with biculturalism, so with bilingualism: ASL signers are commonly sign-language dominant but most have some command of English (or other oral language). Bilingualism expert François Grosjean points out some similarities between spoken-language bilinguals and ASL bilinguals. In the first place, individuals in both groups vary greatly in their command of their two (or more) languages. Further, some Deaf bilinguals, like their spoken-language counterparts, do not think they are bilingual, either because they are not aware that sign language is a separate language, unrelated to the majority language, or because they have not mastered the oral language. Nevertheless, these bilinguals are able to switch language repertories to talk with different people about different topics, as appropriate.

The larger public often misconstrues the attachment of ethnic groups to their minority language, be it spoken or signed. Critics insist needlessly that the ethnic group should master the majority language, as if the group wanted their children to speak only their minority language. On the contrary, the leaders of ethnic groups generally advocate multiethnicity and its attendant ability to move easily between two or more repertories, both linguistically and culturally. The disagreement is not about goals but about means—the role of the minority language in achieving multiethnicity.

SUMMARY

We undertook to compare ethnic groups and ASL signers with respect to language, bonding to one's own kind, culture, social institutions, the arts, history, territory, kinship, socialization, and boundary maintenance. The language of an ethnic group plays many roles: it is the vehicle for transmission of cultural patrimony through the generations; it expresses traditions, rituals, norms, and values; it is a symbol of ethnicity and a means of social interaction. These are indeed also the roles fulfilled by ASL. Deaf people tend to feel strong and protective ownership of their language. There is no higher priority for the Deaf-World than the flourishing of its language, the more so as it has been the target of repressive language policy over many years, including efforts at outright replacement. This is the fate of many ethnic minority languages, as we have seen.

A deep feeling of belonging characterizes many ethnic groups and that is surely a property of the Deaf-World. After all, many of its members found in the Deaf-World surrogate parents, easy communication, access to information, and a positive identity. The solidarity of Deaf-World members is expressed in many ways; among the most striking are the stress it places on collective action and on marriage partners chosen from the Deaf-World.

The culture of ethnic groups includes rules for behavior based on distinctive values, starting with a high value placed on ethnic membership itself. This is true of the Deaf-World, whose central values include being Deaf and allegiance to the group. The values of ethnic groups underlie their rules of behavior in such matters as appropriate use of language and discourse, conferring names and introducing people, decision making, and pooling of resources. We found each of these behavioral repertories in the Deaf-World.

Ethnic groups have social institutions and we found many of those in examining the Deaf-World, including a network of schools, Deaf clubs, churches, athletic organizations, publishing houses and theater groups, as well as associations focused on profession, leisure, politics, and socializing.

The arts enrich the lives of ethnic groups, bind their members, and express ethnic values and knowledge. The Deaf-World has a rich literary tradition including such forms as legends and humor. There are also theater arts, and plastic arts that recount the Deaf experience.

History and ethnicity are intimately bound up in ethnic groups. The Deaf-World has a rich history that is recounted in many forms—books, films, theater, narratives, and so on. As with ethnic groups, much of that history concerns oppression and it has a familiar rhetorical structure. In the beginning, we were dispersed and isolated; but then our people gathered and built our institutions; there was a Golden Age in which we flourished, followed by the dark ages of oppression; but we rose up victorious and recovered our lost values and prestige.

Ethnic kinship practices vary widely from one ethnic group to the next. In some, kinship is based on a belief in shared ancestry. In others, kinship includes persons who clearly have no genealogical connection but only a physical or cultural resemblance, if that. What is common to various kinship practices is the diffuse enduring solidarity that each individual in the ethnic group owes to the others. Kinship in the Deaf-World is based on physical and cultural resemblance and is characterized by diffuse enduring solidarity. That is true both of members who are hereditarily Deaf and those who are not. In addition, hereditarily Deaf people, who constitute the majority of the Deaf-World, have shared ancestry as Parts II–IV illustrate with some lineages of founding Deaf families.

Socialization of ethnic children may be conducted by other than their biological parents and this, too, is a property of Deaf-World ethnicity. What may be peculiar to the Deaf-World is the commonplace delayed start of socialization, including delayed language acquisition, when parents are unable to inculcate Deaf values and language in their Deaf children.

Ethnic groups frequently have a code of conduct governing encounters with other ethnic groups. Many characteristics of the Deaf-World and of the enveloping dominant ethnicity serve to maintain the boundaries between them. To single out a few issues that sustain boundaries, there are the language barrier, radically different understandings of what it means to be a Deaf person, stigma, employment discrimination, the tendency of hearing people to take charge of Deaf affairs, endogamous marriage, the Deaf code of conduct with hearing people, and the propensity of Deaf people to look to the Deaf-World to meet many of their needs.

Finally we spoke of multilingualism and multiculturalism, properties of most ethnic groups. Deaf people are indeed multilingual and multicultural. Virtually all command at least two languages and cultures and many several more.

We conclude that the Deaf-World in the U.S. is aptly included among the nation's ethnic groups. This conclusion is based on self-ascription, bonding language and culture, societal institutions, boundary maintenance, kinship, and shared physical characteristics.[31]

*

We wish to acknowledge our presumption in offering to ASL signers a conception of their minority status and one that may seem far-fetched at that, since it reflects a paradigm change in our understanding of Deaf people. It is only in recent decades that Deaf people in the United States have come to see themselves as the possessors of a distinct natural language and culture.[32] The reader may well ask why we are introducing for discussion a different, although related, conceptualization. In part our answer is that we believe in "getting it right"—that appropriate conceptualizations will help Deaf people and their hearing allies to achieve their goals. Was that not the case when ASL was shown to be a natural language? "Ethnicity" is not a rhetorical flourish, any more than "natural language" is. An ethnic group by any other name—for example, "linguistic and cultural minority"—remains an ethnic group.

We live in a pluralistic society, one formed by many ethnic groups, so if it is suitable to include ASL signers in that classification, they stand to gain by traditions and laws protecting ethnic groups and ensuring that they and their languages and cultures flourish. Of course, we are not creating an ethnic group where there was not one, nor would we be able to do so; we are merely calling attention to it. If our Deaf colleagues find merit in construing the Deaf-World as an ethnic group, and decide to make that information more widely accessible to Deaf people (as they did with the concept of "Deaf culture"), we will be very pleased. However, we certainly do not claim to speak for the Deaf. Deaf writers tell about the Deaf-World in numerous articles, books and other media, many cited in the text and endnotes of this essay.

"Mainstream ethnicity," as we have called it, was in the beginning White Anglo-Saxon Protestant ethnicity.[33] WASP settlers, just as a matter of course, imprinted their ethnicity on America's social institutions, including their English language, cultural rules and values, and religion. Thus, the first Deaf settlers to gather and affirm their Deaf consciousness, the founders of the American Deaf-World, were, with some exceptions, WASPs. In Parts II through IV, we report on the ancestors and descendants of these founders of the American Deaf-World.

First, however, Chapter 3 addresses some opposing arguments, as well as questions and concerns that the reader may have about our conclusion that the Deaf-World is an ethnic group.

3

Yes, But

Having just concluded that *ethnic group* is an apt conceptualization for the linguistic minority of ASL signers, we take on the responsibility of considering countervailing arguments (boldface below) and evaluating each in turn.

On Assimilation

You have said nothing about hearing loss. Not hearing explains a lot about the Deaf-World. For example, it explains why Deaf people commonly do not learn spoken English and become assimilated.[1] **Doesn't that make them different from ethnic groups?**

Some ASL signers can and occasionally do speak English aloud, yet few of them are assimilated by the dominant ethnicity. One obvious reason is that Deaf bodies are suited to visual communication, not oral. But there are other reasons: Deaf ethnics have great group loyalty and surveys indicate they are generally happy with the way they are. Moreover, assimilation often involves marrying out of the minority ethnicity but Deaf people usually marry other Deaf people.

Granted that the descendants of many American immigrants have assimilated—but many have not. Ethnicity has proven more enduring in the United States and elsewhere than many scholars anticipated. Resistance to assimilation is not unique to the Deaf-World. We cited earlier the Amish and Gypsies.[2] We may add the Mennonites, Chinese residents of older Chinatowns, Native American tribal groups, the Chinese diaspora in Southeast Asia, the Old Believer diaspora in North and South America. Other ethnic groups, such as those in the Swat Valley of northern Pakistan, co-exist in a symbiotic relationship without significant assimilation.[3] So the Deaf-World may be among those ethnic groups whose culture and circumstances disfavor assimilation.

If the Deaf-World is limited in assimilation, does that make it less of an ethnic group or more of one? Perhaps more of one as it possesses such a robust boundary with the dominant ethnicity. In any case, all ethnic groups have significant features that differ one to the next. Gypsies (Romas) are a diaspora group and stigmatized; Greek and Chinese ethnic groups in Africa resist assimilation; Chinese-Americans are increasingly marrying outside their ethnic group but this is rare for ASL signers.[4] Many Native American languages are dying out or have disappeared; this is not true of ASL which is unlikely ever to die out. So it is not enough to challenge Deaf-World ethnicity based on differences from other ethnic groups. You have to say why such differences are incompatible with viewing the Deaf-World as an ethnic group, based on its physical traits, language, culture, and boundary maintenance. These differences can provide important insights into the nature of ethnicity. In this first stage we have examined the Deaf-World through the lens of ethnicity but in a later phase scholars must look at ethnicity through the lens of the Deaf-World: What does social science have to learn from the unique properties of Deaf ethnicity such as its base in vision?

On Deaf Bodies

Okay, let's say that limited assimilation to mainstream ethnicity is not unique to the Deaf-World. Still, all the members of this group cannot hear, doesn't that make them less of an ethnic group?

Many ethnicities have distinguishing physical traits; you need only look around you. But to get some perspective on this issue, let's go farther afield. Consider the case of the Pygmies of Central Africa whose ethnicity incorporates a distinct physical makeup—as does that of Deaf people and other ethnic groups. The Pygmies' stature, some four-and-a-half feet on average, allows them modest caloric requirements, easy and rapid passage through dense jungle in search of game, and construction of small huts that can be rapidly disassembled and reassembled for self-defense and hunting. Wild game is captured with bows and arrows and hunting nets. A half-dozen families in a forest camp link their individual hunting nets end to end and the women and children drive the game into the nets; the take is shared. Law enforcement, worship, marriage, social events, art, and architecture are all communal, which reflects the collaborative hunt, which reflects in turn the pygmy's physical makeup and environment. The Bantu villagers, farming at the edge of the forest, have contempt for the hunter-gatherer Pygmies because of their "puny" size, and the Pygmies in turn have contempt for the villagers who are "clumsy as elephants" and "do not know how to walk" in the forest, for they are much too tall to move swiftly and silently.[5] Each group considers the other handicapped by the physical size of its members. Each fails to appreciate how physical makeup, culture, and environment are intertwined.

Physical difference is part of ethnicity and not just incidental to it. You cannot say that Pygmy culture could be any other culture, that it is purely socially constructed. The physical facts underpin Pygmy ethnicity just as they underpin Deaf ethnicity. It is the correlation of physical makeup and ethnicity that allows us to recognize a newborn Pygmy as a Pygmy and a newborn Deaf child as ethnically Deaf; in both cases, "The human body itself is viewed as an expression of ethnicity."[6]

How can a newborn Deaf child be ethnically Deaf before he or she knows sign language and Deaf culture?[7]

How are young members of ethnic groups identified? In Western cultures, at least, we see the newborn as launched on a trajectory that, depending on the child's makeup and environment, will normally lead him or her to master a particular language and culture natively. It is this potentiality in the newborn black or Native American child, for example, that leads us to say that the newborn child *is* black or Native American (not *will be*)—although the child has not yet acquired the language and culture that go with that ethnic attribution. In saying that this newborn is African American, for example, we do not need to ask about the parents; it's the *child's* physical makeup that determines his or her ethnic attribution. The parents' physical makeup and their ethnicity usually agree with the child's but that does not itself decide the child's ethnic assignment. Even with Caucasian adoptive parents or a white surrogate mother, the child with African-American constitution would be called black or African American.

Some years ago, the National Association of Black Social Workers came out formally against programs of transracial adoption of black children on the grounds that the children were being systematically deprived of their black heritage, and black culture was being deprived of its new members, and that is ethnocide—the systematic extinction of an ethnic minority's freedom to pursue its way of life. Many of those adopted black children were too young to have already learned black dialect and culture yet it was clear to everyone that these were ethnically black children, that their life trajectories would normally lead them to black culture and dialect.[8] Otherwise, why protest their adoption by whites? On the same principle, Native-Americans have protested transracial adoption of young Native-American children, perceiving them as members of their ethnic group before the children had learned tribal languages and customs.[9]

So the Deaf child of hearing parents, like the Deaf child of Deaf parents, is ethnically Deaf right from birth?

Yes, or from the moment that the Deaf child has the potential to thrive in an ASL environment. Deaf adults say that such a child "has Deaf eyes." No doubt they refer to the Deaf child's characteristic visual scanning of the environment. A little later in life, these children will look Deaf also because they communicate manually, use codified facial gestures, respond readily to visual events and not auditory ones, and so on.

Not all ethnicities have telltale physical traits.

True, but the Deaf do. Just as the physical difference of the Pygmies goes hand in hand with their ethnicity, so the child who is born Deaf or who early becomes Deaf is a member of the Deaf-World, and that child's life trajectory will normally assure that he or she acquires a sign language and Deaf ethnicity. The Deaf child can be deprived of the opportunity to acculturate to the Deaf-World, as black or Native-American children can be deprived of the opportunity to acculturate to their ethnicities. However, the child's potential for acculturation to that unmarked world, rooted in his or her physical difference, remains, so we consider the child with that difference Deaf, black, or Native American right from the start. That explains why members of those ethnicities feel a strong emotional investment in the welfare of young children physically like themselves and why they identify and empathize with them, even when they are not related to them.

What about those who become Deaf in childhood? They started out in some hearing culture, so what are they—bicultural?

Yes, these are the children that are "adopted" into the Deaf-World, on the basis of physical features and language that they share with all the rest. As soon as the language of Deaf ethnicity is what the children require for communication, they are ethnically Deaf. Those children will have two ethnicities at least. A college student who had become Deaf when she was three explained: "I need the hearing world for it is the world in which I was born, but I need the Deaf-World because it is the world that gives my life meaning."[10]

What about hearing spouses and children of Deaf adults? Are they Deaf? Are Codas ethnically Deaf?

Persons at the margins of our fundamental categories usually intrigue us, as they should for they cast light on the categories themselves. In one movie scenario that tests such categories, Indians attack a group of settlers and ride off with an Anglo baby; she is raised among the Indians and learns their language, culture, and values.[11] Is she ethnically Native American or Anglo? Physically she is Anglo but culturally she is Indian. She might be seen as almost Indian, but not Indian plain and simple, no matter how fluent she may be in their language. Her normal Anglo ethnic trajectory had been deflected but her ethnic identity was still Anglo.

Codas, with their native command of both ASL and English and their knowledge of both cultures, are viewed as virtually Deaf, but not Deaf plain and simple. That, at least, is the answer given by numerous Deaf people, although not all, and by many Codas themselves. We are told that Codas do not have the right physical makeup— and that is instructive, confirming that physical makeup is involved in identifying ethnic membership. In addition to lacking the right physical makeup for ethnic membership, Codas have different language and school experiences from Deaf people and they often marry hearing people; Codas march to a different drummer. "The history of Codas suggests they see themselves as part of the Hearing world not the

Deaf-World," writes one Coda scholar.[12] And Tom Humphries[D], expressing the view of other Deaf leaders, writes: "Hearing children of Deaf parents have blood ties to Deaf people, as well as knowledge of the customs and language of the group. However, in matters that really count, they are not considered Deaf people."[13]

On Socialization

Deaf children of hearing parents are in large part socialized by Deaf people and not their parents. In ethnic groups, though, parents and children have the same ethnicity and the parents do the socializing. So doesn't that difference set Deaf ethnicity apart?[14]

As we have seen, some ethnic groups adopt many foster children and socialize them. Among the Iñupiat in Alaska, most adults have been adopted or have lived in a household where children have been adopted; 40 percent of all children are either adopted in or adopted out.[15] In effect, the Deaf-World does likewise, socializing all the Deaf children whose parents cannot play that role. At the same time, the Deaf child receives a measure of socialization into the hearing world from several sources: from Deaf people, who are after all multiethnic; from hearing siblings, parents, and other relatives; and from formal education. The bottom line in socialization is that the Deaf-World assures transmission of its ethnicity from generation to generation. What may well be unique about Deaf-World ethnicity is not foster socialization but the delay in that socialization that often occurs.

On Other Challenges to Deaf Ethnicity

There is more to challenge in Deaf ethnicity. Start with this: compared to other ethnic groups, the Deaf-World is too rarely autonomous and in control of its own institutions.[16]

We gave earlier a list of social institutions conducted by the Deaf-World primarily for its members, institutions such as Deaf-run schools, churches, places of business, and Deaf athletic and political organizations. But autonomy has its limits; few ethnic minorities in the United States (and many other countries) can be said to "control" their own primary institutions. Take the Francophone ethnic group in the United States, for example. More than 1.5 million Americans speak French at home, most of them in New England. Typically, they celebrate their ethnic identity and traditions but their children attend mainstream schools and places of worship and work in mainstream businesses and there is no central authority structure.

Okay, limited autonomy is not unique to the Deaf-World but here is a feature that is unique—Deaf ethnicity is only one generation "thick."[17] **It is not intergenerational and historically deep, as are other ethnic groups.**

We disagree. Let's go back to the fact that a majority of ethnically Deaf people are hereditarily Deaf. In Parts II through IV we trace numerous Deaf people to their seventeenth-century ancestors who settled in New England. Many of those progenitors came from the English county of Kent. For countless Americans who are hereditarily Deaf today, there is evidence that the trait has been passed down to them through the generations for more than 400 years. The physical component of Deaf ethnicity can be found in every generation of their ancestry, sometimes expressed—those ancestors are visual people, sometimes underlying—those ancestors are hearing people, carriers of the Deaf trait. Granted, it may seem odd to count carriers as evidence of intergenerational transmission, yet their role in transmitting Deaf ethnicity is indisputable.

Deaf language and culture are also passed down through the generations. Deaf children with Deaf parents receive that cultural heritage from their parents. Deaf children with hearing parents receive Deaf heritage from their peers and Deaf adult role models. But who transmits the heritage is less important than that it be transmitted. If the Deaf trait is expressed in the Deaf child but not in his or her parents, there is nonetheless a means for socializing that child to the Deaf-World, where a sense of common history, language, and culture unites successive generations.

Where in Deaf ethnicity are such ethnic properties as traditional clothing, distinctive cuisine, marriage and burial rites, and an ethnic homeland?[18]

In many ethnic groups today, distinctive dress, cuisine, and rituals are absent or greatly diminished, overwhelmed by those of mainstream ethnicity. We have cited some Deaf-World rituals earlier, but there is no reason to expect ASL signers to have developed an exotic cuisine or ethnic clothing, the more so as they do not live gathered together in any specific region or locale and they grow up in hearing homes where they have little opportunity to develop distinctive dress and cuisine. Put it down as a difference if you will, but is it criterial? We would argue that these ethnic properties are not prerequisites for identifying an ethnic group. What features are prerequisite? A sense of belonging, a distinctive culture, and ethnic boundaries.

Belief in a common ethnic homeland is linked to another, related belief, namely that members share an ancestry; both beliefs should be understood as cultural symbols and both are changeable. For example, many immigrants to the United States saw their significant territory as their village; they did not embrace a European nation as their homeland until after living in the United States. The Deaf-World, comprised of ASL signers, has its homeland in North America, as do Native Americans. Some American ethnic groups have no single associated homeland—such as Jewish Americans and Hispanic Americans.

On Scholarly Recognition

If there is such an excellent fit between the Deaf-World and ethnicity, why wasn't that accepted long ago?

Some scholars did advance the concept of Deaf ethnicity as many as fifty years ago (see the Introduction), but many have been misled, it seems, by ethnocentrism. For centuries, speakers of signed languages in the Western world were not considered to be using a natural language, in part because the modality was unfamiliar—using hands and eyes instead of tongues and ears—and in part because sign-language structure was so unfamiliar, so unlike the grammars of Romance and Germanic languages (of which English is the fruit). Linguists know that grammars can take many forms, so when hearing and Deaf linguists became interested in the study of ASL, they were open to discovering that ASL is an independent natural language, unrelated to English. Note how they did it: they started with criteria for "natural language," such as evidence for rules of word and sentence formation; they applied those criteria to ASL, and found that it conforms. Then, they passed on the word of their discovery and Deaf people began to talk about it publicly.[19]

In the same vein, due to ethnocentrism, we failed to see how Deaf children who were not hereditarily Deaf could still be considered kin to those who were because we missed the cultural component to kinship found most markedly in other societies; that is, we failed to realize that kinship in ethnic groups need not be based exclusively on procreation.[20] Again, socialization by other than one's parents troubled some scholars because they failed to see that it is one means among others to ensure intergenerational transmission of language and culture, a means to be found in other ethnic groups.[21] Once we recognize that ethnicity takes many forms worldwide, we can see that the Deaf-World, although its ways are unfamiliar, can be characterized as an ethnic group. We started with the criteria for "ethnic group"; we applied them to ASL signers in Chapters 1 and 2, and we found that their culture conforms.

There are further reasons for the delay in recognizing Deaf ethnicity. There was all along a competing construction of Deaf identity among hearing scholars and laymen—namely, disability, which we turn to next. Then, too, those concerned with shared ancestry in ethnic groups asked about heredity in Deaf children generally, rather than about the heredity of ASL signers and they did not recognize hereditary transmission in the Deaf-World when some of a Deaf child's forebears were carriers of Deaf genes but not Deaf themselves.[22]

Finally, since the case for Deaf ethnicity had not been presented fully, these obstacles were enough to leave unchanged the practice of referring to Deaf people as the "Deaf linguistic and cultural minority."

On Disability

Most people think of Deaf people not as members of an ethnic group but as people with a disability. Surely the inability to hear is a disability.

It is widely accepted among scholars that disability categories are socially constructed; in other words, disabilities arise when a society fails to accommodate its physical and social environment to the range of human variation that it contains. Despite all the evidence that disabilities vary from one culture to the next and, within a culture, from one era to the next,[23] some writers, apparently unaware of disability studies and medical anthropology, simply adopt the naive materialist view when it comes to disability and hearing.[24] An ethicist writes: "I maintain that the inability to hear is a deficit, a disability, a lack of perfect health."[25] States one ear surgeon: "Almost by definition deaf persons . . . have a disability."[26] And another states that Deaf people must have a disability for "deafness is the loss of one of the most important adaptations . . . to improve survival."[27] The effort to decide disability status outside of culture with speculations about survival value is not likely to be helpful and is too close for comfort to eugenic theories.[28] The fact that a biological function such as hearing is typical of our species today may reflect, more than any present survival value, the prehistoric vicissitudes of evolution.

So it's naive to think that Deaf people have a disability?

In Deaf cultures being Deaf is seen as normal human variation, while in hearing cultures it is seen as a disability.[29] There is no point in asking who is right. Is it better to have three gods and one wife or one god and three wives?[30] We suspect that all ethnic groups find in their cultures a positive value assigned to their unique physical traits. If a group of Pygmies were to visit the United States, would their entire ethnic group be considered disabled by short stature? No, in their eyes and in ours, they would be seen as short compared to us but normal for their ethnic group, not disabled. Likewise for Deaf ethnics; most are gifted in vision and limited in hearing, but normal for their ethnic group, not disabled.

It is not necessary to add disability to Deaf ethnicity in order explain, for example, why the Deaf speak a visual language. Deaf people are "The People of the Eye"—that given is a foundation of their ethnicity. In societies where signed language use is widespread because of a substantial Deaf population—on Martha's Vineyard and Bali for example— being Deaf was apparently seen as a trait, not a disability.[31] Deaf scholars nowadays such as MJ Bienvenu$_D$, Tom Humphries$_D$, and Katherine Jankowski$_D$ in the United States and Paddy Ladd$_D$ in Britain are among those who are on record as rejecting the disability construction of ethnically Deaf people.[32] The National Association of the Deaf portrays accurately the view of Deaf-World members that "there is nothing wrong with them, and that their culture, language, and social institutions are just as fulfilling as the ones experienced by the mainstream society."[33] Urban and rural Deaf interviewees in six countries of the European Community have called for recognition of Deaf people as a linguistic minority rather than as a disabled group.[34] The World Games for the Deaf (now "Deaflympics") has, for much of its history, declined incentives to join the Paralympics. For most Deaf ethnics, as Tom Humphries[D] so aptly put it, the idea that all Deaf people are deficient "simply does not compute."[35] Humphries[D] explains:

> "Disabled" is not a label or self-concept that has historically belonged to Deaf people. "Disabled" is a way of representing yourself, and it implies goals that are unfamiliar to Deaf people. Deaf people's enduring concerns have been these: finding each other and staying together, preserving their language, and maintaining lines of transmittal of their culture. These are not the goals of disabled people. Deaf people do know, however, the benefits of this label and make choices about alignment with these people politically.[36]

Perhaps the Deaf deny they have a disability to avoid stigma.[37]

There are numerous reasons, without invoking avoidance of stigma, to expect Deaf people to reject the idea that they all have a disability. The key to understanding why "disabled" is a poor fit to "Deaf" is found in the distinctive language and culture of ASL signers who are, in this respect, unlike any group of disabled people. Deaf people are aware that when they are together, or with hearing people who know ASL, there is no impediment but when they are with other ethnic groups, the impediment is based on language. Language changes everything. It was the catalyst that created an ethnic group out of a visual people and that created a culture with myths, memories, and symbols—a culture that values its ethnic identity. During the civil rights era in America, when Deaf people came to see that they speak a natural language, they also came to see their identity in a different light, one that exposed self-derogatory talk about ASL "gestures" and Deaf "afflictions" and "impairments"—talk that had been, in any case, borrowed from hearing people or addressed to them. Many in the Deaf-World say they are content to be Deaf despite the burdens of minority status, and they welcome having Deaf children.[38] All ethnic groups want to see their group perpetuated. In contrast, many disability leaders say that, although they want their physical difference valued as a part of who they are, they welcome measures that attenuate or remove their disability and reduce the numbers of disabled children.[39]

At least ethnic Deaf people could support the disability movement without actually including themselves.

Yes, and that happens. However, the Deaf were not deeply involved with disabled people in lobbying for the passage of the Americans with Disabilities Act, and disabled people were not deeply involved in the Deaf event of the century in the United States, the revolution known as Deaf President Now.[40] The two groups, disabled and Deaf, have different priorities. People differ widely within each group, but here, much compressed, are the basics: Whereas the disability rights movement seeks independence for people with disabilities, Deaf people cherish interdependence with other Deaf people. Whereas the disability rights movement seeks total integration into society at large whenever possible, Deaf ethnics cherish their unique identity and seek integration that honors their distinct language and culture; they find integration of Deaf children into hearing schools and classes an anathema. Whereas disabled people seek better medical care and rehabilitation services, greater physical access, and personal assistance services (help with personal hygiene, dressing, and eating), Deaf people's priorities concern language acceptance, interpreters, and a spectrum of educational settings including residential schools.[41]

Some disability advocates maintain that the gap between Deaf and disabled is narrowing as, in recent years, people with disabilities have to a degree forged a group identity and a disability culture–"artifacts, beliefs and expressions"—to describe their life experiences.[42] However, disabled people are surely not an ethnic group – where are the language, the sense of belonging, the distinctive culture, and ethnic boundaries? Moreover, transmitting the fruits of shared experience is not the same as the transmission of language, history, and culture across the generations by ethnic groups such as African Americans, Native Americans, and Deaf Americans. Other disability experts do recognize the tension between understanding Deaf people as an ethnic group and understanding them in terms of disability.[43]

Bear in mind that the people with disabilities, whom Deaf ethnics are asked to join in a common category are, for the most part, hearing people of various ethnicities, especially the dominant one. These are just the people who are on the other side of the ethnic boundary from the Deaf-World. It is not straightforward for Deaf people to belong both to their own ethnic group (us) and at the same time to a disabled hearing group with mainstream ethnicity (them).[44]

If the Deaf-World's ties to the disability community are slight, its ties to other ethnic groups are even slimmer. What aid can Deaf people expect from, say, black Americans, in their struggle for their human rights?

The Deaf-World has received a lot from black Americans. In the first place, black Deaf Americans are in its ranks and leadership, as are other multiethnic Deaf people. Moreover, it was black Americans who launched the civil rights era that so greatly re-empowered Deaf Americans. Black Americans, hearing and Deaf, were involved in the Deaf President Now movement. But hearing ethnic groups could not appreciate what they have in common with the Deaf-World—a distinctive language, a history of struggle, pride in an under esteemed heritage, and multiethnic Deaf members—as long as those commonalities were masked by presenting Deaf people as disabled. Interethnic alliances are difficult to forge but when the ethnic basis of the Deaf-World is understood, Deaf leaders can expect more from other ethnicities. After all, Deaf children need what the children of other ethnic groups need: parents who take joy in their arrival and who model language for their children from the outset; peers to promote socialization; teachers who are not only competent in their specializations and skillful in their practices, but also fluent in the children's best language, knowledgeable about their culture, and adept as role models.

If Deaf ethnics insist that they are not disabled, why do they accept the perquisites of disability, such as disability payments, interpreter services, and the like?

That is indeed the Deaf dilemma: To exercise some important rights as members of society at the expense of being mischaracterized by that society and government, or to refuse some of those rights in the hope of gradually undermining that misconstruction and gaining rights that are truly appropriate and broader. On the one hand, Deaf people have an obligation to accept provisions that enhance their full participation in our society—that is an obligation but also a human right.

On the other hand, the price of compliance with alien bureaucratic categories is high. Because of the disability misrepresentation, Deaf people are more vulnerable to measures aimed at reducing Deaf births, to surgery where the risks and costs outweigh the benefits, to delayed language acquisition, to monolingual education in an oral language, to social isolation in the local school, and to marginalization when lacking both the dominant ethnicity of their parents and the minority ethnicity of their Deaf peers.[45] Because of the disability misrepresentation, the deinstitutionalization movement so precious to disability advocates has swept Deaf children into the local public schools and into a communication vacuum. The schools for the Deaf, whatever the drawbacks of boarding schools, were nevertheless a place of ethnic awakening, language development, education, and formation of positive identity. Because of the disability misrepresentation, Deaf ethnics have not sought collaboration with other ethnic groups in efforts, for example, to promote bilingual education. Because of the disability misrepresentation, ethnically Deaf Americans enjoy neither the protections in law for ethnic minorities, nor the democratic traditions that would give them greater control over the destiny of their own ethnic group.[46] Many Deaf citizens seek a middle ground; they wish to retain their rights under the disability umbrella while agitating for reforms based on their ethnicity, reforms such as the promotion of their human rights and of their sign language.[47] Clearly, the reconceptualization of Deaf people as an ethnic group must not deprive them of provisions for their full participation in society; those provisions will be more effective if matched to Deaf people's true status and needs.

On Deaf Diversity and American Pluralism

So many different categories of people called *deaf*! Those born Deaf, those who early became Deaf, those who were deafened as adults; those with Deaf parents and those with hearing parents; those who acquired ASL from birth on, others when they entered school, still others in their teens; those who attended schools where their language was used, others where it was not; those with disabilities and those with multiple ethnicities. Wouldn't it be better just to sweep all these divisive categories away and simply say that anyone who doesn't hear well enough to communicate orally is deaf?[48] Period.

The all-embracing disability category you just defined—doesn't hear well enough to communicate orally– sounds appealing but there are few significant issues all the members could agree on. More often we must recognize that the members of the different categories see themselves differently and have different needs and different agendas. Moreover, the Deaf-World has an ethnicity that is so strikingly unlike the mainstream, one founded on the positive value of being Deaf, that it serves few purposes to merge it with self-identified disability groups.

If you could in principle sweep away socially divisive categories, they would promptly come back. It is true that where there are categories there are often fuzzy boundaries and marginal cases. But we cannot do away with "us" and "them." Ethnocentrism is human nature; our identities are bound up with the fate of the significant groups to which we belong. Moreover, categories help us to make sense of the world around us; they give it a degree of predictability; they speed mental processing and facilitate memory. The danger of category-based responses such as stereotypes is to rely on them even when better information is available. Within Deaf ethnicity, some of the cross-cutting categories have received study, such as black and Deaf,[49] and others await it.

Why do we need the category of Deaf ethnicity? Wasn't "linguistic and cultural minority" sufficient?

There are so many linguistic and cultural parallels between the Deaf-World and ethnic groups, one must ask what the reason is for denying that classification to the Deaf. We have examined such parallels as self-ascription, endogamous marriage, resistance to assimilation, Deaf institutions, boundary maintenance, the use of different sign-language varieties with in-group and out-group members, Deaf acclaim of the positive value of being Deaf despite stigmatized identity, Deaf pleasure at the birth of a Deaf child, Deaf customs such as group decision making, indirect reciprocity, ritualized naming practices and introductions; the sense of commitment and obligation toward former and future generations; the desire to maintain and protect Deaf linguistic, symbolic, and cultural heritage. You can call the ethnic group by another name, such as a "linguistic and cultural minority," but where do we find such minorities that are not also ethnic groups? Moreover, if being a member of the Deaf-World is only a matter of language and culture why are the Deaf "The People of the Eye" and why do the Deaf have a sign language rather than an oral one?

Ethnic Hispanics, ethnic blacks, ethnic Deaf—the way you talk about them and their "physical correlates" seems close to racism.

We disagree. Sex roles are not the same as sexism, religious beliefs not the same as bigotry, ethnicity not the same as racism.[50] True, ethnicity, like race, often involves ancestry, endogamous marriage, and biological differences. But race is a category imposed by outsiders seeking dominance; it is often the fruit of imperialism, accompanied by exploitation based on claims about superior and inferior races. And racial classifications are utterly discredited scientifically. Ethnicity, on the contrary, is about insiders who voluntarily find identity and strength in their group, an antidote to racism.[51] Racism derogates, ethnicity elevates.

Still, I think America needs to overcome all this fractionation if we are to succeed as a nation.

Polyethnic states are frequently dominated by a single ethnic group that seeks to incorporate smaller and weaker ethnic groups.[52] Is that your agenda? When you imagine a homogeneous America with only one ethnicity, one language, one culture, is it by chance your own? In any case, it is not going to happen. Forty-seven million Americans—about one in five adults—speak a language at home other than English according to the 2000 census, and the numbers are growing.[53] Immigration will continue to support ethnic identity. Even assimilated Americans have been turning to their ethnic roots.[54] With the development of ever more sophisticated tools for information processing, ethnic groups are better able to mobilize and to make their case to one another and the general public. This has been especially true of Deaf ethnicity in America where email, texting, instant messaging, blogs, vlogs, video telephones, and websites have greatly enhanced communication.

An important element in the success of the Deaf President Now movement was the rebel students' use of the media.

> **But should our government be in the business of promoting ethnic differences? In asking for the recognition of Deaf ethnicity, Deaf people are asking just that.**

It is true that ethnicity can be divisive—especially when manipulated by political and religious forces. But ethnicity is a basic human good and a natural right. Ethnicity provides continuity, a basis for collective action, intimate attachment to others, the rewards of culture. It is an antidote to the depersonalizing forces of modernity. There is a body of research showing that preserving a tie to one's own group and culture fosters self esteem, life satisfaction, and well-being generally.[55] As a nation we must encourage our ethnic groups if we are to talk with the rest of the world.[56] Fishman has put it well: "The American dream includes the promise of assimilation, the promise of ethnolinguistic self-maintenance, and the promise of freedom to choose between them."[57]

> **Yet for Deaf people to insist on separateness when it is a hearing world—is that really the right way to go?**

There is a pluralistic vision for America, in which each ethnicity contributes to the nation with some fusing and some intermingling.[58] Fishman, querying activists in three ethnic groups found that they had a strong desire to maintain their ethnicity alongside their Americanism.[59]

According to Deaf scholars, this is what the Deaf-World, too, is seeking—integration with a measure of autonomy. And that is not at all peculiar to the Deaf. Integration with autonomy is characteristic of many ethnic groups who participate both "in intimate networks of familiar ethnie [ethnicity] and the broad open but impersonal ties of citizenship in the state and its public community and the professional world of work."[60] Psychologist John Edwards calls integration with autonomy "modified pluralism"—allowing both participation in mainstream society and maintenance of group cohesion.[61] It is mistaken to think that the route to successful participation is the denial of self. Bahan_D speaks of a "safe harbor" where Deaf people can anchor their connections to one another after traveling on the high seas with the rest of humanity.[62] Historian Joseph Murray_D explains that the Deaf have traditionally expected both to participate in a society not tailored to Deaf norms and to have a separate space of being Deaf; he calls the joint expectation *co-equality*. Humphries_D has expressed it as follows:

> Deaf people have a vision of integration that is different from what hearing people envision for them. Deaf people see grounding in the culture and signed language of the deaf community in which they

live as the most important factor in their lives. Integration comes more easily and more effectively from these roots.[63]

*

In the following sections (Parts II–V) we examine the rise of American Deaf ethnicity from Deaf ancestry in New England. When the full story of American Deaf ethnicity is told, it will include other regions of the United States and other immigrant groups. Although the diffuse enduring solidarity of the Deaf-World can be read as ethnic kinship, as we explained earlier, in the view of many ethnologists shared ancestry is the litmus test for ethnicity. We present evidence of shared ancestry that also describes Deaf lives in early America and throws light on the formation of Deaf clans through Deaf intermarriage. Part II describes two prominent Deaf enclaves, those located in southeastern New Hampshire and on Martha's Vineyard, Massachusetts. A contrast between those two Deaf communities reveals differences in ethnic boundaries that we trace to differences in the genetic transmission of the Deaf trait.

Notes

Part I

1   A. D. Smith, *The Ethnic Origins of Nations* (Oxford: Oxford University Press, 1986).
2   S. Fenton, *Ethnicity, Key Concepts* (Malden, Mass.: Blackwell, 2003). "There are no ethnic minorities without an ethnic majority" (quotation from p. 165). J. R. Edwards, *Language, Society, and Identity* (New York: Blackwell, 1985): "All people are members of some ethnic group but dominant groups rarely define themselves as ethnic" (quotation from p. 6); "Ethnic identity does not mean minority identity—we are all ethnics" (quotation from p. 45); T. H. Eriksen, "Ethnicity, Race, Class and Nation," in J. Hutchinson and A. D. Smith, eds., *Ethnicity* (Oxford: Oxford University Press, 1996): "Majorities and dominant people are no less ethnic than minorities" (quotation from p. 28). J. A. Fishman, *The Rise and Fall of the Ethnic Revival: Perspectives On Language and Ethnicity* (New York: Mouton, 1985): "Perhaps when the mainstream will recognize its ethnicity, it will be less likely to view ethnicity as equivalent to either marginality or provincial uncouthness in others" (quotation from p. 37). M. Verkuyten, *The Social Psychology of Ethnic Identity* (Hove, U.K.; New York: Psychology Press, 2005): "The term ethnicity also applies to the identity of the majority" (p. 76).
3   C. Geertz, *The Interpretation of Cultures* (New York: Basic Books, 1973).
4   A. D. Smith, *The Ethnic Revival* (Cambridge, U.K.: Cambridge University Press, 1981). For a discussion of primordialism, see: Fenton, *Ethnicity*; J. A. Fishman, *Language and Ethnicity in Minority Sociolinguistic Perspective* (Philadelphia: Multilingual Matters, 1989); J. A. Fishman, *Rise and Fall*; Hutchinson and Smith, *Ethnicity*; R. Jenkins, *Rethinking Ethnicity: Arguments and Explorations* (Thousand Oaks, Calif.: Sage, 1997); A. D. Smith, *Ethnic Origins*. There is only partial agreement among scholars on how to define ethnicity, to enumerate its traits, or to assign relative importance to each of them.

Chapter 1

[1] D. Horowitz, "Symbolic Politics and Ethnic Status," in Hutchinson and Smith, *Ethnicity*, 285–291; S. Rutherford, "The Culture of American Deaf People," *Sign Language Studies* 59 (1988): 129–147; "Since language is the prime symbol system to begin with and since it is commonly relied upon . . . to enact and call forth all ethnic activity, the likelihood that it will be recognized and singled out as symbolic of ethnicity is great indeed." J. A Fishman, "Language and Ethnicity," in H. Giles, ed., *Language, ethnicity and intergroup relations*. (New York: Academic Press, 1977); quotation from p. 15.

[2] B. Bahan, "Comment on Turner," *Sign Language Studies* 84 (1994): 241–249. By convention, English glosses on ASL signs are written in capital letters. However, for readability we adopt *Deaf-World* and *Deaf* to refer to the language minority and its members, respectively. For an early published use of the terms *Deaf* and *Deaf-World* see C. Padden, "The Culture of Deaf People," in C. Baker and R. Battison, eds., *Sign Language and the Deaf Community: Essays in Honor of William Stokoe* (Silver Spring, Md.: National Association of the Deaf, 1980).

[3] S. Fischer and H. van der Hulst, "Sign Language Structures," in M. Marschark, ed., *Oxford Handbook of Deaf Studies, Language, and Education*. (Cary, N.C.: Oxford University Press, 2003), 319–331; C. Valli and C. Lucas, *Linguistics of American Sign Language* (2nd ed.) (Washington, D.C.: Gallaudet University Press, 1995).

[4] K. Emmorey and H. Lane, *The Signs of Language Revisited* (Mahwah, N.J.: LEA, 2000); O. Sacks, *Seeing Voices* (Los Angeles, Calif.: Univ. California Press, 1989); H. Poizner, U. Bellugi, and E. S. Klima, "Biological Foundations of Language: Clues From Sign Language," *Annual Reviews of Neuroscience* 13 (1990): 283–307.

[5] B. Bahan, "Memoir Upon the Formation of a Visual Variety of the Human Race," in B. K. Eldredge, D. Stringham, and M. Wilding-Diaz, eds., *Deaf Studies Today* (Orem, Utah: Utah Valley State College, 2005), 17–35.

[6] H. Lane, R. Hoffmeister, and B. Bahan, *A Journey into the Deaf-World* (San Diego, Calif.: DawnSignPress, 1996).

[7] E. Newport, "Maturational Constraints on Language Learning," *Cognitive Science* 14 (1990): 11–28.

[8] MJ. Bienvenu and B. Colonomos, *An Introduction to American Deaf Culture: Social Interaction Workbook* (Burtonsville, Md.: Sign Media, 1985).

[9] C. Padden, "The Deaf Community and the Culture of Deaf People," in S.Wilcox, ed., *American Deaf Culture* (Burtonsville, Md.: Linstok Press, 1989), 1–16.

[10] Ibid.

[11] B. Kannapell, "Inside the Deaf Community," in Wilcox, *American Deaf Culture*, 21–28; quotation from p. 27.

[12] J. D. Schein, *At Home Among Strangers* (Washington, D.C.: Gallaudet University Press, 1989), quotation from p. 39.

[13] Native American Languages Act 1990, PL 101–477.

[14] Kannapell, "Deaf Community," quotation from pp. 22, 25.

[15] Fishman, *Rise and Fall*.

[16] H. Kloss, "Bilingualism and Nationalism," *Journal of Social Issues* 23 (1967): 39–47; quotation from p. 46.

[17] W. B. Gudykunst, *Language and Ethnic Identity* (Philadelphia, Pa.: Multilingual Matters, 1988).

[18] L. Clerc (1785–1869) also apparently brought la Langue des Signes Française (LSF). He cofounded the Hartford school with T. H. Gallaudet (1787–1851).

[19] H. Lane, *When the Mind Hears: A History of the Deaf* (New York: Random House, 1984). It has not been established that there was in Clerc's time, a single sign language in broad use in France that was the precursor of modern LSF.

[20] C. Lucas and C. Valli, *Language Contact in the American Deaf Community* (New York: Academic Press, 1992); W. C. Stokoe, "Sign Language Diglossia," *Studies in Linguistics* 21 (1970): 21–41; T. S. Supalla and P. Clark, *Sign Language Archeology: Understanding the Historical Roots of American Sign Language* (Washington, D.C.: Gallaudet University Press, in press.).

[21] Kloss, "Bilingualism and Nationalism"; Fenton, *Ethnicity*.

[22] B. Greenwald, "Taking Stock: Alexander Graham Bell and Eugenics, 1883–1922," in J. V. Van Cleve, ed., *The Deaf History Reader* (Washington, D.C.: Gallaudet University Press, 2007), 136–152; R. Winefield, *Never the Twain Shall Meet: The Communications Debate* (Washington, D.C.: Gallaudet University Press, 1987).

[23] Bell quoted in: National Education Association of the United States, *Proceedings of Meeting Held in the Senate Chamber, Madison, Wis., Wednesday, July 16th, 1884, To Consider the Subject of Deaf-Mute Instruction in Relation to the Work of the Public Schools* (Washington, D.C.: Gibson Brothers, 1885), quotation from p. 21. There were contemporary efforts to take Native American children off the reservations to teach them English and majority customs. A. Leibowitz, "Language and the Law: The Exercise of Political Power Through Official Designation of Language" in W. O'Barr and J. O'Barr, eds., *Language and Politics* (The Hague: Mouton, 1976), 449–466. Concerning Bell, see B. Greenwald, "Taking Stock."

[24] D. Baynton, *Forbidden Signs* (Chicago: University of Chicago Press, 1996).

[25] T. S. Supalla and P. Clark "*Infancy of American Sign Language.*" Unpublished manuscript, University of Rochester, 2008. The hearing son of Thomas Hopkins Gallaudet, Edward Minor Gallaudet, was also among the orators in ASL.

[26] Edwards, *Language, Society*; N. Glazer and D. P. Moynihan, *Ethnicity: Theory and Experience* (Cambridge, Mass.: Harvard University Press, 1975); Jenkins, *Rethinking Ethnicity*; M. Marger, *Race and Ethnic Relations: American and Global Perspectives* (5th ed.) (San Diego, Calif.: Wadsworth, 2003); Smith, *Ethnic Origins*.

[27] Verkuyten, *Social Psychology*, quotation from p. 41.

[28] Henri Tajfel, *Social Identity and Intergroup Relations* (New York: Cambridge University Press; 1982).

[29] Glazer and Moynihan, *Ethnicity*; Jenkins, *Rethinking Ethnicity*.

[30] Fishman, *Language and Ethnicity*; Glazer and Moynihan, *Ethnicity*; L. Vail, "Ethnicity in Southern African History," in R. Grinker and C. Steiner, eds., *Perspectives on Africa: A Reader in Culture, History and Representation* (Oxford,: Blackwell Publishers, 1996), 52–68.

[31] B. Kannapell, "Personal Awareness and Advocacy in the Deaf Community," in C. Baker and R. Battison, eds., *Sign Language and the Deaf Community, Essays in Honor of William Stokoe* (Silver Spring, Md.: National Association of the Deaf, 1980), 105–116, quotation from p. 112.

32   Fenton, *Ethnicity*.

33   T. Humphries, Personal communication. 2009. Adapted.

34   S. J. Carmel, "A Study of Deaf Culture in an American Urban Deaf Community" (Ph.D. dis. American University, 1987); Schein, *Home Among Strangers* (Washington, D.C.: Gallaudet University Press, 1989), quotation from p. 39.

J. Schein, *The Deaf Population of the United States* (Silver Spring, Md.: National Association of the Deaf, 1974). These data are not recent and the percentages may have changed.

35   A. Mindess, *Reading Between the Signs: Intercultural Communication for Sign Language Interpreters* (2nd ed.) (Boston, Mass.: Intercultural Press, 2006).

36   Hutchinson and Smith, *Ethnicity*; Smith, *Ethnic Origins*. For a meta-discussion of how to approach characterizing Deaf culture, see G. Turner, "How is Deaf Culture?" *Sign Language Studies* 83 (1994): 127–148.

37   V. N. Parrillo, *Understanding Race and Ethnic Relations* (Boston, Mass.: Pearson/Allyn and Bacon, 2005).

38   S. Cornell and D. Hartmann, *Ethnicity and Race: Making Identities in a Changing World*. (Thousand Oaks, Calif.: Sage, 1998).

39   Fishman, *Language and Ethnicity*.

40   This discussion draws from P. Ladd, *Understanding Deaf Culture: In Search of Deafhood* (Clevedon, U.K.: Multilingual Matters, 2003); Mindess, *Reading Between the Signs*; C. Padden and T. Humphries, *Deaf in America: Voices from a Culture* (Cambridge, Mass.: Harvard University Press, 1988); C. Padden and T. Humphries, *Inside Deaf Culture* (Cambridge, Mass.: Harvard University Press, 2005); Rutherford, *Deaf Folklore*; T. Smith, *Deaf People in Context* (Ph.D. diss., University of Washington, 1996).

41   R. E. Johnson and C. Erting, "Ethnicity and Socialization in a Classroom for Deaf Children," in C. Lucas, ed., *The Sociolinguistics of the Deaf Community* (New York: Academic Press, 1989), 41–84.

42   Padden, "Deaf Community."

43   C. Baker, "Regulators and Turn-Taking in ASL Discourse," in L. Friedman, ed., *On the Other Hand* (New York: Academic Press, 1977); S. Hall "Train-Gone-Sorry: The Etiquette of Social Conversations in American Sign Language" *Sign Language Studies* 41 (1983): 291–309.

44   Padden and Humphries, *Inside Deaf Culture*.

45   Mindess, *Reading Between the Signs*; S. Supalla, *The Book of Name Signs: Naming in American Sign Language* (San Diego, Calif.: DawnSignPress, 1992); Y. Delaporte, *Les Sourds, C'Est Comme Ça: Ethnologie de la Surdimutité* (Paris: Maison des Sciences de l'Homme, 2002).

46   Ladd, *Understanding Deaf Culture*, see p. 364

47   Smith, "Deaf People In Context," quotation from p. 143.

48   C. J. Erting "Cultural Conflict in a School for Deaf Children," *Anthropology and Education Quarterly* 16 (3) (1985): 225–243. Reprinted in P. Higgins and J. Nash, eds., *Understanding Deafness Socially* (Springfield, Mass.: Charles C. Thomas, 1987); C. J. Erting, *Deafness, Communication, Social Identity: Ethnography in a Preschool for Deaf Children*. (Burtonsville, Md.: Linstok Press, 1994).

49   Mindess, *Reading Between the Signs*; Smith," Deaf People in Context."

50   S. A. Hall, *"The Deaf Club is Like a Second Home": An Ethnography of Folklore Communication in American Sign Language*. (Philadelphia: University of

Pennsylvania, Department of Folklore and Folklife, 1989); Padden and Humphries, *Inside Deaf Culture*; C. Padden, "The Decline Of Deaf Clubs in the United States: A Treatise on the Problem of Place," in H-D. Bauman (ed.), *Open Your Eyes: Deaf Studies Talking* (Minneapolis, Minn.: University of Minnesota Press, 2008): 169–176.

51 One Deaf club member explained to a hearing scholar: "For Deaf people, the Deaf club is like a second home." S. Hall, "Door Into Deaf Culture: Folklore in an American Deaf Social Club," *Sign Language Studies* 73 (1991): 421–429. Deaf people feel that their clubs are "a piece of their own land in exile—an oasis in the world of sound," quotation from p. 421; B. Bragg and E. Bergman, *Tales from a Clubroom* (Washington, D.C.: Gallaudet University Press, 1981), compare p. vii.

52 D. A. Stewart, *Deaf Sport: The Impact of Sports Within the Deaf Community* (Washington, D.C.: Gallaudet University. Press, 1991); www.usdeafsports. org (accessed 7/22/2010)

53 Padden and Humphries, *Inside Deaf Culture.*

54 Padden, "Decline of Deaf Clubs." For a discussion of clubs and the British Deaf community, see: J. Kyle, "The Deaf Community: Culture, Custom and Tradition," in S. Prillwitz and T. Vollhaber, eds., *Sign Language Research and Application* (Hamburg, Germany: Signum, 1990), 175–185.

55 Fishman, *Rise and Fall.*

56 T. A. Ulmer, "A Review of the Little Paper Family for 1944–45," in L Bragg, ed., *Deaf-World* (New York: New York University Press, 1945), 257–268.

57 *The Deaf Mute* was a monthly published by the North Carolina Institution for the Deaf, Dumb and Blind. J. Gannon, *Deaf Heritage* (Silver Spring, Md.: National Association of the Deaf, 1991). Newspapers for ethnically Deaf audiences, both national and local, useful for the study of New England Deaf history, are as follows: *American Annals of the Deaf* (1886-present); *American Annals of the Deaf and Dumb* (1847–1886); *American Gazette for the Deaf, Boston, Mass.* (1895); *Association Review* (1899–1909); *Brooklyn Deaf-Mute Leader New York* (1879–1881); *C. Aug. Brown's Copy, Belfast, Maine* (1890); *Deaf Mutes' Friend, Henniker, N.H.* (1869); *Deaf Mutes' Journal, Mexico, New York* (1874–1938); *Deaf-Mute Times* (1888); *Gallaudet Guide and Deaf Mutes' Companion, Boston, Mass.* (1860–1862); *Lantern, Harlem, New York* (1881); *Literary Budget, Boston, Mass.* (1874); *Mexico Independent Deaf Mutes' Journal, Mexico, New York* (1873–1874); *National Deaf Mute Gazette, Boston, Mass.* (1867–1868); *National Deaf-Mute Leader New York* (1879–1885); *Silent People, Lake Village, N.H.* (1880); *Silent Worker, Trenton, N.J.* (1888–1929); *Silent World, Washington, D.C.* (1871–1876).

58 Lane, Hoffmeister and Bahan, *Journey.*

59 Smith, *Ethnic Origins*; Fishman, *Language and Ethnicity.*

60 W. Stokoe, H. R. Bernard, and C. Padden, "An Elite Group in Deaf Society," *Sign Language Studies* 12 (1976): 189–210.

61 Smith, "Deaf People In Context."

62 Hutchinson and Smith, *Ethnicity.* H-D. Bauman, J. Nelson, and H. Rose, eds., *Signing the Body Poetic: Essays on American Sign Language Literature* (Berkeley: University of California Press, 2006).

63 N. Frishberg, "Signers of Tales: A Case for Literary Status of an Unwritten Language," *Sign Language Studies* 59 (1988): 149–170.

64 Padden, "Deaf Community."

65 Supalla, *Book of Name Signs*.

66 Reported by Anna Witter Merrithew in Smith, "Deaf People In Context," pp. 200–201. "There is also the 'One Deaf' railroad coupler story in which 'One Deaf' invents the coupling mechanism that revolutionized the railroads, but the Hearing supervisor stole the plans and used them to his own advantage. The moral: hearing people take advantage of Deaf." (Dennis Cokely, personal communication, 2009).

67 Translated by Carol Padden. Some authors use *de l'Epée*.

68 C. M. de L'Epée, *La Véritable Manière d'Instruire Les Sourds Et Muets Confirmée Par Une Longue Expérience* (Paris: Nyon, 1784).

69 S. Rutherford, "Funny in deaf—not in hearing," *Journal of American Folklore* 96 (1983): 310–322.

70 S. Baldwin, *Pictures in the Air: the Story of the National Theatre of the Deaf* (Washington, D.C.: Gallaudet University Press, 1995).

71 B. Schertz and H. Lane, "Elements of a Culture: Visions by Deaf Artists," *Visual Anthropology Review* 15 (2000): 20–36.

72 Smith, *Ethnic Origins*, quotation from p. 87. Also, J. Nagel, "Constructing Ethnicity: Creating and Recreating Ethnic Identity and Culture," *Social Problems* 41(1994): 152–176.

73 http://83.137.212.42/sitearchive/cre/diversity/ethnicity/index.html (Consulted February 1, 2009). "Other relevant characteristics may (but need not) include common geographical origin or ancestry, a common language (not necessarily peculiar to the group), a common literature, a common religion and the status of either a minority or a dominant group within a larger community."

74 A. Cohen, *The Symbolic Construction of Community*. (New York: Tavistock, 1985), quotation from p. 99.

75 Smith, *Ethnic Origins*

76 Ibid.

77 S. Cornell, "The Variable Ties That Bind: Content and Circumstance in Ethnic Processes," *Ethnic and Racial Studies* 19 (1996): 265–289; Smith, *Ethnic Origins*.

78 C. Krentz, *A Mighty Change: An Anthology of Deaf American Writing 1816–1864* (Washington, D.C.: Gallaudet University Press, 2000), quotation from p. xiii. Krentz explains the various sources for this wording.

79 See, for full legend, Krentz, *Mighty Change*.

80 Legends: J. Gannon, *Deaf Heritage* (Silver Spring, Md.: National Association of the Deaf, 1991); Lane, *Mind;* Padden and Humphries, *Deaf in America;* Padden and Humphries, *Inside Deaf Culture*.

81 See Lane, Hoffmeister and Bahan, *Journey*.

82 L. Rae, "Ceremonies at the Completion of the Gallaudet Monument," *American Annals of the Deaf* 7 (1854): 19–54.

83 Rae, ibid., quotation from p. 19.

84 Anon. "Personal." *Gallaudet Guide and Deaf-Mute's Companion* 1(8) (1860): 30.

85 Krentz, *Mighty Change;* Lane, *Mind*.

86 Padden and Humphries, *Inside Deaf Culture*.

87 T. Humphries, "Scientific Explanation and Other Performance Acts in the Re-organization of DEAF," in D. J. Napoli, ed., *Signs and Voices* (Washington, D.C.: Gallaudet University Press, 2008), 3–20; quotation from page 16.

88 H-D. Bauman, "Postscript: Gallaudet Protests of 2006 and the myths of in/exclusion," in Bauman, *Open Your Eyes*, 327–336.

89 S. N. Barnartt and J. B. Christiansen, "Into Their Own Hands: The Deaf President Now Protest and its Consequences," in L. Bragg, *Deaf-World*, 333–347; J. B. Christiansen and S. M. Barnartt, *Deaf President Now! the 1988 Revolution at Gallaudet University* (Washington, D.C.: Gallaudet University Press, 1995).

90 "This protest helped us find pride—and hope," *USA Today*, March 15, 1988, p. 11a.

91 Smith, *Ethnic Revival*. Quotation from frontispiece attributed to Simon Dubnow in K. S. Pinson, ed., *Nationalism and History* (Philadelphia: Jewish Publication Society of America, 1958).

92 Verkuyten, *Social Psychology*, quotation from p. 122; F. Barth, *Ethnic Groups and Boundaries* (Boston: Little Brown, 1969).

93 Louder and Waddell point out that "The true locus of the continuity of the Quebecois ethnic group is more temporal than spatial: it is the family; Quebecois are scattered over Louisiana, New England, Quebec, the Maritime Provinces and in Western Canada." D. R. Louder and E. Waddell, *French America: Mobility, Identity, and Minority Experience Across the Continent* (Baton Rouge: University of Louisiana Press, 1993), quotation from p. 27.

94 M. W. Hughey and J. Vidich, "The New American Pluralism: Racial and Ethnic Solidarities and Their Sociological Implications," in M. W. Hughey, ed., *New Tribalisms: the Resurgence of Race and Ethnicity* (New York: New York University Press, 1998), 173–196, quotation from p. 181; S. Schalk, "Multicultural Foreign Policy," in Hughey, *New Tribalisms*, 299–316.

95 D. Bullard, *Islay* (Silver Spring Md.: TJ Publishers, 1986); Lane, Hoffmeister, and Bahan, *Journey*; Lane, *Mind*; J. Levesque, "Its a Deaf Deaf Deaf-World," *D.C.ARA News* 15 (1994): 2; J. Van Cleve and B. Crouch, *A Place of their Own; Creating the Deaf Community in America* (Washington, D.C.: Gallaudet University Press, 1989); M. A. Winzer, "Deaf-Mutia: Responses to Alienation by the Deaf in the Mid-Nineteenth Century," *American Annals of the Deaf* 131 (1986): 29–32.

96 Fishman, *Language and Ethnicity*. J. Krejci and V. Velìmsky, "Ethnic and Political Nations in Europe," in Hutchinson and Smith, *Ethnicity*, 209–221; Hughey and Vidich, "New American Pluralism." American scholars have posited a transnational identity of Afrocentricity that binds all people of African descent.

97 A Smith, "Chosen Peoples," in Hutchinson and Smith, *Ethnicity*, pp.189–197; Smith, *Ethnic Origins*; Smith, "Deaf People in Context."

98 J. Murray, "One Touch of Nature Makes the Whole World Kin: The Transnational Lives of Deaf Americans," 1870–1924 (Ph.D. diss., University of Iowa, 2007).

99 Smith, "Deaf People in Context," quotation from p. 57.

100 There are, however, striking similarities between Deaf culture in the United States and that in Great Britain; see J. Kyle, "The Deaf Community: Culture, Custom and Tradition," in Prillwitz and Vollhaber, *Sign Language Research*, 175–185.

101 Lane, *Mind*, quotation from p. 219.

102 Berthier and others on universality of sign: F. Berthier, *Sur l'Opinion du feu le Dr. Itard. Relative aux Facultés Intéllectuelles et aux Qualités Morales des Sourds-Muets* (Paris: Lévy, 1852); Ladd, *Understanding Deaf Culture*;

B. Mottez, "The Deaf-Mute Banquets and the Birth of the Deaf Movement," in R. Fischer and H. Lane, eds., *Looking Back: A Reader on the History of Deaf Communities and their Sign Languages* (Hamburg: Signum, 1993), 143–155; T. Supalla and R. Webb, "The Grammar of International Sign: A New Look at Pidgin Languages," in K. Emmorey and J. S. Reilly, eds., *Language, Gesture, and Space* (Hillsdale, N.J.: Lawrence Erlbaum Associates, 1995), 333–354; see p. 334.

[103] R. Rosenstock, "An Investigation of International Sign: Analyzing Structure and Comprehension" (Ph.D. diss., Gallaudet University, 2004); B. Moody, "International Sign: A Practitioners Perspective," *RID Journal of Interpretation,* [n.v.] (2002): 12–13; Murray, "One Touch of Nature." "I[nternational] S[ign] users combine a relatively rich and structured grammar with a severely impoverished lexicon." Quotation from: L. Alsop, B. Woll, and J. M. Brauti, "International Sign: The Creation of An International Deaf Community and Sign Language," in H. Bos and T. Schermer, eds., *Sign Language Research: International Studies on Sign Language and Communication of the Deaf* (Hamburg: Signum, 1994), quotation from p. 187; T. Supalla and R. Webb, "The Grammar Of International Sign: a New Look at Pidgin Languages," in Emmorey and Reilly, *Language.* We thank Rachel Rosenstock for her helpful observations on International Sign.

[104] Murray, "One Touch of Nature," quotation from p. 46.

[105] J. Carsten, *Cultures of Relatedness: New Approaches to the Study of Kinship* (Cambridge, Mass: Cambridge University Press, 2000); D. M. Schneider, *A Critique of the Study of Kinship.* (Ann Arbor: University of Michigan Press, 1984), quotation from p. 191.

[106] J. Carsten, "The Substance of Kinship and the Heat of the Hearth: Feeding, Personhood, and Relatedness among Malays in Pulau Langkawi," *American Ethnologist* 22 (1995): 223–241.

[107] B. Malinowski, *Coral Gardens and their Magic* (Bloomington: Indiana University Press, 1965), quotation from p. 199.

[108] Barth, *Ethnic Groups;* H. Jonsson, "Does the House Hold? History and the Shape of Mien (Yao) Society," *Ethnohistory* 48 (2001): 613–654.

[109] B. Bodenhorn, "'He Used to be My Relative': Exploring the Bases of Relatedness Among the Iñupiat of Northern Alaska," in Carsten, *Cultures,* 128–148.

[110] G. Witherspoon, *Navajo Kinship and Marriage* (Chicago: University of Chicago Press, 1975).

[111] Marger, *Race and Ethnic Relation,* quotation from p.13; S. Cornell, "Ties That Bind"; D. M. Schneider, "What is Kinship all About?" in P. Reining, ed., *Kinship Studies in the Morgan Centennial Year* (Washington, D.C.: Anthropological Society of Washington, 1972), 32–64;

[112] Fishman, *Language and Ethnicity, see* p. 25.

[113] I. Prattis, "Barthing Up the Wrong Tree," *American Anthropologist* 85 (1) (1983): 103–109. "To be Pathan is based on criteria that range from patrilinear descent, Islam, and the maintenance of Pathan custom with regard to hospitality, council structure, and domestic organization," quotation from p. 107; Barth, *Ethnic Groups;* Fenton, *Ethnicity, see* p. 149. Smith, *Ethnic Origin;* "At the centre of every ethnie . . . stands a distinctive complex of myths, memories, and symbols, with peculiar claims about the group's origins

and lines of descent. These claims and this complex provide the focus of a community's identity and its mythomoteur or constitutive political myth," quotation from p. 57.

114 Smith, *Ethnic Origins,* see p.58; Cornell and Hartmann, *Ethnicity and Race.*

115 Jenkins, *Rethinking Ethnicity,* see p.150.

116 W. Connor, "Beyond Reason: The Nature Of The Ethnonational Bond," in Hutchinson and Smith, *Ethnicity,* 69–75, quotation from p. 71.; D. Horowtiz, "Ethnic Identity," in Glazer and Moynihan, *Ethnicity,* 111–140; D. M. Schneider, "Kinship, Nationality and Religion In American Culture: Toward a Definition of Kinship," in R. F. Spencer, ed., *Forms of Symbolic Action* (Seattle, Wash.: University of Washington Press, 1969), 116–125; Schneider, "What Is Kinship"; Fishman, *Language and Ethnicity.*

J. Carsten, "Substance Of Kinship"; Carsten, *Cultures*; D. M. Schneider, *American Kinship: A Cultural Account* (Englewood Cliffs, N.J., Prentice-Hall, 1968); D. M. Schneider, "Kinship, Nationality and Religion In American Culture: Toward a Definition of Kinship," in R. F. Spencer, ed., *Forms of Symbolic Action* (Seattle: University of Washington Press, 1969), 116–125; Schneider, "What Is Kinship?"; D. M. Schneider, *The American Kin Universe: A Genealogical Study, Series in Social, Cultural, and Linguistic Anthropology* (Chicago: Dept. of Anthropology, University of Chicago, 1975). Sociologist Mary Waters observes, "One may know that the Normans, the Franks, the Burgundians and the Gauls were once separate groups who came to be known as French, but that does not necessarily make the [ethnic] category French any less 'real' to a particular individual." M. C. Waters, *Ethnic Options: Choosing Identities in America.* (Berkeley, Calif.: University of California Press, 1990), quotation from p. 17.

117 Cornell and Hartmann, *Ethnicity and Race*; Verkuyten, *Social Psychology*. On biological resemblance, see Johnson and Erting, "Ethnicity and Socialization." When genealogic facts were uncovered and disseminated they had no effect on kinship myths, suggesting that the myths are rooted elsewhere. See Schneider, "What is Kinship?"

118 Ibid. M. Marshall, "The Nature of Nurture," *American Ethnologist* 4(4) (1977): 643–662.

119 Smith, *Ethnic Origins,* quotation from p. 49.

120 Fenton, *Ethnicity*; W. Petersen, "Concepts Of Ethnicity," in S. Thernstrom, ed., *Harvard Encyclopedia of American Ethnic Groups* (Cambridge, Mass.: Harvard University Press, 1980), 234–242.

121 Fishman, *Language and Ethnicity*; T. Parsons, "Some Theoretical Considerations on the Nature and Trends of Change of Ethnicity," in Glazer and Moynihan, *Ethnicity,* 53–83.

122 W. Connor, "Beyond Reason: The Nature of the Ethnonational Bond," in Hutchinson and Smith, *Ethnicity,* quotation from p. 71.

123 Fenton, *Ethnicity: Racism, Class and Culture* (Lanham, Md.: Bowman and Littlefield, 1999); Waters, *Ethnic Options*; M. Weber, "Ethnic Groups," in Hughey, *New Tribalisms,* 17–30.

124 gri.gallaudet.edu/Demographics/2008_National_Summary.pdf. (accessed 4/5/09). Gallaudet Research Institute, *Regional and National Summary Report of Data from the 2007–2008 Annual Survey of Deaf and Hard of Hearing Children and Youth* (Washington, D.C.: GRI, Gallaudet University, 2008).

[125] M. L. Marazita et al., "Genetic Epidemiological Studies of Early-Onset Deafness in the U.S. School Age Population," *American Journal of Medical Genetics* 46 (1993): 486–491, quotation from p. 486.

An enumeration of all Deaf people born Deaf and become so in Northern Ireland found only six cases of Deaf at birth owing to maternal illness. In that study, 424 persons were born Deaf and 183 became Deaf before age six; thus the incidence of hereditary Deaf in this sample was 70 percent. Seventy percent hereditary Deaf may be an underestimate since a child who is Deaf due to heredity may be mistakenly thought Deaf due to some environmental incident or may simply be discovered Deaf belatedly. A. C. Stevenson and E. A. Cheeseman, "Hereditary Deaf Mutism, With Particular Reference to Northern Ireland," *Annals of Human Genetics* 20 (1956): 177–207; Chung et al. further analyzed these data and report 24 percent dominant, 74 percent recessive, and 2 percent x-linked. C. S. Chung D. W. Robinson and M. E. Morton, "A Note on Deaf-Mutism," *Annals of Human Genetics* 23 (1959): 357–366.

An analysis of the 1898 Fay survey–in an era when many more people were Deaf as a sequel to illness—yielded 55 percent of all Deaf people who were hereditarily Deaf. E. A. Fay, *Marriages of the Deaf in America* (Washington, D.C.: Volta Bureau, 1898); K.S. Arnos et al., "A Comparative Analysis of the Genetic Epidemiology of Deafness in the United States in Two Sets of Pedigrees Collected More Than a Century Apart." *American Journal Of Human Genetics* 83 (2008): 200–207. A survey of the student body at Gallaudet yielded 76 percent hereditarily Deaf. W. E. Nance et al., "Opportunities For Genetic Counseling Through Institutional Ascertainment of Affected Probands," in H. A. Lubs and F. de la Cruz, eds., *Genetic Counseling* (New York: Raven Press, 1977), 307–331. Y. Delaporte states that the percent of hereditarily Deaf in France is 70 percent. Delaporte, *Les Sourds*.

[126] W. Reardon, "Genetic Deafness," *Journal of Medical Genetics* 29 (1992): 521–526; quotation from p. 524; C. Morton and W. Nance, "Newborn Hearing Screening–a Silent Revolution." *New England Journal of Medicine.*" 354(20) (2006): 2151-2164: "Genetic causes account for at least 50 to 60 percent of childhood hearing loss in developed countries and can be classified according to the pattern of inheritance, the presence (syndromic) or absence(nonsyndromic) of distinctive clinical features, or the identification of the causal mutation" quotation from p. 2151. For incidence at birth, before oral language learning can proceed, the authors estimate 68 percent genetic causes.

[127] When two people are known to carry or express the same gene for the Deaf trait, it is often assumed that if the gene is rare, the couple are likely to have a common ancestor. However, even a common gene associated with the Deaf trait can signal a shared ancestor if one traces the lineage back far enough– with the proviso that the same mutation may arise in two unrelated individuals.

[128] Jenkins, *Rethinking Ethnicity*. Johnson and Erting, "Ethnicity and Socialization."

[129] S. Foster, "Communication Experiences of Deaf People: An Ethnographic Account," in I. Parasnis, ed., *Cultural and Language Diversity and the Deaf Experience* (New York: Cambridge University Press, 1996), 117–135.

[130] C. Erting, "Socialization in Families with Deaf Children," *Gallaudet Encyclopedia of Deaf People and Deafness* (New York: McGraw-Hill, 1987), 141–147;

C. J. Erting and M. Kuntze, "Language Socialization in Deaf Communities," in P. Duff and N.H. Hornberger, eds., *Encyclopedia of Language and Education*, (2nd ed)., Vol. 8: *Language and Socialization* (New York: Springer, 2008), 287–300.

Chapter 2

1   Johnson and Erting, "Ethnicity and Socialization."
2   For a discussion of the constructivist perspective, see: D. Bell, "Ethnicity and Social Change," in Hutchinson and Smith., *Ethnicity*, 138–146; Cornell, "Ties That Bind"; Cornell and Hartmann, *Ethnicity and Race*; Fenton, *Ethnicity*; Hutchinson and Smith, *Ethnicity*; Jenkins, *Rethinking Ethnicity*; Johnson and Erting, "Ethnicity and Socialization"; Nagel, "Constructing Ethnicity"; To say that we are "deploying ethnicity" in this book in order to facilitate Deaf people achieving their goals is to view the issue solely from a constructivist point of view. In fact, Deaf-World language and culture are centuries old and are the precursor of what is "deployed."
3   Cornell, "Ties That Bind"; Fenton, *Ethnicity*; Hutchinson and Smith, *Ethnicity*; Jenkins, *Rethinking Ethnicity*; Smith, *Ethnic Origins*. For a discussion of primordialism in relation to constructivism, see: J. L Comaroff, "Of Totemism and Ethnicity: Consciousness, Practice and the Signs of Inequality," in Grinker and Steiner, *Perspectives on Africa*, 69–85; Cornell and Hartmann, *Ethnicity and Race*.
4   Cornell and Hartmann, *Ethnicity and Race*.
5   Carmel, "Deaf Culture"; H. Lane, "Ethnicity, Ethics and the Deaf-World," in L.R. Komesaroff, ed., *Surgical Consent: Bioethics and Cochlear Implantation* (Washington, D.C: Gallaudet University Press, 2007), p. 6; Padden and Humphries, *Deaf In America*; Padden and Humphries, *Inside Deaf Culture*.
6   T. K. Holcomb, "Social Assimilation Of Deaf High School Students: The Role of School Environment," in Parasnis, *Cultural and Language Diversity*, 181–200; H. Lane, "The Education of Deaf Children: Drowning in the Mainstream and the Sidestream" in J. Kauffman and D. Hallahan, eds., *The Illusion of Full inclusion: A Comprehensive Critique of a Current Special Education Bandwagon* (Austin, Tex.: Pro-Ed, 2004), 275–287; J. V. Van Cleve, "The Academic Integration of Deaf Students An Historical Perspective," in J. Van Cleve, *Deaf History Reader*, 116–135.
7   C. Padden, "Folk explanation in language survival," in Bragg, *Deaf-World*, 104–115.
8   A. B. Crammatte, *Meeting the Challenge: Hearing-Impaired Professionals in the Workplace* (Washington, D.C.: Gallaudet University Press, 1987); C. Padden, "From The Cultural To The Bicultural: The Modern Deaf Community," in Parasnis, *Cultural and Language Diversity*, 79–98.
9   Cornell and Hartmann, *Ethnicity and Race*. Eldredge describes four ways in which members of the Deaf-World signal their unity and six ways in which they may marginalize others when communicating: Eldredge, Stringham, and Wilding-Diaz, *Deaf Studies Today*.
10 A. Portes and R. Schauffler, "Language Acquisition and Loss Among Children of Immigrants," in S. Pedraza and R. G. Rumbaut, eds., *Origins and Destinies: Immigration, Race and Ethnicity in America* (New York: Wadsworth, 1996), 432–443.

11 S. Steinberg. *The Ethnic Myth: Race, Ethnicity, and Class in America* (Boston: Beacon Press, 2001).

12 J. Edwards, "Symbolic Ethnicity and Language," in Hutchinson and Smith, *Ethnicity*, 227–229; C. Erting, "Language Policy and Deaf Ethnicity in the United States," *Sign Language Studies* 19 (1978): 139–152; Fishman, *Language and Ethnicity*; Johnson and Erting, "Ethnicity and Socialization"; Waters, *Ethnic Options*. However, the contact variety of ASL, used primarily with outsiders to the Deaf-World, is another mechanism for maintaining the boundary between Deaf and non-Deaf. Erting, "Language Policy"; F. Grosjean, *Studying Bilinguals* (Oxford: Oxford University Press, 2008).

13 N. Groce, *Everyone Here Spoke Sign Language* (Cambridge, Mass.: Harvard University Press, 1985); H. Lane, R. Pillard, and M. French, "Origins of the American Deaf-World: Assimilating and Differentiating Societies and Their Relation to Genetic Patterning," *Sign Language Studies* 1 (new ser.) (2000): 17–44.

14 T. Humphries, "Of Deaf-mutes, the Strange and the Modern Deaf Self.," in Bragg, *Deaf-World*, 348–364; see p. 356.

15 Ibid.; see p. 359; paraphrased and abridged.

16 Murray," One Touch of Nature."

17 Smith, "Deaf People In Context"; Schein, *Home Among Strangers*.

18 V. Achim, *The Roma in Romanian History* (New York: Central European University Press, 2004).

19 Quotes from Deaf parents on the merits of having a Deaf child will be found in C. J. Erting "Cultural Conflict in a School for Deaf Children," *Anthropology and Education Quarterly* 16 (3) (1985): 225–243. Reprinted in P. Higgins and J. Nash, eds., *Understanding Deafness Socially*. (Springfield, Mass.: Charles C. Thomas, 1987).

20 S. Fenton, *Ethnicity*.

21 Dr. Joseph Murray called this adaptiveness to our attention.

22 Carmel, "Deaf Culture."

23 T. Humphries, "Of Deaf-mutes," quotation from p. 358.

24 Carmel, "Deaf Culture."

25 Ibid. See p. 124: Deaf are hostile to oralists and to hearing society; p. 130; that is, the segment of hearing society that impinges on the Deaf-World. Compare p. 339.

26 Erting, "Language Policy."

27 F. Bowe, "Deaf and Hard of Hearing Americans' Instant Messaging and E-Mail Use: A National Survey" *American Annals of the Deaf* 147 (2002): 6–10.

28 Fishman, *Language and Ethnicity*; F. Grosjean, *Studying Bilinguals*; see "The Bilingualism And Biculturalism Of The Deaf."

29 Cornell and Hartmann, *Ethnicity and Race*.

30 Delaporte, *Les Sourds*.

31 The British social scientist Paddy Ladd developed the related concept of Deafhood to capture the process by which Deaf people live out and explain their way in the world given their evolving culture. He describes it further as "collective culture; collective history; collective arts; collective spiritual issues." Ladd documents and analyzes the struggle of Deaf people to counter oppressive forces. All in all, the properties of Deafhood appear to us to

flow from Deaf ethnicity. P. Ladd, *Understanding Deaf Culture: In Search of Deafhood* (Clevedon, U.K.: Multilingual Matters, 2003).

32 Padden and Humphries, *Deaf in America*; Padden and Humphries, *Inside Deaf Culture*.

33 Hughey, *New Tribalisms*, see p. 3. Some authors describe mainstream ethnicity as WASP—White Anglo-Saxon Protestantism. Others speak of Euro-American; however that term appears to regroup several ethnicities. D. A. Hollinger, *Postethnic America* (New York, N.Y.: Basic Books, 1995); Hughey and Vidich, "New American Pluralism"; Hutchinson and Smith, *Ethnicity*; S. Shain, "Multicultural Foreign Policy," in Hughey, *New Tribalisms*, 299–316; Steinberg, *Ethnic Myth*. "Long before the onset of mass migration there was a deeply rooted consciousness of the nation's Anglo-Saxon and Protestant origins. From the beginning, the nation's political institutions, culture, and people all had an unmistakable English cast and despite denominational differences Protestantism was the near universal creed." Quotation from p. 13.

Chapter 3

1 D. Baynton, "Beyond Culture: Deaf Studies and the Deaf Body," in Eldredge, Stringham, and Wilding-Diaz, *Deaf Studies Today*, 37–56; D. Baynton, "Beyond Culture: Deaf Studies and the Deaf Body," in Bauman, *Open Your Eyes*, 293–313; J. Harris, *The Cultural Meaning of Deafness* (Aldershot U.K.: Avebury, 1995); Kyle, "Deaf People,"; J. Nash, "Who Signs To Whom: The American Sign Language Community," in P. C. Higgins and J. E. Nash, eds., *Understanding Deafness Socially* (Springfield, Ill.: Thomas, 1987), 81–100; J. E. Nash, "Policy and Practice in the American Sign Language Community," *International Journal of the Sociology of Language* 68 (1987): 7–22; D. Parratt, "The State, Social Work and Deafness," in S. Gregory and G. M. Hartley, eds., *Constructing Deafness* (London: Pinter, 1991), 247–252.

2 E. Gellner, *Thought and Change* (London: Weidenfeld and Nicholson, 1978); Nash, "Who Signs to Whom"; Smith, *Ethnic Revival*.

3 F. Barth, "Ecologic Relations of Ethnic Groups in Swat, North Pakistan," in Y. Cohen, ed., *Man in Adaptation: The Cultural Present* (Chicago: Aldine, 1958), 324–331; M. W. Hughey and J. Vidich, "The New American Pluralism: Racial and Ethnic Solidarities and Their Sociological Implications," in M. W. Hughey, ed., *New Tribalisms: the Resurgence of Race and Ethnicity* (New York: New York University Press, 1998), 173–196.

4 N. Kristoff, "Love and Race," *New York Times*, December 6, 2002, A35.

5 BaMbuti of the east of Zaire: C. M. Turnbull, *The Forest People* (New York: Simon and Schuster, 1962), quotation from p. 14. See also: R. Bailey and N. R. Peacock, "Efe Pygmies of northeast Zaïre: Subsistence Strategies in the Ituri Forest," in I. De Garine and G.A. Harrison, eds., *Coping with Uncertainty in Food Supply* (New York: Oxford University Press, 1988), 88–117; L. L. Cavalli-Sforza, ed., *African Pygmies* (Orlando, Fla.: Academic Press, 1986); L. L. Cavalli-Sforza, *The Great Human Diasporas: The History of Diversity and Evolution* (Reading, Mass.: Addison-Wesley, 1995); P. Schebesta, *My Pygmy and Negro Hosts* (New York: AMS Press, 1936); D. S. Wilkie, "Hunters and Farmers of the African Forest," in J. S. Denslow and C. Padoch, eds., *People of the Tropical Rain Forest* (Berkeley: University of California Press, 1988), 111–126.

[6] J. Fishman, "Ethnicity as Being, Doing and Knowing," in Hutchinson and Smith, *Ethnicity*, 63–69; quotation from p. 63.

[7] Baynton, "Beyond Culture"; N. Cohen, "The Ethics of Cochlear Implants in Young Children," *American Journal of Otology* 15 (1994): 1–2.

[8] A. Chimezie, "Transracial Adoption of Black Children," *Social Work* 20 (1975): 296–301; H. Lane and M. Grodin, "Ethical Issues in Cochlear Implant Surgery: An Exploration into Disease, Disability and the Best Interests of the Child," *Kennedy Institute of Ethics Journal* 7 (1997): 231–251.

[9] as this deprived the children of their heritage and deprived the tribe of a more open future. The Supreme Court ruled that lower courts must consider the best interests of the particular Native American tribe as well as the best interests of the child Indian Child Welfare Act of 1978. Passed at a time when the survival of Native American cultures was considered threatened by very high rates of transracial adoption, the act was designed to prevent the undermining of Native American tribes; it states that "it is the policy of this nation to protect the best interests of Indian children and to promote the stability and security of Indian tribes. . . ." The Supreme Court has ruled that lower courts must consider the best interests of the particular Indian tribe as well as the best interests of the child. R. J. Simon and H. Altstein, *Adoption, Race and Identity: From in fancy Through Adolescence* (New York: Praeger, 1992).

[10] Quoted in H. Markowicz, "La Langue Des Signes et l'Education Des Sourds: Une Perspective Sociolinguistique" (Mémoire de Diplôme d'Etudes Approfondies, U.E.R. de Linguistique, Université de Paris V, 1989–1990), quotation from p. 99.

[11] See, for example, the 1956 movie "The Searchers," with John Wayne.

[12] R. Hoffmeister, "Border Crossings by Hearing Children of Deaf Parents: The Lost History of Codas," in Bauman, *Open Your Eyes*, 189–218; quotation from p. 202.

[13] T. Humphries, "An Introduction to the Culture of Deaf People in the United States: Content Notes and Reference Materials for Teachers," *Sign Language Studies* 72 (1991): 209–240. See also: Baynton, "Beyond Culture"; Davis, "Postdeafness"; L. Davis, "Deafness and the Riddle of Identity," *Chronicle of Higher Education*, January 12, 2007, B6; Padden and Humphries, *Deaf in America*; Padden, "Deaf Community"; Smith, "Deaf People In Context"; but see B. Bahan, "Comment on Turner."

[14] Kyle, "Deaf People"; Ladd, *Understanding Deaf Culture*.

[15] B. Bodenhorn, "'He Used to be My Relative': Exploring the Bases of Relatedness among the Iñupiat of Northern Alaska," in Carsten, *Cultures*, 128–148; see p. 139.

[16] J. Fishman, "A Critique of Six Papers on the Socialization of the Deaf Child," in J. B. Christiansen, ed., *Conference Highlights: National Research Conference on the Social Aspects of Deafness* (Washington, D.C.: Gallaudet College, 1982), 6–20.

[17] R. Hoffmeister, quoted in: L. Davis, "Postdeafness," in Bauman, *Open Your Eyes*, 314–326.

[18] Davis, "Postdeafness"; Kyle, "Deaf People"; J. G. Kyle, "Deaf People and Minority Groups in the U.K," in B. Tervoort, ed., *Signs of Life*. (Amsterdam: Dutch Foundation for the Deaf, 1986); Ladd, *Understanding Deaf Culture*; Padden, "From the cultural."

[19] E. Klima and U. Bellugi, *The Signs of Language* (Cambridge, Mass.: Harvard University Press, 1979); W. C. Stokoe, D. Casterline, and C. Croneberg, *A Dictionary of American Sign Language on Linguistic Principles* (Silver Spring, Md.: Linstok Press, 1976); T. Humphries, "Scientific explanation and other performance acts in the re-organization of DEAF" in D. J. Napoli, ed., *Signs and Voices* (Washington. D.C.: Gallaudet University Press, 2008).

[20] The anthropologist Ladislav Holy states: "The most significant development in the study of kinship has been the growing awareness of the cultural specificity of what were previously taken to be the natural facts on which all kinship systems were built." L. Holý, *Anthropological Perspectives on Kinship* (Ann Arbor, Mich.: Pluto Press, 1996), quotation from p.165.

[21] Fishman, "A Critique"; Harris, *Cultural Meaning*, see p. 13; J. E. Nash, "Policy and Practice in the American Sign Language Community," *International Journal of the Sociology of Language* 68 (1987): 7–22; J. Ree, *I See a Voice: Language, Deafness and the Senses: A Philosophical History* (London: HarperCollins, 1999).

[22] "Deaf genes." We will use this phrase of convenience when we mean an allele, giving rise to the Deaf trait. An allele is one of several possible DNA sequences at a given physical gene location. The correspondences between the transmission of the Deaf trait and Mendelian laws of inheritance suggest the effects of a single gene but many traits are influenced by variation at several genes.

[23] P. Conrad and J. Schneider, *Deviance and Medicalization: From Badness to Sickness* (Columbus, Ohio: Merrill, 1980).

[24] H. T. Engelhardt, "The Concepts Of Health And Disease," in A. Caplan, H. T. Engelhardt, and J. J. McCartney, *Concepts of Health and Disease* (Reading, Mass.: Addison Wesley, 1981) pp. 31–45; R. Selzer, "Against Devices for the Deaf [a review of H. Lane, *Mask of Benevolence*]," *Washington Post*, July 2, 1992.

[25] D. S. Davis, "Cochlear Implants and the Claims of Culture? A Response to Lane and Grodin," *Kennedy Institute of Ethics Journal* 7 (1997): 253–258; quotation from p. 254.

[26] T. P. Gonsoulin, "Cochlear Implant/Deaf-World Dispute: Different Bottom Elephants," *Otolaryngology Head and Neck Surgery* 125 (2001), 552–556; quotation from p. 554.

[27] T. Balkany, A. Hodges, and K. Goodman, "Ethics of Cochlear Implantation in Young Children," *Otolaryngology—Head and Neck Surgery* 114 (1996): 748–755; quotation from p. 753.

[28] R. Hofstadter, *Social Darwinism in American Thought* (Philadelphia: University of Pennsylvania Press, 1944)

[29] H. Lane, "Do Deaf People have a Disability?" in Bauman, *Open Your Eyes*, 277–292.

[30] R. Shweder, "Anthropology's Romantic Rebellion Against the Enlightenment," in R. Shweder and R. A. LeVine, eds., *Culture Theory* (New York: Cambridge University Press, 1984), 27–66.

[31] Groce, *Everyone Here*. When Groce asked her informant to say who were "handicapped by deafness when she was a girl on the Island," she replied emphatically: "Oh, those people weren't handicapped. They were just deaf"; quotation from p. 5. See also: Lane, Pillard, and French, "Origins."

[32] MJ Bienvenu, "Disabled: Who?" *The Bicultural Center News* 13 (April 1989): 1; K. A. Jankowski, *Deaf Empowerment: Emergence, Struggle and Rhetoric* (Washington, D.C.: Gallaudet University Press, 1997); Ladd, *Understanding Deaf Culture.*

[33] http://www.nad.org/issues/technology/assistive-listening/cochlear-implants (accessed 7/22/2010).

[34] L. Jones and G. Pullen, "'Inside We Are All Equal': A European Social Policy Survey of People Who are Deaf," in L. Barton, ed., *Disability and Dependency* (Bristol, Penn.: Taylor and Francis Falmer Press, 1989), 127–137.

[35] T. Humphries, "Deaf Culture and Cultures," in K. M. Christensen and G. L. Delgado, eds., *Multicultural Issues in Deafness* (White Plains, N.Y.: Longman, 1993), quotation from p. 6.

[36] Humphries, "Reference Materials," quotation from p. 220.

[37] D. Baynton, "Beyond Culture"; V. Finkelstein, "'We' Are Not Disabled, 'You Are,'" in Gregory and Hartley, *Constructing Deafness*, 265–271; Gonsoulin, "Cochlear Implant/Deaf-World Dispute"

[38] M. Mills, "I Am Happy My Child Is Deaf: Many Are Horrified by a U.S. Couple Deliberately Choosing to Have Deaf Children. Here, Sharon Ridgeway, Who Is the Deaf Mother of a Deaf Child Sympathises With Their Decision," *The.Guardian* (April 9, 2002): 8. A survey of Deaf and hard-of-hearing participants found no preference about the hearing status of their children: S. J. Stern, K. S. Arnos, L. Murrelle, K. Welch, W. Nance, and A. Pandya, "Attitudes of Deaf and Hard-of-Hearing Subjects toward Genetic Testing and Prenatal diagnosis of Hearing Loss," *Journal of Medical Genetics* 39 (2002): 449–453; M. Miller, D. Moores, and D. Sicoli, "Preferences of deaf college students for hearing status of their children." *Journal of the American Deafness and Rehabilitation Association* 32 (2003): 1-8.

[39] P. Abberley, "The Concept of Oppression and the Development of a Social Theory of Disability," *Disability, Handicap and Society* 2 (1987): 5–19. Baynton presents the case that many disabled persons have no desire to join the disabled "other": D. Baynton, "Beyond Culture." "What needs to be stated is that disability—while never wished for—may simply not be as disastrous as imagined": M. Fine and A. Asch, "Disability Beyond Stigma: Social Interaction, Discrimination, and Activism," *Journal of Social Issues* 44 (1988): 3–21; quotation from p. 11. J. Gusfield writes: "We must take care not to parody and reject lightly either the naive materialist or the constructivist positions. Naive materialists do recognize that their actions can affect the 'real' social problem they are trying to remedy. And constructivists do not claim that social problems are invented out of thin air; some disease and disabilities—some—have biological as well as social determinants of their categorization": J. Gusfield, "On the Side: Practical Action and Social Constructivism in Social Problems Theory," in J. Schneider and J. Kitsuse, eds., *Studies in the Sociology of Social Problems* (Rutgers, N.J.: Ablex, 1984), 31–51. "Every disabled person would welcome such an operation (or other form of personal intervention) which guaranteed successful elimination of the impairment": V. Finkelstein, "We Are Not Disabled, You Are.," in Gregory and Hartley, *Constructing Deafness*, 265–271; quotation from p. 265; H. Lane, "Constructions of Deafness," *Disability and Society* 10 (1995): 171–189. While it is true that barriers of many kinds are disabling, strong

constructionism fails to take into account the "difficult physical realities faced by people with disabilities," arising from factors "such as chronic pain, secondary health effects, and ageing derive from the body." T. Siebers, *Disability Theory* (Ann Arbor: University of Michigan Press, 2009), 25, 57.

40 S. N. Barnartt and J. B. Christiansen, "Into Their Own Hands: The Deaf President Now Protest and Its Consequences," in Bragg, *Deaf-World*, 333–347.

41 J. P. Shapiro, *No Pity: People with Disabilities Forging a New Civil Rights Movement* (New York: Times Books, 1993).

42 S. E. Brown, "What is Disability Culture?" *Independent Living Institute Newsletter* 12 (2001): 1.

43 Baynton, "Beyond Culture."; Lennard Davis has written: "Instead of calling the Deaf a nationality, one might consider them as occupying the place of an ethnic group."; "Thus the Deaf became a new subgroup within each state throughout Europe: like Jews and Gypsies, they were an ethnic group in the midst of a nation." L. Davis, *Enforcing Normalcy: Disability, Deafness and the Body.* (New York: Verso, 1995): 77, 83. However, Davis questions the wisdom of "identity politics"; "Postdeafness." In, H-D. Bauman, ed., *Open your Eyes: Deaf Studies Talking.* (Minneapolis, University of Minnesota Press, 2008): 314-325; L. Davis, "The End of Identity Politics," in L. Davis (ed.) *The Disability Studies Reader.* (3rd ed.) (New York: Routledge, 2010): 301-315. This is a matter of considerable debate; see, for example, Tobin Siebers, who writes: "Identity politics remains in my view the most practical course of action by which to address social injustices against minority peoples and to apply the new ideas, narratives and experiences discovered by them to the future of progressive democratic society." In Davis, *Disability Studies Reader,* p. 321.

44 In both France and the United States, Deaf sports federations have declined to participate in the Paralympics, despite the funding that would provide. See also: H-D. Bauman, "Postscript: Gallaudet Protests of 2006 and the myths of in/exclusion," in Bauman, *Open Your Eyes,* 327–336; Baynton, "Beyond Culture."

45 Lane, "Constructions of Deafness"; Lane, "Disability"; Lane, "Ethnicity, Ethics."

46 R. Dunbar and T. Skutnabb-Kangas "Forms of Education of Indigenous Children as Crimes Against Humanity?" Expert paper written for the United Nations Permanent Forum on Indigenous Issues, 2008. "It is important to remember that indigenous peoples also include Deaf individuals and communities who use sign languages as their mother tongues" (p. 1). http://www.un.org/esa/socdev/unpfii/documents/E_C19_2008_7.pdf (accessed 7/22/2010).

47 The Americans with Disabilities Act provides that the widespread perception of disability is itself a handicapping condition. See interpretive guidance for the ADA regulations, page I-35. The Supreme Court ruled (480 U.S. at 284) that a similar provision was included in the 1973 Rehabilitation Act because "Congress acknowledged that a society's accumulated myths and fears about disability and diseases are as handicapping as are the physical limitations that flow from actual impairment."

48 Davis, "Postdeafness."

[49] G. Anderson, C. Grace, and V, "Black Deaf Adolescents: A Diverse and Underserved Population," *Volta Review* 93 (1991): 73–86; G. B. Anderson and D. Watson, eds., *The Black Deaf Experience: Excellence and Equity. Proceedings of a National Conference March 12–14, 1992* (Little Rock: University of Arkansas RRTC, 1992); G. B. Anderson, "Tools for a Wiser, Healthier, Black Deaf Community," *Deaf American Monographs*. 44 (1994): 1–4; H. Anderson, "Perspectives on Discrimination and Barriers Encountered by Black Deaf Americans," in Anderson and Watson, *Black Deaf Experience*, 49–51; A. Aramburo, "Sociolinguistic Aspects of the Black Deaf Community," in C. Erting et al. *The Deaf Way: Perspectives From the International Conference on Deaf Culture* (Washington, D.C.: Gallaudet University Press, 1994), 474–482; K. M. Christensen and G. L. Delgado, *Multicultural Issues in Deafness* (White Plains, N.Y.: Longman, 1993); College for Continuing Education, *Empowerment and Black Deaf Persons Conference Proceedings April 6–7, 1990* (Washington, D.C.: Gallaudet University, 1992); L. Dunn, "Setting the Pace In Black Deaf America," in G. Olsen, ed., *A Kaleidoscope of Deaf America* (Silver Spring, Md.: National Association of the Deaf, 1989), 22–23; C. Farrell, "Students Who Are Black and Deaf Say They Face Dual Discrimination," *Black Issues in Higher Education*. (1989): 14–15; E. Hairston and L. Smith, *Black and Deaf in America* (Silver Spring, Md.: TJ Publishers, 1983); H. Joyner, *From Pity To Pride: Growing Up Deaf in the Old South* (Washington, D.C.: Gallaudet University Press, 2004); Padden and Humphries, *Inside Deaf Culture*; C. McCaskill, C. Lucas, R. Bayley, and J. Hill. *Hidden Treasure: The History and Structure of Black ASL* (Washington, D.C.: Gallaudet University Press, in press); R. K. Rittenhouse et al., "The Black and Deaf Movements in America Since 1960: Parallelism and an Agenda for the Future," *American Annals of the Deaf* 136 (1987): 392–400; V. Valentine, "Listening to Deaf Blacks," *Emerge*. (1996): 56–61; J. Woodward, "Black Southern Signing," *Language in Society* 5 (1976): 211–218.

[50] J. Fishman, "Ethnicity as Being, Doing and Knowing," in Hutchinson and Smith, *Ethnicity*, 63–69. Fenton, *Ethnicity: Racism*. On racism and audism see: H-D. Bauman, "Audism: Exploring the Metaphysics of Oppression," *Journal of Deaf Studies and Deaf Education* 9 (2004): 239–246.

[51] Davis, "Postdeafness"; Fishman, *Rise and Fall*; Glazer and Moynihan, *Ethnicity*; Jenkins, *Rethinking Ethnicity*; Verkuyten, *Social Psychology*.

[52] Smith, *Ethnic Origins*.

[53] "In 2000, 18 percent of the total population aged 5 and over, or 47.0 million people, reported they spoke a language other than English at home. These figures were up from 14 percent (31.8 million) in 1990 and 11 percent (23.1 million) in 1980. The number of people who spoke a language other than English at home grew by 38 percent in the 1980s and by 47 percent in the 1990s." www.census.gov/prod/2003pubs/c2kbr-29.pdf (accessed 7/22/2010).

[54] Waters, *Ethnic Options*.

[55] Verkuyten, *Social Psychology*.

[56] Cornell and Hartmann, *Ethnicity and Race*.

[57] Ibid.; Fishman, *Language and Ethnicity*; Fishman, *Rise and Fall*; quotation from p. 516; L. Vail, "Ethnicity in southern African History."

[58] Smith, *Ethnic Revival*; Verkuyten, *Social Psychology*.

59 Fishman, *Rise and Fall.*
60 Smith, *Ethnic Revival*; Verkuyten, *Social Psychology.* The Arab European League in the Netherlands stated: "We want to remain who we are, participate in the broader society, while keeping our own cultural identity"; quotation from p. 131.
61 Edwards, *Language, Society.*
62 Bahan, "Comment on Turner"; Lane, Hoffmeister, and Bahan, *Journey.*
63 T. Humphries, "Deaf Culture and Cultures," in K. M. Christensen and G. L. Delgado, *Multicultural Issues in Deafness* (White Plain, N. Y.: Longman, 1993), 3–15.

Part II

Deaf Ancestry: Henniker, NH, and Martha's Vineyard, MA

Three Deaf enclaves that flourished in the nineteenth century stand out in an analysis of how the Deaf-World was founded in New England: Henniker, New Hampshire, Martha's Vineyard, Massachusetts, and southern Maine.[1] Deaf ancestry in America has roots in the English settlers of the seventeenth century. What the settlers found and created together is the backdrop for a consideration of the individual Deaf families.

4

Context: Settling the New World

Early in the 1600s, the postmaster in the village of Scrooby, Nottinghamshire, William Brewster, illegally convened a little Separatist church in his home. The Separatists, or Puritans as they came to be called derisively, were Calvinist. They were opposed to all ritual not plainly required by the word of God, and they believed that God predestined some souls for salvation, others for damnation. But these Calvinists sought to carry the Protestant Reformation further than the Church of England was willing to carry it; they opposed the cross in baptism, the ring in marriage, kneeling at communion, and ecclesiastical vestments. Queen Elizabeth and her archbishop saw in this movement a grave threat to the Church of England and were determined to stamp it out; numerous clerics were suspended for being tainted by it. The Scrooby congregation attempted to flee by ship to the Netherlands but was betrayed by the ship's captain; their leader was jailed for heresy. At his release, the congregation regrouped in Amsterdam but then, finding no work and fearful of becoming involved in an ongoing dispute among other Separatist congregations there, they settled in Leiden, in the Netherlands, where other Englishmen joined them and the congregation grew to more than two hundred.

The congregation then passed over a decade in exile, engaged in manual labor, while many of its children were drawn into the military or merchant marine, imperilling the future of the community. Yearning for their native English language and culture, the congregation debated its future and prayed, prayed and debated, and decided to send an initial group, led by Brewster, to America. They applied for funding to a London stock company. Boarding the ship *Speedwell*, they sailed to Northampton on the English coast where they met up with other Separatists, who had come from London on the *Mayflower*, and the two ships set out for the New World. However, the *Speedwell* proved unseaworthy. After putting into port to exchange passengers with the *Mayflower*, it headed back to London with those too old, too ill, or with too many children to brave the voyage and the harsh conditions reputed to await them in America. Many families were separated but about one hundred set sail, a third of them Separatists, the rest sent by investors. The pioneers dropped anchor in Plymouth Harbor on December 16, 1620, where they created a "church without a bishop and a state without a king."[2]

These early settlers, called Pilgrims, built log hovels, and survived the first freezing winter by stealing grain from Native American stores. Although there were farmers among these pioneers, they had no knowledge of New World agriculture and had neither plow nor ox. It has been truly said of them that they lacked everything but virtue. By the following autumn, half the original colonists were dead, killed by cold, sickness, and famine. The survivors begged food from a fishing settlement on the Maine coast. Friendly Native Americans showed them how to plant native crops and to fertilize the ground with fish. The first harvest was sufficient for a thanksgiving feast. Elder William Brewster and his fellow Pilgrims had established the first colony that would ratify the Constitution of the United States.

In the next two years, additional settlers came without provisions, sent by the colony's London investors. The enlarged community counted thirty-two cabins and 180 settlers. Some labored to exhaustion to convert the communal meadows and marshes into cornfields but others were unwilling to do so, and the harvests proved insufficient, leading to a time of starvation. When the colony dropped communal farming and assigned to each family its own parcel of land, the harvest improved greatly and trading soon commenced with Native American tribes. Fur proved the best way the Pilgrims found to pay their debts contracted for the voyage; the *Mayflower* had been rented. Livestock was distributed, so each family had its own supply of dairy and meat. Nevertheless, life remained very hard. These were constant concerns: securing enough firewood to withstand the bitter winters and to prepare food; transporting enough water; planting, tending, and harvesting fields, maintaining gardens and orchards; mowing meadowland and storing hay; caring for livestock.

Meanwhile, it had become clear to the Puritans, who had remained in England seeking to reform the church from within, that the crown was determined to move the church back toward Catholicism. Many more Puritans decided to immigrate to New England. In 1628, a group of Puritan businessmen formed a venture for profit named the *Governor and Company of Massachusetts Bay*. Initial voyages that year and the next created a small colony on Cape Ann and later at Salem, Massachusetts. Beginning in 1630, nearly one thousand colonists came to the New World, establishing a settlement on Massachusetts Bay in what is now Boston. The Great Migration had begun. Some two hundred settlers died the first year and as many again returned to England. As living conditions improved, new colonists came, mainly English Puritans— more than 20,000 over the next decade. New settlements soon fanned out from Boston—Newtown (later Cambridge), Lexington, Concord, Watertown, Charlestown, Dorchester, and others. After 1640 there was little immigration until after the Revolution, with the result that for a long time the ancestors of most New Englanders were English Puritans.

This homogeneity of the small population of settlers made it more likely that marriages would be among people with similar genetic backgrounds, favoring the birth of Deaf children, as we explain later.

The result of the Great Migration was a new society, forged not as European societies had been through long evolution around fortress towns and markets, but forged—without peasants and without landlords—by shared beliefs and a theocratic government. The Massachusetts Bay Colony organized immigrants into towns of two to four square miles and some thirty to fifty families, generally from the same region, exception made for essential tradesmen, such as blacksmiths, who might hail from a different region. A surveyor would designate a main street with lots laid out on both sides. This arrangement facilitated contacts among neighbors, attendance at the meetinghouse (as the Puritan churches were called), mutual protection, and supervision by authority. For example, Andover, Massachusetts, ancestral seat of the great Lovejoy Deaf clan (on whom, more later), was founded in this way in 1646. Everybody farmed, including the minister and the artisans. Everybody paid taxes to support the established church. All members of the church signed a covenant: one had to avow and defend the faith, live a godly life and, since all mankind was born in sin, experience spiritual rebirth (and prove it to the minister and the congregation). The inherent hardships of frontier life became ethical values: the Puritans favored plain style in life and plain speech in sermons; their homes were plainly furnished, their meetinghouses unadorned.

The Plymouth Colony founded by the Pilgrims merged with its larger and more successful neighbor, the Massachusetts Bay Colony, in 1691. Together they built the society and government that ultimately gave rise to the New England states. Puritanism became a "tribal cult"— *cult* because of shared religion, *tribal* because some two-thirds of all church members from 1630 to 1800 were either original founders or their descendants.[3] The transmission of property and of family names linked one generation with the next. If a child died, the same first name was normally given to the next infant of the same sex. Moreover, some two-thirds of first sons and daughters were given their parents' names. (These practices make tracing New England ancestries particularly challenging.) Thus, the Puritans, by virtue of their language, culture, religion, ancestry and bonding to one another, comprised an ethnic group, one that would do battle with Native-American ethnicities.

The first immigrants found marshland for the most part from the Connecticut coast north as far as Saco, Maine. There were also meadows bordering the great rivers that various Native-American tribes had cleared; these allowed the Pilgrims at Plymouth and the Puritans in Massachusetts Bay to survive their first years in the New World by cultivating wheat and roots. Increasingly, the pioneers grew livestock feed in the salt and fresh marshes. For home consumption, every farmer tried to keep a few cows. By the late 1600s, most farmers also had a family horse, an ox or a pair of oxen, a pig or two, and in some areas sheep and goats. They harvested a few tons of English cultivated hay to feed them. The early farmer sowed his seed by hand, plowed and harrowed with primitive tools, harvested with a sickle, threshed his grain with a flail. Agricultural historians have estimated what a farm family of five required in acreage in those times: six to eight acres of cultivated land including a kitchen garden and an orchard (barley for the customary English beer grew poorly, but apples for cider grew well); fifteen acres of pasture for grazing and as many again for mowing to yield winter hay; thus, some forty acres of improved land, plus woodland to yield wood for the fire. Many farmers had less, and about half were unable to sustain themselves. Destitute, they went to work for other farmers and were paid with livestock; or they fished and trapped; or moved north to Maine or west to hill country, where land was cheaper or even, in later years, free (some had been confiscated from British loyalists).

The settler's first priority, on arriving at the land he had acquired, was shelter. One-room log cabins were the quickest solution. Low ceilings, few windows, and large hearths helped to keep houses warm despite the bitter cold. The successor to the log cabin in the Maine countryside, from the mid-1700s until a century later, was one or one-and-a-half stories and one or two rooms deep, with all living spaces arranged around a central chimney. The average colonial house had a simple bed, a large wooden table with benches, some stools, and a chest and chamber pots. There were knives and wooden spoons but no forks; there were dishes, earthenware bowls, and cups. All the activities of the house took place in one large room, the "hall" on the first floor. Food was basic and unvaried—fried pork and corn meal. Beans, potatoes, apples, eggs, butter and cheese; fish and game. Water, coffee, cider, beer.[4]

Families worked from sunrise to sunset. It was expected and it was necessary for survival. Supporting a family of, say, nine members with just a hoe, a scythe, an axe, and a spinning wheel was daunting and yielded only the essentials: shelter, food, fuel, and clothing. Farming obeyed the dictates of the seasons: spring, planting; summer, cultivating; fall, harvesting. Winter: flail grain, shell corn, cure tobacco; repair fences, tools, and harnesses; cut wood and pull stumps; cut ice; increase home manufacturing. Farmers and their sons might take jobs in town in winter. Much of the home manufacturing was done by women and their daughters. This included fabricating all the family clothing in linen, wool, or blend. Shoes were prohibitively expensive and many families were unshod, even in winter. Child labor was needed to survive in this unmechanized rural society. For example, it took twenty procedures and sixteen months to turn flax into linen.[5] Girls participated in most stages of that process and also learned sewing, quilting, cooking, candle-making, and dairying; boys tended the livestock, cut wood, mended fences, cleared ground. Girls often joined other families to do household work and often stayed on there until married. Nearly all women married while they were still quite young, and they had many children—seven births per family on the average.[6]

We said that nearly everyone was engaged in farming in the early years of the new republic. Each farmer was highly dependent on his neighbors, and this no doubt reinforced the importance for Deaf people of finding one another and of forming small enclaves. When bringing in the harvest or corn husking, as many as a dozen neighbors might participate. Neighbors might lend the farmer a man and a horse or a set of tools. They would often help with digging a cellar, moving boulders, felling trees, logging, threshing grain, house raising and barn raising, dressing flax. The neighbor would ordinarily be paid back in labor and produce. Those who did not have the means to own a farm (this was true of many Deaf people) worked as hired hands. Like the Deaf hands employed at the Brown$_D$ homestead in Henniker, New Hampshire (about whom more later), workers were treated as family dependents. In addition there were public works where neighbors were expected to labor together in order to protect against fire and disease, to create water supply and waste-disposal, and to build harbors.

Early farmers also traded with their neighbors and they hunted, fished, visited and quilted with them. Many of the collaborative events were recreational as well as utilitarian. County fairs, started in 1811, gathered people at a distance from town for socializing, agricultural education, and modest sales of farm surplus. Neighbors also provided emotional support. They helped with births, weddings, illnesses and death. Entire families might arrive in the evening and remain overnight. Married children, nephews, aunts, the minister and deacons of the church might all stop by. Residents frequently attended the same church. Furthermore, marriages among townspeople made many neighbors into relatives, reinforcing those bonds. All this intimacy meant that everyone knew their neighbor's home and affairs, inside and out.

Although the record shows that Deaf people participated in this system of broad interdependence, their numbers in many towns were few. In 1850 the average Maine town with Deaf inhabitants had fewer than three Deaf people among 2500 citizens (See "Where Deaf people lived" in Chapter 9); most towns had none. Consequently, to enjoy the company and collaboration of their own kind, and to find a spouse, Deaf people had to leave town to visit or live with Deaf relatives, or move to a town or city with other Deaf people.[7] The earliest travel was on foot along Indian trails, painfully slow, arduous, and dangerous.[8] Most towns were beside the sea or on navigable rivers. In winter, when the rivers froze, travel between towns was rapid by sleigh.[9] In warmer weather, the river traffic used canoes, small sailing vessels, flatboats poled along, and later steamboats. With improvement in the roads came wagons and stagecoaches. Finally, after 1835, the railroad arrived.

Everyone who lived in the same household was family: old or young widows, children and stepchildren, elderly grandparents, maiden aunts and uncles, nieces and nephews, hired men and hired girls; apprentices, servants; orphans and cousins of all ages. In the 1700s, family and kin connections were at the core of village life. A Connecticut history explains: "All of the families of old timers seemed to be related to each other."[10] Thus hearing and Deaf families in this era were extended families: not in the sense that two or more married couples would be found in the same household, but rather that every household was part of a kinship network. The Puritan conception of the ancient Hebrew family allowed marriage between first cousins. The same tradition provided equal shares of inheritance for the children and a double share for the oldest son, thus favoring the bonds of kinship more than those of marriage (though the widow would normally be provided for). The practice of marrying kin—especially first cousin marriage with a blood uncle's daughter—favored strong ties between male kin, and yielded more opportunities for children to be hereditarily Deaf. The patriarchal Puritan family subordinated women: they were seen as minors, unable to make most contracts and required to give their property to their husband on marriage.

Birth took place at home with a midwife and female kin and neighbors, but physicians like Mason Fitch Cogswell, sponsor of the American Asylum for the Deaf and Dumb, were increasingly challenging the practice, determined to make obstetrics a medical specialty.[11] If the infant survived pregnancy and delivery, its life was threatened by scarlet fever, measles, mumps, whooping cough, smallpox, yellow fever, cholera, diphtheria, typhoid, typhus, respiratory and intestinal disorders, and quack medicine (bleeding, leeching, purging, induced vomiting). If a child did not succumb to one of these illnesses he or she might become Deaf, like Mason Cogswell's Deaf daughter, Alice$_D$ (on whom more later). One in every seven infants died before age one.[12] One in three died before age twenty![13] The likelihood that parents would bury a child was increased by the high birth rate. Death was common in the eighteenth and nineteenth century and not romanticized.

New England farmers put a high value on education for their children. A 1647 law of the Massachusetts Bay Colony required every town with more than fifty families to have a reading and writing school and those with more than one hundred, a high school. These schools were open only for the four winter months. Most pupils were between six and twelve; apprenticeship began at age fourteen.[14] Girls were admitted to school in most communities but not all. Not until 1817 did the New England states sponsor education for Deaf children.

There were few markets at first to encourage the growing of surplus crops; but as rural agricultural towns evolved, they became trading centers for an entire agricultural area. The first towns and villages tended to aggregate around water power (used for sawmills and grist-mills) and around transportation routes. Those towns became hubs for gathering the products of trapping, farming, and foresting, which they shipped out of the region, and for receiving manufactured goods, which they distributed in the region. A large portion of surplus produce was transported to seacoast towns, there to be sold in coastal and interna-tional trade. The Massachusetts seacoast had three hundred whaling vessels at the time of the Revolution, over one hundred of them har-bored at the island of Martha's Vineyard, site of a large Deaf enclave, many of whom were fishermen. Whalers set forth on perilous voyages in search of spermaceti wax for candles and blubber for whale oil, the best means of domestic lighting then available. Seacoast towns also exploited forest wealth. Profiting from its immense forests, Maine developed a vast shipbuilding industry where Deaf laborers found work. Oaks yielded ship planking; pine trees provided masts and pitch for waterproofing; both kinds of wood went into the construction of barrels for shipping agricultural produce. Although trading with England was reduced just after the Revolution, in the following years England's demand for American products resumed, fueled by its war with France. In 1800, four out of five Americans were engaged primar-ily in agriculture; farmers consumed most imported products and pro-vided most exported ones. Federal policy encouraged agriculture.

The export-import trade flourished. Merchants pushed their activi-ties inland, thereby buttressing the growing agriculture. They brought in imported goods and brought out farmers' surplus productions. Furthermore, farmers sold some of their produce in local markets. In addition to the farmers and the merchant class, there was an artisan class closely related to both. A family in the artisan class passed on a symbolic property, such as a highly skilled occupation, to the members of the next generation who usually remained in the same area. This practice fostered stable extended families; it helped children with ambi-tion to move up in the world; and it generated surplus wealth, for such apprentice labor was cheap. Among the artisan class were itinerant portrait painters, such as John Brewster_D Jr. and Augustus Fuller_D, both of whom attended the American Asylum. Other Deaf artisans were cabinetmakers, shoemakers, printers, mechanics, and dressmakers—to name just a few.

The Napoleonic wars at the dawn of the nineteenth century origi-nally helped but then hurt American shipping. France bought from America products that originated in the British West Indies that she could no longer buy from her adversary. And England used the neutral American fleet to trade with hostile nations. However, thousands of

American ships were seized by French or British warships or priva-
teers. In response, President Thomas Jefferson, hoping to show the
combatants how much they needed a neutral carrier, imposed a four-
teen-month embargo on shipping to foreign ports, which stifled foreign
trade. In the War of 1812 the British blockaded New England shipping,
drying up the market for farm produce. When the war ended, factories
sprung up at every waterfall but then cheap foreign goods poured in
and the nascent prosperity was extinguished. By 1819 all the textile
mills had closed. On the island of Martha's Vineyard, the sheep flock,
reduced during the Revolution, had been built up again only to be
depleted once more when commandeered by the army in the War
of 1812.

Thanks to the coming of the railroad in the mid-nineteenth century,
new mills sprung up in places like Lowell and Lawrence, Massachusetts,
and Manchester, New Hampshire, providing farmers with customers
for food and fiber right near home. These water-powered machines
freed farm women from spinning and weaving. Released from that
labor, many farm girls, some of them Deaf, flocked to the mills. With
mill rather than farm labor, girls could afford much better clothes as
well as comforts and luxuries previously out of reach. The rails also
drastically reduced rural isolation. Because rail transportation in New
England was widespread, rapid and relatively inexpensive, it made
possible the gathering of more Deaf people than ever before, allowing
them to form a critical mass for socializing and political action. The
gatherings that led to the first institutions of the American Deaf-World
had their forerunners in the Deaf enclaves of southern New Hampshire
and the island of Martha's Vineyard, Massachusetts, which we
examine next.

5

The Brown Family of Henniker, NH

The first great American Deaf leader was Thomas Brown$_D$ (1804–1886), who was born in Henniker, New Hampshire, thirteen years before the American Asylum for the Deaf and Dumb opened in Hartford, Connecticut, and who died in Henniker six years after the 1880 congress of Milan. Our story begins with his because he founded important institutions for the Deaf in America and because his family, with Deaf people in every generation, was central to the Deaf enclave in Henniker. (See a portrait of Thomas Brown$_D$ in Fig. 1.)

Figure 1 Thomas Brown portrait. Courtesy, Gallaudet University Archives.

To the best of our knowledge, the Brown – Swett – Sanders clan of Henniker was one of only two early American Deaf founding families in the northeast. By "founding," we understand three or more consecutive generations of Deaf people, starting before 1800.[1]

We use the term *clan* to refer to a group of Deaf lineages linked by Deaf marriage. We make the presumption, for which there is often evidence, that the Deaf members share a signed language and "feel knit to one another."[2] We have made the case in Part I that common ancestry is not necessary for kinship; Deaf people are kin based on a shared physical trait, shared language and culture, and diffuse enduring solidarity. However, the members of many Deaf clans do share ancestry, as was the case with the Brown$_D$ clan. Thomas Brown$_D$'s grandfather, also named Thomas, lived in Stow, Massachusetts, with his wife, eight daughters, and a son, Nahum$_D$–the first Deaf-mute in the family, as far as anyone knew. (See Fig. 2, Brown$_D$ Pedigree.) In the figures, circles stand for females, squares for males, diamonds for multiple children, filled symbols for Deaf, and open symbols for hearing. See Appendix C, Pedigree Methods, for details.)[3] The progenitor of this Brown family in America, Thomas Browne, left Suffolk County in England and settled in Cambridge, Massachusetts[4] His grandson, Jabez, moved to Stow where son Joseph was born. Joseph's son, Thomas Brown, was born and raised in Stow, where he took up the trade of blacksmith and, in 1763, married Persis Gibson. The Gibson line originated in the United States with John Gibson, who settled in the Massachusetts Bay Colony about 1634; his birthplace in England is not known.

In 1785 Thomas Brown fled Stow with his family to Henniker, New Hampshire, a virtual wilderness some hundred miles away. It seems that Thomas had contracted a hard-currency debt that he was unable to pay. At the time of the Revolution, the colonial states printed their own money, "fiat money," not backed by coin. Too much of this money was printed, and Thomas's money lost its value. According to his son, Nahum$_D$, he once took a bushel of fiat money and dumped it into a grain bin in the attic.[5] Increasingly lenders wanted repayment in British gold, pounds, or other hard currency. Fearing debtors' prison, Thomas set out for Henniker where his wife's family, former residents of Stow, had moved. Henniker is located on the Contoocook River; the early settlers would have been drawn there by the numerous large ponds teeming with fish, the dense forests with abundant game, the large meadowlands and waterfalls that could be harnessed to power mills.

On arriving, Thomas made a clearing and built a log cabin, which stood for nearly a century and was known as the Brown House. Then, according to one account, he sent word to Nahum$_D$ (it is not clear how, at a distance, he would have instructed his thirteen-year-old Deaf son to do this) to hitch two yoke of oxen to a sled, load the furniture and food, bundle his mother and sisters atop the load and, armed with a goad, prod the oxen a hundred miles through the snow to Henniker.[6] According to another account, Nahum_D preceded his father to Henniker and was living with his uncle, Captain Timothy Gibson, Jr. (Gibson was a sergeant in the French and Indian War). In that case, it was probably Nahum_D's father, Thomas, who brought the family.[7]

The contemporaries of Nahum_D's father described him as smart, energetic, and fond of books; he held minor elected posts in later years. His eight daughters, tall, blue-eyed, good-looking, were said to be brilliant, witty, and well educated; most became teachers. Neighbors and relatives had a harder time judging son Nahum_D's intellect since he was Deaf; he was called plucky, a skillful axman and hunter, a model farmer, and a first-rate teamster of oxen and horses. Of course, no one thought of his becoming a teacher or even of his going to school.

Curiously, the first deed of land to the Browns on record was for 100 acres to Nahum_D, who was only 17. Perhaps his father could not afford to buy land some four years after moving to Henniker, and it was Nahum_D's mother's family who bought the land and gave it to Nahum_D, endeavoring to provide for their Deaf grandchild. Or perhaps, given his debts, Nahum_D's father thought that deeding the land to his son was safer. Thomas Brown died when he was eighty-two–old enough to outlive two of his three wives; to attend the marriage of his son Nahum_D to Abiah Eastman, a hearing woman of the town; to witness the birth of their daughter, Persis_D, in 1800 and their son, Thomas_D, in 1804; and old enough to learn of the opening of the first school for the Deaf (in Hartford, in 1817). His grandson Thomas_D enrolled there five years later.

As a young man in Henniker, Nahum_D did not wear shoes; in order to chop wood, he stood on warm planks in the doorway of his family cabin. The many chores he performed as the lone male child prepared him for a life of responsibility and labor. According to his son Thomas_D, he worked hard from dawn to dusk and was known as a good parent and neighbor.[8] He never learned to read or write. He communicated in pantomime or "natural sign." His wife served as his interpreter and helped him in such activities as buying and selling cattle. Like his father, Nahum_D had a long life, dying at age eighty-eight. He raised his two Deaf children, Persis_D and Thomas_D, saw them marry and give him five grandchildren, three of whom were Deaf. The next generation brought nine great-grandchildren, five of them Deaf. In an era when the arrival of a Deaf child was most often attributed to maternal fright, Nahum_D and his family must surely have been puzzled.[9] Nahum_D saw his son Thomas_D graduate from school, among the first Deaf-mutes in the nation to do so, and emerge as a preeminent Deaf leader, beginning in mid-century. Five years before Nahum_D's death, a group of son Thomas_D's Deaf friends gathered in the Brown household to draft a constitution for the first enduring Deaf organization in America, the New England Gallaudet Association of Deaf-Mutes (NEGA). Nahum$_D$'s sight had begun to fail. He suffered from severe headaches and became blind in one eye and then the other. "During his helpless and blind situation," his son Thomas$_D$ related, "he would sign for [us] to come and see what he wanted. With his arms moving slowly, he understood the movement of our hands."[10] One day, he signaled for his wife to come near; with her hands upon him, the common ancestor of the Brown – Swett –Sanders clan, passed peacefully away.

In 1822, when Thomas Brown$_D$ was eighteen—a slender, powerful man with a large head, gray eyes, and a facial tic from a childhood encounter with an ox—he enrolled at the American Asylum. The town of Henniker voted annually to pay his educational expenses, until the state legislature undertook to pay for Deaf-mute pupils from New Hampshire.[11] Thomas$_D$ and his elder sister, Persis$_D$, were both considered bright—Thomas$_D$ was "shrewd, wild but not vicious"—and both could no doubt have attended the school, but Persis$_D$ was bound by a marriage contract to a hearing carpenter from Henniker, Bela Mitchell Swett, and was not free to join her brother.[12] Thomas$_D$ studied under the cofounders of American Deaf education, Clerc$_D$ and Gallaudet, and under an intellectual leader of the profession, Harvey Peet, who would later direct the New York school for the Deaf.[13] Thomas$_D$, we are told, was an excellent student; at the completion of his five-year course, he agreed to stay on for two years as monitor and carpentry instructor. However, at the end of that period, twenty-five years old, he declined to become a teacher at the Ohio school for the Deaf and returned instead to Henniker to help his parents work their 123 acres.

In view of Thomas$_D$' tireless efforts in later years to organize Deaf people, to honor their leaders past and present, and to promote Deaf interests, one wonders to what extent and in what ways his years at the American Asylum developed his early consciousness of Deaf people as a distinct group. The Central Society of the Deaf in Paris, with its annual banquets celebrating Deaf language, history, and leaders, began shortly after Thomas left school, so he could not have learned about it while he was a pupil of Clerc$_D$'s, though no doubt he learned of it subsequently for it was clear to American educators of the Deaf that their methods derived from the French, and transatlantic visits were made in both directions.[14] Perhaps the sense of Deaf people as a distinct group was in the very air at the American Asylum in the 1820s. After all, a single language was emerging that connected Deaf people despite wide differences among them in region, family circumstances, isolation, and former methods of communication; with it, a sense of we-who-speak-this-language might naturally have emerged. Indeed, the first initiative for creating a Deaf state was organized by a group of seniors at the American Asylum just two years after Thomas$_D$ left.[15] The initiative was, however, short-lived.

One of the scattered enclaves of Deaf people that were gathered and to some extent amalgamated by the schooling of their number at the American Asylum was the Deaf population of Martha's Vineyard; more pupils came from there than from any other single locale.[16] While at school, Thomas$_D$ met Mary Smith$_D$, whose family came from the Vineyard, where Deaf people—especially in some remote communities "up island," such as Tisbury and Chilmark—were quite common. Three years after his return to his father's farm in Henniker, Thomas$_D$ made the journey to the coast, where he took a boat for the Vineyard, six miles off the Massachusetts shore, and then traveled a day on horseback to arrive at the village of Chilmark, where he and Mary$_D$ were married (April 1, 1832) in the presence of her many Deaf and hearing relatives and friends. (More about Mary Smith$_D$ and other Deaf people on the Vineyard in the next chapter.)

Thomas$_D$ and Mary$_D$ settled on his parents' farm; his father was sixty, his mother sixty-six and strong hands were sorely needed. More than that, Thomas brought to the task many natural gifts. He was a good horseman. He drove his own oxen and won prizes at the county fairs in Concord, New Hampshire, for drawing a load with a large boulder, over a ton, the allotted distance. He won awards for plowing, and for his colts, and Mary$_D$ drew a premium of $2 for a nice lot of cheese she had prepared.[17] He raised cattle and poultry, grew fruit, wheat, and hay. Thomas divided the large farm into lots of pasturage, tillage, orchard, woodland, etc., and each lot had a name. Those that have come down to us were figures in Deaf education such as Gallaudet, Clerc$_D$, and Peet.[18] He kept his accounts carefully. He was frugal, practical, methodical.[19] Sometimes it was very hard: there were years of early and severe frosts that killed the crops; there were seasons extremely dry, when small fruit withered and fell from the trees and clouds of grasshoppers settled on the fields, devouring everything.[20]

Deaf people, like their hearing contemporaries, found it beneficial and at times imperative to work together as an extended family. Deaf bonding, based on shared language and way of life, made frontier life bearable, even rewarding. In addition to Thomas$_D$'s father, Nahum$_D$, and sister, Persis$_D$, there were Persis$_D$'s and Bela's two Deaf sons, Thomas B. Swett$_D$ (called Nahum$_D$ in honor of his grandfather), born the year Thomas Brown$_D$ went off to school, and William B. Swett$_D$, two years older (See Fig. 2, Brown$_D$ Pedigree). In 1837, Thomas B. Swett$_D$ went to the American Asylum and Mary Brown$_D$ lost her hearing daughter, Charlotte, to illness, only a year old. Then, two years later, William Swett$_D$ went off to school and Mary$_D$ gave birth to a Deaf son, Thomas Lewis Brown$_D$. On return from Hartford, the Swett boys took Deaf wives. William$_D$ married Margaret Harrington$_D$, from Ireland, whose Deaf brother had also married into a large Deaf family. William$_D$ had a colorful career as an explorer, showman, mechanic, writer, and artist, before settling down. They had three hearing children two of whom died quite young, and two Deaf daughters who married Deaf men. William$_D$'s brother, Thomas Swett$_D$, and his wife Ruth Stearns$_D$ of Bradford, Maine, had three Deaf children and one hearing. Thomas$_D$ was a farmer and mechanic, Ruth$_D$ a factory worker.

As many ethnic groups did, Deaf people tended both to marry within their ethnic group and to hire workers from their group. The Swetts lodged a Deaf carpenter who owned the blind and sash company where William$_D$ B. worked. Sometimes Deaf workmen would live on the Brown farm—for example, Joel Lovejoy, one of the Deaf Lovejoys from Concord, New Hampshire, (see Chapter 8) and Josiah Smith$_D$, with Deaf relatives in Hillsboro, New Hampshire. There was also a Deaf couple nearby, named the Goves$_D$, who were close friends. (Abigail Clark Gove$_D$ was from two towns away, New Boston, where there was the Deaf Smith clan, good friends of the Browns$_D$.) So it was quite a little Deaf society that worked and celebrated together and prayed together at the interpreted services in the Congregational Church.[21] However, the Deaf society centered in Henniker extended into nearby towns. Thomas Brown$_D$ socialized with Thomas Head$_D$ and his family in Hooksett and with NEGA member George Kent$_D$ and others in Amherst (both two towns away from Henniker); Mrs. Head$_D$ was from a large Deaf family in nearby Francestown, one town away from Henniker.[22] In his notebooks devoted to genealogical studies of the Deaf, Alexander Graham Bell lists all the Deaf persons in New Hampshire according to the Seventh Census, conducted in 1850.[23] Including only towns that are contiguous to Henniker, or at one remove, we find an additional thirteen Deaf residents, for a total of twenty-seven including Henniker itself.

A different gauge of the size of the Deaf-World in and around Henniker may be had from the 1887 publication of cumulative enroll-ments at the American Asylum since its opening in 1817. There were six children enrolling from Henniker and an additional thirty-eight from townships contiguous or at one remove, for a total of forty-four. Both the census and enrollment measures are in one respect underestimates of the Henniker Deaf enclave, since participants could certainly live more than two towns away and, indeed, with the coming of the rail-roads, they could live a considerable distance away. On the other hand, presumably not all Deaf people within easy reach of Henniker chose to participate in its social life.

As we recounted earlier, Brown$_D$ had the idea, at mid-nineteenth century, to assemble in Hartford a large gathering of Deaf people to pay tribute to Gallaudet and Clerc$_D$. When he asked for contributions, "the flame of love ran like a prairie fire through the hearts of the whole Deaf-mute band, scattered though they were through various parts of the country" and $600 was soon raised (that's about $17,000 today, according to the Consumer Price Index).[24] Four hundred Deaf people witnessed the presentation of the symbolic pitchers. A few years later, Deaf representatives from each of the New England states gathered in Henniker to write a constitution for the New England Gallaudet Association, as we have told; some were lodged in the Brown_D home, others at the Swetts_D, still others at the Goves_D. Thomas Brown_D was chosen president of the new organization, which convened at the same time as the Gallaudet monument unveiling, in Hartford. The second biennial meeting of the NEGA took place in Concord, New Hampshire, in 1856.[25] There were forty-four members from Massachusetts (including four Mayhews and three Tiltons from Chilmark, Martha's Vineyard; see Chapter 6); thirty-four from New Hampshire (mostly from towns close to Henniker); eleven from Maine, and fifty-eight from other states. It was at this meeting that the eminent Deaf minister and teacher, Job Turner_D, dubbed Thomas Brown_D "the mute Cincinnatus of Americans," since he was so ready to drop his plough and come to the aid of his fellow mutes. The honorific, Mute Cincinnatus, stuck.[26] The third biennial NEGA meeting was held in Worcester Massachusetts, and the fourth in 1860 at the American Asylum, as mentioned earlier.[27] Brown_D gave the presidential oration.

Just at the time when his network of Deaf friends and associates was the strongest yet, Thomas Brown_D, age fifty-six, suffered a series of personal losses. The year before, he had lost his father, Nahum_D, age eighty-seven, who gradually became blind and helpless. Then, two years later, his wife Mary_D died, sixty-one years old, after an excruciating, year-long illness. Some months later, death took his mother, Abiah, age eighty-five. Then Bela Swett_D, and Bela's hearing grandchildren, William B. Swett_D's children, died. Deeply depressed at the loss of his children, William_D left to pursue the life of an adventurer and guide in the White Mountains. Thomas_D' son, Thomas Lewis Brown_D, age twenty, graduated from the American Asylum and accepted a position as teacher in the Deaf and Dumb Asylum at Flint, Michigan. It was not uncommon in that era for a widower to remarry; Thomas_D married Sophia Curtis, a hearing member of one of the large Deaf families in southern Maine. (We'll come back to the Curtises in Chapter 10.)

Thomas continued his life as a farmer—and Deaf leader. In 1866, the NEGA met in Hartford to coincide with the fiftieth anniversary celebration of the American Asylum. Some 500 people saw Brown_D give the presidential address, in which he announced that, after twelve years of service, he would resign in favor of his vice-president, George Wing_D of Bangor, Maine.[28] Two years later, the *Deaf-Mutes' Friend* (successor to the *National Deaf-Mute Gazette*) published a letter from Thomas Brown_D proposing a national convention of Deaf-mutes. According to an eminent Deaf teacher and journalist who endorsed the suggestion in the following issue, Brown_D had first made this proposal "to the convention in Syracuse in 1865"—no doubt the meeting of the Empire State

Association of Deaf-Mutes.[29] A year later, Thomas$_D$' sister, Persis$_D$, died, as did Laurent Clerc$_D$.[30]

Thomas$_D$, sixty-five years old, won awards at the state fair and cattle show. His son, Thomas Lewis$_D$, came home from Michigan to host a large birthday party for his father. Just as the *Gazette* reassured its readers that Brown$_D$'s new wife knew sign language, so the *Friend* explained to its readers that one of the storytellers at the birthday party "although a hearing man, is a very good sign-maker."[31] In 1874, Brown$_D$ took on the presidency of the Clerc Monument Association,.[32] and four years later he founded the Granite State Deaf-Mute Mission and was elected president.[33] William B. Swett$_D$ followed in his uncle's footsteps in promoting Deaf welfare: he published (with William Chamberlain$_D$) the *Deaf-Mutes' Friend*; he was a director of the Deaf-Mute Library Association; he was business manager of the Boston Deaf-Mute Mission[34]; and he founded a school of industrial arts for Deaf adults, which shortly added an educational program for Deaf children; it continues today as the Beverly School for the Deaf (formerly the New England Industrial School for Deaf Mutes).[35] Thomas Brown$_D$ was a trustee of the school in its early years.[36] In 1880, the first national convention of the Deaf in America was convened just as Brown$_D$ had proposed—except for the venue: it was held in Cincinnati, not Hartford; at that meeting was founded the preeminent national organization of the Deaf to this day, the National Association of the Deaf. Brown$_D$, then seventy-six years old, could not attend. He did, however, attend the meeting in New York in 1884, and then traveled to the Vineyard with his son Thomas Lewis$_D$, to visit the friends of his late wife.[37]

Thomas Brown$_D$ died March 23, 1886.

We will return to an examination of the Henniker Deaf enclave in order to contrast it with Deaf lives on Martha's Vineyard, to which we turn now.

6

Martha's Vineyard

Mary Smith$_D$ no doubt found her life quite changed after she married Thomas Brown$_D$, left the Vineyard, and took up residence on the mainland in the intensely Deaf Henniker enclave, far from her hearing family and numerous relatives and friends on the island. She decided to take with her some remembrances of her island home—a whalebone; some beautiful big seashells; and shark teeth with scrimshaw sailor carvings on them.[1] Mary$_D$ and Thomas$_D$'s descendants would have the combined Deaf heritage of the Vineyard, some six generations deep at that time, and of the Henniker Deaf enclave, merely a generation old. Mary Smith$_D$ is representative of numerous Deaf young men and women who grew up on the Vineyard, attended the American Asylum, married a Deaf schoolmate, and created a family with Deaf and hearing children. Mary Smith$_D$ is also representative in that she could trace her ancestry, as could virtually all Deaf people on the Vineyard, to just a few settlers.

VINEYARD LINEAGES

In the following we present our pedigrees for all the major Vineyard Deaf families.[2] Before turning to Mary Smith$_D$'s pedigree, a word is needed here on how these pedigrees were made (see Pedigree Methods, Appendix C). We analyzed the information in Fay's *Marriages of the Deaf in America*, Bell's unpublished notebooks, federal censuses, and Banks' *History of Martha's Vineyard*, among numerous other sources listed in the endnotes. Each pedigree gives the descendants of the named progenitor who are in the line of descent to a Deaf person. Off-island Deaf descendants of Vineyard dwellers were included.

To prepare the Vineyard pedigrees below, we first identified, as far as possible, all the Deaf people and their relations on Martha's Vineyard in the eighteenth and nineteenth centuries. Because intermarriage was so extensive on the Vineyard, often we could not be sure who were the cousins or other relatives of a given Deaf person; consequently, this first stage was as inclusive as possible. Then in the second stage the inclusive group was pruned: we retained only the Deaf people, their ancestors, their descendants, and their siblings—no one else. All of the pedigrees presented in this book appear with more details at our website, http://dvn.iq.harvard.edu/dvn/dv/DEA, where the reader will also find pedigrees for numerous additional families with Deaf members.

A pedigree for Mary Smith$_D$ appears in Fig. 3. (Tilton pedigree; *see arrow*. Also see Fig. 6.) Mary Smith$_D$'s mother, Sarah (Sally) Cottle, was hearing; she was the daughter of Silas Cottle and Jerusha Tilton$_D$. Jerusha $_D$'s mother and father (Mary$_D$'s great-grandparents) were cousins (note the double bar indicating consanguinity).[3] They were both descendants of the island's first governor, Thomas Mayhew. Jerusha$_D$'s great-grandfather was Samuel Tilton, the progenitor of the Tiltons on the Vineyard. Samuel Tilton's father had emigrated from Warwickshire, England, to Lynn, Massachusetts, where Samuel was born. As a young man, Samuel learned the trade of carpenter and, after his father's death, moved with his mother and siblings to his step-father's home in Hampton, New Hampshire, where he married. In 1673, he moved his family to the Vineyard. The five Deaf Tiltons identified in the pedigree, with common descent from Samuel, are all children of consanguineous marriages and all have a Mayhew ancestor in addition.

Governor Thomas Mayhew and his family came from Wiltshire, England, to Medford, Massachusetts, in 1631 (see Fig. 4, Mayhew pedigree).[4] He worked as a business representative and merchant, bought an interest in a mill, and held various local offices. After moving to Watertown, one of the earliest of the Massachusetts Bay settlements, Mayhew bought Martha's Vineyard in 1641 from the two patentees under royal charter then disputing ownership of the island; he moved there six years later. The Mayhews intermarried so extensively with other families and their Deaf descendants were so numerous—thirty-eight counted here—that the pedigree is large and complex. The governor's son, Matthew, married Mary Skiffe in 1674; her family was from Kent. The Mayhew sibship in the eleventh generation is noteworthy for having four hearing and five Deaf members. Three of the siblings and their sister-in-law were members of the NEGA. (A sibship is a set of siblings, children of the same parents.)

Because the Tiltons early intermarried with the Skiffes, Mary$_D$ was also descended from James Skiffe, a native of Kent who came to America on the *Mayflower* (see Fig. 5, Skiffe pedigree) and settled in Sandwich, Massachusetts.[5] His son, James, purchased land on the Vineyard in 1669, settled in Tisbury, and sold the remaining tracts there to friends. (Edgartown in the east part of the island, Tisbury in the central part, and Chilmark in the west, were the three predominant settlements.)

Mary Smith$_D$'s father was Mayhew Smith (Fig. 6, Smith-Parkhurst pedigree, *see arrow*).[6] Her paternal grandfather, Elijah Smith, married a Mayhew; he was descended from the Smith progenitor, John, who was born in Hampton, England, and died in Watertown, Massachusetts, in 1639. His son, also named John, moved to Edgartown, Massachusetts, on the Vineyard, in 1653. Mary Smith$_D$ had eight hearing siblings and an older sister, Sally$_D$, who also attended the American Asylum. Sally$_D$ married a hearing cousin, Hariph Mayhew, who had six Deaf brothers and sisters. Mary$_D$'s brother, Captain Austin Smith, married Levina Poole—the two had a shared ancestor in Samuel Tilton (Fig. 3). They had two hearing children and two Deaf. One of their Deaf children, Freeman$_D$, married a Deaf cousin—Deidama West$_D$ (see Fig. 7, Lambert pedigree). Deidama$_D$ had four Deaf siblings and three hearing. Deidama$_D$'s parents (mother, Deaf; father, hearing) were distant cousins, both descended from Governor Thomas Mayhew, and her father was descended from the first recorded Deaf person on the island, Jonathan Lambert$_D$.[7]

Lambert$_D$ was a carpenter, who had arrived from Barnstable about 1692. Although early Vineyard immigrants were from the Boston area, late in the 1600s many, like Lambert$_D$, came from lower Cape Cod towns of Sandwich, Barnstable, and Falmouth. A Jonathan Lambert was master of the Brigantine *Tyral* and had served under Sir William Phips, Royal Governor of Massachusetts, in an expedition to Quebec in 1690.[8] A Jonathan Lambert$_D$, presumably the same person, left a will that reveals him to be relatively wealthy and literate and the father of two Deaf children.[9] In the following excerpt, spelling errors have been retained.

> Being arrived to old age but of suitable mind and memory to dispose as hereafter the goodness of my God, calling to mind the mortality of my body, do mak and ordain this my last will and testament. [I leave] to Elizabeth my beloved wife the use and improvement of all whatsoever I leave in the world. . . .
>
> I leave to my loving son Jonathan, half of my meadow at Felix Neck in Edgartown and also half a shear in the commons of the town of Tisbury. I give to my loving son and daughter, Ebenezer$_D$ and Beula$_D$, the other half of that meadow . . . together with half of my hous (viz. est end) and land hear at home and also two cowes . . . [gifts to the other four children] . . . and furthermore, by these presents (considering my two poor children that cannot spake for themselves), I earnestly desire that my son Jonathan and my trusty beloved friend David Butler after the understanding hereof would please as they have opportunity to help them in any lawful way as they shall have need.
>
> March 23, 1737. Witness: Samuel Luce, David Butler,
> Jonathan Farnum

Evidence that Lambert$_D$ was Deaf comes from a diary entry of a Boston judge, who was visiting the Vineyard: "We were ready to be offended that an Englishman, Jonathan Lumbard, in the company spake not a word to us, and it seems he is Deaf and Dumb."[10] Jonathan Lambert$_D$'s grandfather, Thomas, was born in Tenderton, Kent, in 1600 and migrated to Scituate, on Cape Cod, in 1630, part of the Great Migration. This progenitor had numerous Deaf descendants on the Vineyard. In the 1700s three of them were children or grandchildren of Jonathan$_D$, two by his wife Elizabeth Eddy; her grandfather, Samuel, emigrated from Kent to Barnstable, Massachusetts. She married Jonathan Lambert$_D$ in 1683 and the couple moved to Tisbury. Deaf Lamberts, Mayhews, and others follow but that is the last we hear of the Eddy name in Deaf ancestry.

Jonathan Lambert$_D$'s sister, Abigail, had three Deaf grandchildren. Many more Deaf Lambert descendants were born in the following century, stemming from intermarriage with members of the West family in Chilmark.[11] The progenitor of the West clan, Francis, moved from Wiltshire, England, where he was a carpenter, to Duxbury, Massachusetts, in 1639 (see Fig. 7, Lambert pedigree). His son Thomas, an attorney and doctor—the first physician on the Vineyard—was associated with the Skiffe family and about 1673 he moved to Tisbury. There were no Deaf children in the West clan until after the seventh generation, when Lydia West married her relative, Thomas Lambert in Chilmark; they had a Deaf daughter Prudence$_D$. Lydia's brother, George West, married his second cousin, Deidama Tilton$_D$. George had ancestors from the Butler family, whose progenitor was Nicholas, and from the Athearn family, whose progenitor was Simon; both progenitors emigrated from Kent. Nicholas Butler and wife have two lines of descent on the Vineyard: son John married Priscilla Norton and settled in Edgartown; daughter Mary married Simon Athearn and settled in West Tisbury.[12] Descendants of John and Priscilla intermarried as did those of Simon and Mary but their Deaf descendants are all Mayhews and Wests six and seven generations later.

George West and wife Deidama$_D$ had eight children, five of whom were Deaf. Among the Deaf children, Joseph ("Josie") West$_D$ was reportedly the only illiterate Deaf person in Chilmark. He was a farmer, gardener and axman. His portrait, painted by Thomas Hart Benton, is in the Martha's Vineyard Museum.[13] Josie$_D$ married a hearing woman and they had no children. Josie$_D$'s brother, George$_D$, a farmer and fisherman, married Sabrina R. Rogers$_D$—she from a large Deaf clan (Fig. 14). The couple had three children, one of whom was Deaf, Eva$_D$; she married a hearing man. Another of Josie$_D$'s brothers, Benjamin$_D$ married a hearing woman; on her death he married an Asylum graduate like himself, Catherine ("Katie") Dolan$_D$.

We find evidence of what it meant to be Deaf on the Vineyard, and how this differed from the views of the general public, in a newspaper article of the day. George West, husband of Deidama$_D$, when interviewed for a Philadelphia newspaper in 1895, stated that he had thirty-three grandchildren of whom ten were Deaf.[14] The reporter comments: "The kindly and well-informed people whom I saw, strange to say, seemed to be proud of the affliction—to regard it as a plume in the hat of the stock. . . Anyone who should . . . offer to wipe out the affliction from the place and to prevent its recurrence, would almost be regarded as a public enemy and not as a benefactor."

A KENTISH ENCLAVE

In his testimony to the *Royal Commission of the United Kingdom on the Condition of the Blind, the Deaf and Dumb, Etc.,* Bell stated that he had identified seventy-two Deaf individuals who had been born on the Vineyard or whose ancestors came from the Vineyard. Of those, thirty-two had Samuel Tilton as an ancestor, forty-one Governor Mayhew, and sixty-three James Skiffe.[15] Most of the island Deaf had all three of these colonists in their pedigrees. Now for a child with hearing parents to be Deaf, in what is called recessive transmission, each parent must pass on the same gene associated with being Deaf. Since there are numerous such genes, when they match we infer that the parents were related—that is, that they had a common ancestor who gave each of them the same gene. However, the known Deaf Vineyarders could not be traced to a single Vineyard ancestor.

In her classic study of the Deaf on Martha's Vineyard, *Everyone Here Spoke Sign Language,* anthropologist Nora Groce concludes, then, that the Deaf people on the Vineyard had a common ancestor back in England. In view of the Kentish origins of so many Vineyarders, it was likely their ancestors had lived in Kent, in particular the isolated and forested region of Kent known as the Weald, where inbreeding was common.[16] Indeed, by the 1840s, nearly everyone on the Vineyard had two or more Kentish ancestors.[17]

Here is how that came to pass. In 1634, a minister named John Lothrop and some two hundred members of his congregation and their servants, all from parishes in the Weald in Kent, arrived in Boston harbor. Lothrop had been born in 1584 in Yorkshire and married a woman of Kent, Hannah House, in 1610. He had served as curate of a church in Kent for five years before becoming a Puritan Separatist in 1623. In so doing, Lothrop joined an outlawed movement that had been strong in Kent since the early 1400s. Nine years later he accepted leadership of a congregation of Separatists in London for which he was promptly imprisoned for two years. On release, he sailed with a portion of his London and Kentish flocks to Boston and then traveled to Scituate, where a new home had been prepared for him and where half the population was from the Weald. Indeed, there was a Kent Street in Scituate, so-called from the many "Men of Kent" who lived there.[18] Five years later Lothrop moved with many of his flock to Barnstable,

Massachusetts (on Cape Cod), and founded a church there, serving as minister of both Scituate and Barnstable.[19]

In 1670 several of the families in Lothrop's congregation, most from Kent, moved from Barnstable to the Vineyard when James Skiffe, who was from Kent, sold land in the village of Tisbury. In the ensuing decades, more of these families, Tiltons, Lamberts, and others, moved across Vineyard Sound, settling in the Chilmark area.[20] Thus, the progenitors of Deaf families on the Vineyard who had emigrated from Kent—James Skiffe, John Smith, and Thomas Lambert—joined by other Kentish settlers from Scituate and Barnstable, combined with extensive intermarriage on the island, created the conditions for an uncommonly large Deaf population there. Groce reports that the ancestries of Deaf Vineyarders almost always lead back to Scituate (the second oldest town in Plymouth Colony). It follows that the pattern of migration was Kent to Scituate, to Barnstable and the Cape Cod area, to Martha's Vineyard. Thus it is very likely that all the Deaf people on Martha's Vineyard, and all their descendants scattered over America right down to the present, have a common ancestor in Kent, the Ur ancestor in whom the original genetic mutation occurred.

One bit of evidence that there was indeed a Deaf population in the Weald in that era comes from Samuel Pepys's famous diary that gives an account of upper-class life in London in the early 1600s. Pepys relates what happened when a messenger arrived bearing news of a fire that was threatening large parts of the capital:

> There comes in that dumb boy . . . who is mightily acquainted here and with Downing; and he made strange signs of the fire, and how the king was abroad, and many things they understood but I could not, which I wondering at and discoursing with Downing about it, 'Why,' says he, 'it is only a little use and you will understand him and make him understand you, with as much ease as may be.'[21]

Sir George Downing, the English politician for whom Downing Street is named, was an Anglo-Irish soldier and diplomat whose mother was a sister of Massachusetts Bay Governor John Winthrop. According to one source, he grew up in the heart of the Kentish Weald at the same time as emigration to the Vineyard began but that connection has yet to be confirmed. We infer that Downing could communicate with a Deaf boy, but where did he learn how to do that? As a child in Kent or elsewhere in England; as a young man in Massachusetts, or as an adult in England?[22] Another report, consistent with the idea that a sign language used in Kent reached New England in the seventeenth century, comes from the noted divine, Increase Mather, who in an essay of 1684 relates that a Deaf woman and her Deaf husband in Weymouth, Massachusetts, engaged in fluent sign communication; her guardian had lived among immigrants from the Weald in Scituate, fifteen miles away.[23]

LIFE AND MARRIAGE ON MARTHA'S VINEYARD

The colonizers were drawn to the Vineyard by availability of farmland, the long growing season, the surrounding sea that abounded in fishes and shellfish of vast variety and the numerous woods and ponds, where game and birds were to be found. The sandy soil was adapted to sheep raising. The Native Americans were friendly and taught the islanders how to catch whales—nearly every family on the Vineyard had a member aboard a whaler by the time of Mary Smith's$_D$ wedding there.[24] In 1700, there were 400 people on the Vineyard; the population stopped growing about 1800 at some 3000.[25] Not surprisingly for this relatively isolated populace, whose ancestors were from the same parishes, most people married someone to whom they were already related and who was from their own village on the island.[26] A symptom of this practice was the proliferation of the same family names: an 1850 census counted 132 Mayhews and 87 Tiltons in Tisbury and Chilmark.[27] In 1807, 32 names comprised three-fourths of the island population![28]

Marrying a man who was from off island, as Mary Smith$_D$ did, was thus an anomaly brought about by the opening of the American Asylum and the desire of families on the Vineyard to see their Deaf children educated. After the school opened, Groce reports, all but one of the Vineyard Deaf of school age attended.[29] With so many Deaf Vineyarders enrolled, their Vineyard sign language must have had a profound influence on the developing ASL and ASL may well have affected the sign language on the Vineyard.[30] Deaf Vineyarders often met their future spouses at the Asylum, many of whom were from the mainland.

The Deaf graduates of the Asylum were among the most literate people on the Vineyard in that era; less educated townspeople would bring them documents for explanation. The number of Deaf people born on the island gradually rose, peaking around the time of Thomas$_D$' marriage at 45. Groce estimates that, later in the nineteenth century, one in every 155 people on the Vineyard was born Deaf (0.7 percent), about twenty times the estimate for the nation at large (.03 percent).[31] An 1830 census found twelve Deaf people in Chilmark; no doubt Mary Smith$_D$ was one of them. The town's population was 694; hence 1.7 percent of the town was Deaf, while only 0.01 percent of the population in the neighboring islands was Deaf—a ratio of more than 100 to one.[32] In the 1840s, some fourteen Deaf children were born in Chilmark; by the 1870s only one Deaf child was born there, Katie West$_D$ She was the last of the hereditarily Deaf in Chilmark, twelve generations deep, and died in 1952.[33] The gradual decline in the numbers of Deaf people on the island was due to off-island marriages, in part the result of meeting mainland Deaf at the Asylum. The flourishing of Deaf ancestry had moved to the mainland, especially to Maine (see Chapter 8).

Mary Smith$_D$'s marriage to Thomas Brown$_D$ was anomalous in a second sense: Not only did she marry a man from off-island but also she married a Deaf man, whereas most Deaf people like her on the Vineyard married hearing people, while those on the mainland predominantly married Deaf people. On the Vineyard nearly two-thirds of marriages were "mixed" (they were even more common before the opening of the American Asylum.)[34] On the mainland, only about one-fifth of Deaf marriages were to hearing people. The high rate of mixed marriages on the Vineyard was probably a reflection of, and contributor to, a broader feature of life on the island—the blending of Deaf and hearing lives. Like Mary Smith$_D$ (and her maternal grandmother, Jerusha Tilton$_D$), most children born Deaf on the Vineyard had both parents hearing, as well as many hearing siblings, the more so as birth rates were high on the island.[35]

Another reflection of, and contributor to, this blending of hearing and Deaf lives was the widespread use of a sign language among both Deaf and hearing people (no doubt with varying degrees of fluency). A reporter who visited Chilmark in 1895 recounted that "every resident of Chilmark learns to talk with his fingers as early as with his tongue." This may be an overstatement as by one account "Some of the deaf would carry little notebooks around with them, and when they wanted to communicate they would write their messages down on paper."[36] The reporter goes on to report that distant neighbors communicated by sign language using spy glasses; sign language also served for boat to boat communication and for "whispering" in church. Folks were so bilingual, he claimed, that they passed from English to sign almost unconsciously.[37] The sign language on the Vineyard may have come from England to America with the colonizers: When Martha's Vineyard signs, elicited from elderly hearing residents in 1977, were recorded and presented to a British Sign Language speaker, he identified 40 percent of the signs as cognates. (The British two-handed alphabet was also in use on the Vineyard, unlike the one-handed manual alphabet on the mainland.)[38] Two and a half centuries had passed from the arrival of the first Deaf person on the Vineyard to the test with the British Sign Language speaker, so there had been ample time for Martha's Vineyard sign language to diverge from its origins, and to converge toward ASL, which Asylum students presumably brought back with them to the Vineyard if they settled there. An ASL informant, tested about the same time, found 22 percent overlap of ASL signs with Vineyard signs.

Linguists Ben Bahan$_D$ and Joan Poole-Nash make the case that Deaf people on the Vineyard were thoroughly assimilated and, as with Deaf people in the Mayan community studied by linguist Robert E. Johnson,[39] they valued their village more than they valued the company of other Deaf people: "Being Deaf itself is irrelevant," Johnson wrote, "as Deaf people have access to everyone in the village"[40] In accord with this "village-first" value in assimilative societies, the Mayan villagers, according to Johnson, tended to identify first with their family, then with the village, and then with Mayan society. When Johnson gave a party for all the Deaf people in the village and their families, he learned that it was the first event in the village that singled out Deaf people. Similarly, Groce relates that on the Vineyard "All these [Deaf] people were included in all aspects of daily life from their earliest childhood. . . . One of the most striking aspects of this research is the fact that rather than being remembered as a group, every one of the Deaf islanders who is remembered is remembered as a unique individual."[41] From this perspective, the Deaf on Martha's Vineyard were not a distinctive ethnic group; instead, they conformed to the dominant ethnicity, they were almost totally assimilated – to a society that valued them and used their language.[42]

The next chapter contrasts the very different Deaf enclaves in Henniker and on the Vineyard. It hypothesizes that the differences between these communities in language barriers and marriage practices are due to differences in genetic transmission of the Deaf trait; those differences give rise, in turn, to differences in ethnic consciousness.

7

Assimilating and Differentiating Societies

The story of Thomas Brown_D and the emergence of the first American organizations of and for Deaf people that he led can be seen as the story of emerging Deaf ethnic consciousness, which surfaced clearly in the mid-nineteenth century. Consider this evidence: The formation of the numerous societies of Deaf people over which Brown_D presided; the explicit goals of the first enduring Deaf organization, the NEGA, which he founded ("We, Deaf-mutes, desirous of forming a society in order to promote the intellectual, social, moral, temporal and spiritual welfare of *our mute community.* . ." [italics added]); the ritual-like rehearsal at meetings of the great events in Deaf history; the raising of monuments to important figures—all these testify that Brown_D and his associates saw the Deaf as a distinct group with a language and way of life that should be fostered. "That these conventions [of the Deaf] tend to keep alive the feelings of brotherhood and friendship among the mutes at large cannot be disputed," wrote William Chamberlain_D, an eminent Deaf journalist.[1] Consequently, Chamberlain_D supported the gatherings of "the children of silence." In the silent press, Brown_D was referred to as the "patriarch of the silent tribe"[2] and his eulogist stated that Brown_D was always ready to do his share "for any plan which promised to promote the welfare of his class."[3] *Class, our mute community, children of silence, silent tribe*—these are all forms, we submit, of ethnic self-ascription.

In stark contrast, the accounts available to us of the lives led by Deaf and hearing people in Tisbury and Chilmark during the same era are marked by an apparent absence of events and structures that would set Deaf people apart from hearing people. These accounts do not reveal any leader, any organization, any distinctive gathering place, any banquet or other ceremony, any monuments—indeed anything at all that suggests that Deaf people on the Vineyard had ethnic consciousness. Now that we have made this bald claim, something contrary may well come to light but it seems unlikely that the difference in degree will be eliminated by future discoveries.

The pedigrees that we have presented (Figs. 2 through 7) have led us to the hypothesis that a difference in the incidence and distribution of Deaf people in the two locations, Henniker and the Vineyard, is responsible for the difference in the emergence of ethnic consciousness. Other possible explanations of that difference come to mind, foremost among them, perhaps, differences between the two locations in language and marriage practices. We believe that those differences, like ethnic consciousness itself, are heavily influenced by genetic patterning.

The hereditary difference between hearing and Deaf people can be traced to any of numerous genes, most often acting singly. As a result, the occurrence of Deaf and hearing people in the family tends to follow the laws of heredity first spelled out by Austrian botanist Gregor Mendel in the mid-nineteenth century (but not widely recognized until the early twentieth century). Mendel identified two main patterns of genetic transmission, called dominant and recessive.

The Brown—Swett—Sanders clan of Henniker exemplifies the dominant pattern of inheritance. To the best of our knowledge, the Deaf trait was not expressed in any of Nahum Brown$_D$'s ascendants among the twenty-three we ascertained but Nahum$_D$ and some of his descendants in every generation expressed that trait, indicating that the genetic difference in this family began with Nahum$_D$ (see Fig. 2, Brown pedigree). If the pattern of genetic transmission was dominant in Nahum$_D$'s family, then on average half of his offspring would inherit that genetic difference and be born Deaf, while the other half would be born hearing. The proportion of offspring that can be expected to have a particular trait is called the "segregation ratio." Of Nahum$_D$'s eighteen descendants, twelve were Deaf and six hearing: this is statistically within range of the expected half-way split. All Deaf members of the family had a Deaf close relative and all Deaf members who married had at least one Deaf child. Thus the Deaf trait was expressed in each generation: Each Deaf person receives a Deaf heritage and may pass it on. Marriage between relatives (that is, spouses with the same gene) is not necessary for such generational depth.

The Tilton, Mayhew, Skiffe, Smith, and Lambert families of Martha's Vineyard (Figs. 3 through 7), exemplify, on the other hand, the recessive pattern of inheritance. In this pattern, many people in the family may possess the critical gene but the trait will not be expressed—it remains hidden or latent. This is because with a recessive trait two copies of the gene, one from each parent, are needed to produce a Deaf child. Parents who carry but do not express the gene are called simply "carriers." According to recessive transmission, hearing parents who are carriers will have, on the average, a segregation ratio of three-fourths hearing children. Deaf adults who marry hearing people who are not carriers will have only hearing children. Hence, with recessive transmission, there are lots of hearing people in families with Deaf members. Contrast that with dominant transmission where at least one parent is Deaf, and fully half of all their children are Deaf in every generation.

As our lineages for families with recessive transmission demonstrate, the hearing parents of a recessively Deaf person very frequently have an ancestor in common (see Parts III and IV). The odds of unrelated parents having exactly the same recessive gene (so that their child will receive the pair and be Deaf) are much greater if those parents are related to one another, as we explained. Intermarriage among relatives is most likely in a community that is isolated—on an island, say. This was indeed the picture on Martha's Vineyard.

Thus on the Vineyard, the overtly Deaf person must have felt a part of a rather extended family that included numerous hearing people in his or her immediate family and numerous hearing relatives. That Deaf person may not have felt like a crucial link in the chain of Deaf heritage from the past down to the future, as in dominant transmission.

The numerous *hearing* children of Deaf parents (Codas) on the Vineyard would be likely to acquire sign language as a native language; they and their Deaf siblings would thus form a critical mass within the family for sign language use. The *Deaf* children of hearing parents would learn the language from their parents, if they knew it, or, if not, from Deaf peers, elders and Codas, and they would seek to use sign language with their own parents and hearing siblings. Numerous hearing relatives on the island might also be motivated to master the sign language, at least to some extent, to communicate with their Deaf relatives. Thus the difference between Henniker and the Vineyard in the spread of sign language into the hearing environment may be traceable, in part, to the difference between them in genetic patterning. One Vineyard "old timer," interviewed in the 1950s, gave this account of the spread of sign language over much of the island:

> We would sit around [the post office–general store] and wait for the mail to come in and just talk. And the deaf would be there, everyone would be there. And they were part of the crowd, and they were accepted. They were fishermen and farmers and everything else. And they wanted to find out the news just as much as the rest of us. And often times people would tell stories and make signs at the same time so everyone could follow him together. Of course, sometimes, if there were more deaf than hearing there, everyone would speak sign language—just to be polite, you know.[4]

Recall that the incidence of mixed hearing and Deaf marriages on the Vineyard was more than triple that on the mainland. This difference may be attributable, at least in part, to the more widespread use of the sign language among hearing people on the Vineyard. Vineyarders born Deaf encountered a much lower communication barrier then their mainland peers. Since a common language greatly facilitates meeting one's life partner in the first place and then developing a deep interest in and affection for that person, it is not surprising that mixed marriages were common on the Vineyard.

Table 7.1 Factors in Ethnic Consciousness in Two Deaf Enclaves

	Henniker	Vineyard
Genetic Patterning	Dominant	Recessive
Hearing carriers of Deaf trait	–	+
Deaf people in every generation	+	–
Ethnic language boundary	+	–
Predominantly Deaf-Deaf marriages	+	–
Ethnic consciousness	+	–

Finally, we hypothesize that the differences in language use and marriage practice, which are underpinned in part by the differences in genetic patterning, mediate in turn differences in ethnic consciousness. Table 7.1 schematizes this line of reasoning.

What we are suggesting is that it takes a "them" for an "us" to develop, and the blending of hearing and Deaf lives on the Vineyard, because of shared family life and language (underpinned by genetics), discouraged the construction of hearing people as "them." Conversely, many members of the Henniker Deaf enclave had parents, grand-parents, and great-grandparents in whom the Deaf trait was expressed, and the boundary with the surrounding hearing population was rather sharply demarcated. That said, other factors may also have fostered Chilmark blending, such as a sense of isolation on a remote island and an awareness of shared ancestry. Blending is a matter of degree. No matter how cohesive and ethnically conscious Henniker's Deaf com-munity, for example, its members interacted with their hearing siblings and other relatives, and with hearing officials and commerce in the town.

THE BALI EXAMPLE: DESA KOLOK

Findings concerning the Deaf and hearing residents of a village in Bali help to evaluate the claim that Deaf genetic patterning, marriage and language practices, and ethnic consciousness are related. (Additional studies of assimilating sign-language communities are cited in the notes.[5]) A 1995 report states that there were 2185 people in this village, of whom 2.2 percent were Deaf.[6] The genetic patterning in "Desa Kolok" (not its official name) is recessive as on the Vineyard and, as on the Vineyard, marriages between hearing and Deaf people are completely acceptable.[7] There were sixteen families in Desa Kolok with two hear-ing parents and at least one Deaf child, so it is clear that there was more blending of hearing and Deaf lives in the Desa Kolok nuclear family than in Henniker where there were no families with hearing parents and Deaf children. However, the blending of hearing and Deaf lives in

Desa Kolok may not have been as great as on the Vineyard, since, in Desa Kolok, the twenty families with a Deaf parent (or two) had 75 percent Deaf children. Thus, there were more Deaf families with a Deaf parent than without, and the children in those Deaf families predominantly expressed the trait.

Beyond the blending of hearing and Deaf lives within the nuclear family in Desa Kolok, there are also cultural and social forces there that ensure widespread contact between Deaf and hearing people. Of particular note, Balinese villages are kin based and Deaf people grow up in house yards shared with their hearing relatives. Thus, with respect to the mixing of hearing and Deaf lives, the extended family of the Desa Kolok house yard may be more like Vineyard families than Henniker families. Perhaps for this reason, the use of a sign language in Desa Kolok is nearly universal and Deaf people are integrated in many facets of social life including groups organized for work and for some religious practices. Moreover, hearing attitudes toward the Deaf, many of whom are relatives, are generally positive.[8] Thus, the evidence from Desa Kolok suggests that the mixing of hearing and Deaf people in the family determines their mixing in community life, as we hypothesize was the case on the Vineyard.

It is not clear to us whether Deaf people in Desa Kolok lack ethnic consciousness, as we hypothesize was the case on the Vineyard. On the one hand, certain activities in Desa Kolok are associated with Deaf villagers who also have specific roles with regard to certain festivals and musical events. These distinctive activities would presumably be conducive to ethnic consciousness. On the other hand, as on the Vineyard, "the Deaf villagers interact freely and equally with other villagers."[9] Perhaps the mixed evidence for ethnic consciousness is a reflection of an intermediate status for Desa Kolok between Henniker and the Vineyard with regard to the blending of hearing and Deaf lives.

Although our inquiry has focused so far on southeastern New Hampshire and the Vineyard, there were many other clusters of Deaf people in other New England towns in the early years of our republic. We selected for a case study of Deaf ethnicity and ancestry the state of Maine. Part II examines Deaf families in a northern grouping of towns and Part III in a southern grouping.

Notes

Part II

Chapter 4

[1]   Works consulted for Chapter 4: "Settling the New World": S. Brant and E. Cullman, *Small Folk: A Celebration of Childhood in America* (New York: EP Dutton, 1980); D. B. Danbom, *Born in the Country: A History of Rural*

America (Baltimore: Johns Hopkins University Press, 1995); M. B. Davidson, *Life in America* (New York: Houghton Mifflin, 1951); B. Farber, "Family And Community Structure: Salem In 1800," in M. Gordon, ed., *The American Family in Socio-Historical Perspective* (New York: St. Martins, 1973), 100–110; J. A. Henretta, "Families and Farms: Mentalité in Pre-Industrial America," *William and Mary Quarterly* 35 (1978): 3–32; C. M. Jedrey, *The World of John Cleaveland: Family and Community in Eighteenth C. New England* (New York: Norton, 1979); E. B. Jones, *The Brewster Genealogy* (New York: Grafton, 1908); A. Kulikoff, "The Transition to Capitalism in Rural America," *William and Mary Quarterly* 46 (1989): 120–144; J. Larkin, *The Reshaping of Everyday Life: 1790–1840* (New York: Harper Row, 1988); K. Lockridge, "Land, Population, and the Evolution of New England Society: 1630–1790," *Past. and Present* 39 (1968): 62–80; J. C. Nylander, *Our Own Snug Fireside: 1760–1860* (New Haven, Conn.: Yale University Press, 1994); J. G. Palfrey, *History of New England* (Boston: Little Brown, 1877); B. H. Pruitt, "Self-Sufficiency and the Agricultural Economy of Eighteenth Century Massachusetts," *William and Mary Quarterly* 41 (1984): 333–364; J. O. Robertson and J. C. Robertson, *All Our Yesterdays* (New York: Harper Collins, 1993); H. S. Russell, *A Long Deep Furrow: Three Centuries of Farming in New England* (Hanover, N.H.: University Press of New England, 1976); D. S. Smith, "The Demographic History of Colonial New England," in Gordon, *The American Family*, 397–415; P. Smith, *As a City Upon a Hill* (New York: Knopf, 1971); L. Sprague, *Agreeable Situations: Society, Commerce and Art in Southern Maine 1780–1830* (Boston: Brick Store Museum, Northeastern University Press, 1987); L. T. Ulrich, *A Midwife's Tale: The Life of Martha Ballard Based On Her Diary 1785–1812* (New York: Knopf, 1990).

2 Palfrey, *History*. The first English colony in New England, Popham Colony, built a fort at the mouth of the Kennebec River, Maine, in 1607. However, after a year of many hardships, the settlement was abandoned and the surviving settlers returned to England. J.P. Brain, "Popham, Colony: The First English Colony in New England," *New England Ancestors* (2007): 31–33.

3 Henretta, "Families and Farms."

4 Danbom states that milk was not included in the diet but other authors disagree. Danbom, *Born in the Country*.

5 S. Brant and E. Cullman, *Small Folk: A Celebration of Childhood in America* (New York: E. P. Dutton, 1980).

6 Smith, *As a City Upon a Hill*.

7 A. J. Boyce, C. F. Kuchemann and G. A. Harrison, "Neighborhood Knowledge and the Distribution of Marriage Distances," *Annals of Human Genetics* 30 (1967): 335–338.

8 R. Wright, *Hawkers and Walkers of Early America* (Philadelphia: Lippincott, 1927).

9 "Report on an Exploration and Survey of the Territory on the Aroostook River" (Augusta, Me.: Smith and Robinson, 1839).

10 Robertson and Robertson, *All Our Yesterdays*.

11 Ulrich, *Midwife's Tale*.

12 Larkin, *Reshaping*.

13 Jedrey, *World of John Cleaveland*.

14 Ibid.

Chapter 5

1   T. W. Jones, "America's first multi-generation deaf families (A genealogical perspective)," *Deaf American Monographs* 46 (1996): 49–54; T. W. Jones, "Deafness-Focused Records for Genealogical Research," *National Genealogical Society Quarterly* 81 (1993): 5–18.

2   A. D. Smith, *Ethnic Origin of Nations* (Oxford: Oxford University Press, 1986), quotation from p. 49.

3   For the methods employed in researching the pedigrees, see Appendix C, Pedigree methods. In this and all other pedigrees, the following conventions are observed. Squares represent men; circles women; diamonds, individuals without regard to gender. Filled symbols indicate Deaf. Double bars indicate a consanguineous marriage. Dates are given in the form birth-death. "AA" indicates that this person attended the American Asylum. A superscript 0 indicates the person is not an ancestor of a Deaf person.

4   Wilson, *John Gibson of Cambridge, Mass and his Descendants 1634–1899* (author, 1900).

5   E. P. Thwing, "White Mountain Memories," *National Deaf Mute Gazette* 16 (April 1868): 8–9.

6   Ibid.

7   G. C. Braddock, *Notable Deaf Persons* (Washington, D.C.: Gallaudet College Alumni Association, 1975); L. Cogswell, *History of the Town of Henniker* (Concord, N.H.: Republican Press, 1880. Reprinted, 1973: Somersworth, N.H.: New Hampshire Publishing Co.)

8   T. Brown, [Sketch of Nahum Brown], *Gallaudet Guide and Deaf-Mutes' Companion* 1 (3) (1860): 12.

9   N. Groce, "Hereditary Deafness on the Island Of Martha's Vineyard: An Ethnohistory of a Genetic Disorder" (Ph.D. diss., Brown University, 1983).

10   T. Brown, [Sketch of Nahum Brown]; W. B. Swett, "Obituary of Nahum Brown," *American Annals of the Deaf and Dumb* 11 (1859): 237–240.

11   T. L. Brown, *In Memoriam: A Tribute To the Memory of Thomas Brown* (Flint, Mich.: School for the Deaf, 1888)

12   S. Childs, [Sketch of Nahum and Thomas Brown], *Gallaudet Guide and Deaf-Mutes' Companion* 2 (4) (1861): 14–15.

13   H. Lane, *When the Mind Hears: A History of the Deaf* (New York: Random House, 1984.)

14   B. Mottez, "The Deaf-Mute Banquets And The Birth Of The Deaf Movement," in R. Fischer and H. Lane, eds., *Looking Back: A Reader on the History of Deaf Communities and their Sign Languages* (Hamburg: Signum, 1993), 143–155.

15   W. M. Chamberlain, "Proceedings of the Third Convention of the New England Gallaudet Association of Deaf-Mutes," *American Annals of the Deaf* 10 (1858): 205–219.

16   Groce, *Everyone Here*, p. 73.

17   Anon. (1869). [Annual fair]. *Deaf-Mutes' Friend* 1 (11) (1869): 344.

18   W.M. Chamberlain, "Thomas Brown," *American Annals of the Deaf* 31 (1886): 204–210.

19   Anon., "In Memoriam" [Thomas Brown], *Gallaudet Guide and Deaf Mutes' Companion* 2 (4) (1861): 14.

20   Cogswell, *Henniker*.

21 R. E. Colby, "On The Thomas Brown Place" (Handwritten Ms., Henniker Historical Society, 1961).

22 Anon., Letter from New Hampshire, *Deaf-Mutes' Friend* (1) (1869): 26–27; Anon. "A Festival of Deaf-Mutes" *Literary Budget* 1 (1) (1874): 3; J. Turner, "Biographical Sketch of Thomas Brown," *Deaf-Mutes' Journal* 9 (43) (1880): 2.

23 A. G. Bell, *Unpublished Notebooks* (Washington, D.C.: Volta Bureau, 1888).

24 L. Rae, "Presentation of Silver Plate to Messrs. Gallaudet and Clerc," *American Annals of the Deaf* 3 (1851): 41–64. "It also bespeaks a critical mass of people, and a level of achievement to have the resources of time and money to conceive of and implement such a gathering" (Theresa Smith, personal communication, 2009). In this period farmers earned about fifty cents a day, artisans three times as much. Six hundred dollars in 1850 corresponds to $15,000 in 2007 according to the Consumer Price Index.

25 W. M. Chamberlain, "Proceedings of the Convention of the New England Gallaudet Association of Deaf-Mutes," *American Annals of the Deaf* 9 (1857): 65–87.

26 Romans regarded Lucius Quinctius Cincinnatus as a model of Roman virtue and simplicity. George Washington was often referred to as the Cincinnatus of the Americans.

27 Anon., "Fourth Convention of the New England Gallaudet Association of Deaf-Mutes," *American Annals of the Deaf and Dumb* 12 (1860): 236–243; W. M. Chamberlain, "Proceedings of the Fourth Convention of the New England Gallaudet Association of Deaf-Mutes, *Gallaudet Guide and Deaf-Mutes' Companion* 1 (10) (1860): 1–2.

28 W. M. Chamberlain "Celebration of the Fiftieth Anniversary," *National Deaf-Mute Gazette* 1 (1) (1867):1–4.

29 T. Brown [signed T.B.], "Letter," *Deaf-Mutes' Friend* 1 (6) (1869): 188–190. The Deaf teacher and journalist was Henry C. Rider.

30 W. M. Chamberlain, "Obituary of Laurent Clerc," *Deaf-Mutes' Friend* 1 (1869): 216–217.

31 W. B. Swett, "A Birth Day Party" *Deaf Mutes' Friend* 1(4) (1869): 123.

32 Brown, *In Memoriam*.

33 J. T. Tillinghast, "Gathering of Mutes at Amherst, New Hampshire," *Michigan Deaf-Mute Mirror* 4 (1878): 3.

34 Anon., "Meeting of Deaf-Mutes" [Boston Deaf-Mute Mission]. *Silent World* 4 (1874): 5.

35 W. B. Swett, *Adventures of a Deaf-Mute* (Boston, Mass.: Deaf-Mute Mission, 1874).

36 T. L. Brown, *In Memoriam*.

37 T. Brown, [Address by Thomas Brown at his 80th birthday]. *Hillsboro Messenger*, March 6, 1884.

Chapter 6

1 Colby, "Thomas Brown place."

2 Dr. Nora Groce informs us that she has deposited a set of Vineyard pedigrees with the Library of Congress and also with the Martha's Vineyard Historical Society in Edgartown, Mass. (Personal communication, April 2009.)

The following were the primary sources of data that included multiple Vineyard families:

C. E. Banks, *The History of Martha's Vineyard*. (Edgartown, Mass.: Dukes County Historical Society, 1911, reprinted 1966); Bell, *Unpublished Notebooks;* Cogswell, *Henniker;*

E. A. Fay's census of Deaf marriages: E. A. Fay, *Marriages of the Deaf in America* (Washington, D.C.: Volta Bureau, 1898). The data forms for Fay's census are in the Gallaudet University Archives. J. C. Gordon, *Education of Deaf Children: Evidence of Edward Gallaudet and Alexander Graham Bell Presented to the Royal Commission of the United Kingdom On the Condition of the Blind, Deaf and Dumb, etc.* (Washington, D.C.: Volta Bureau, 1892); W. Haygood, "The Mystery of Martha's Vineyard," *Boston Globe*, July 20 (1986): A1, A4; C. M. Mayhew, *Vital Records of Chilmark Massachusetts to the Year 1850 with Birth Marriage and Death additions* (Bowie, Md.: Heritage Editions, 1991).

3 Pedigrees shown at the website provide a coefficient of relatedness—see Method appendix.

4 Banks, *History*, see vol. 1, p. 125; D. C. Poole, *A New Vineyard* (Edgartown, Mass.: Dukes County Historical Society, 1976); D. C. Poole, "Vineyarders Down East," *Dukes County Intelligencer* 22 (1980): 3–14.

5 N. Groce, *Everyone Here Spoke Sign Language* (Cambridge, Mass.: Harvard University Press, 1985); p. 35 states that Skiffe was from Kent. Banks, *History*, see vol. 2, p. 8, "Annals of West Tisbury," states it was James Skiffe Jr. who purchased the land. Tisbury first had the name Takemmy, then Middletown.

6 Inspecting the pedigrees, the reader may have noticed that a Martha Parkhurst (1595–1635) wed Gov. Thomas Mayhew while a Deborah Parkhurst (1619–1678) married John Smith. Martha is not a proven name; she is sometimes referred to as Ann or Abigail. Her father has been identified as Matthew (b. 1575). One source gives as Matthew's wife, Ann Newcomb, m. 1594. Since nothing is known of Matthew's parents or siblings, it has not been possible to evaluate the hypothesis that Deborah is the daughter of a brother of Matthew. www.conovergenealogy.com/ancestor-p/p160.htm (accessed 7/23/2010).

7 Lambert references: A. Otis, "The Lumbert or Lombard Family," *Library of Cape Cod History and Genealogy* #54 (Yarmouthport, Mass.: C.W. Swift, 1914); S. Rich, "The Lombards of Truro," *Library of Cape Cod History and Genealogy* #76 (Yarmouthport, Mass.: C.W. Swift, 1912). We appreciate Del Wynne's sharing family genealogy with us for the Lambert family.

8 H. G. Lang, "Genesis of a Community: The American Deaf Experience in the Seventeenth and Eighteenth Centuries," in J. V. Van Cleve, ed., *The Deaf History Reader* (Washington D.C.: Gallaudet University Press, 2007), 1–23.

9 Groce, *Everyone Here.*

10 Banks, *History*, quotation from vol. 2, p. 53, "Annals of West Tisbury."

11 Butler clan: W. Butler, "Martha's Vineyard, a Diary by William Butler," *Dukes County Intelligencer* 8 (2) (1966): 23–32; F. G. Butler, *A History Of Farmington Maine 1776–1885* (Farmington, Me.: Moulton, 1885); W. C. Hatch, *A History of the Town of Industry, Franklin County, Maine. Embracing the Cessions of New Sharon, New Vineyard, Anson and Starks* (Farmington, Me: Press Of Knowledge, 1893); New Sharon, *New Sharon, Maine, Historical Collections* (1977). Poole, *New Vineyard.*

[12] Athearn: Town of Tisbury, *Vital Records of Tisbury, Massachusetts, to the Year 1850* (Boston, Mass.: New England Historic Genealogical Society, 1910).

[13] Personal communication, Joan Poole-Nash, 2009.

[14] Anon., "Deaf and Dumb of Squibnocket," *Deaf-Mutes' Journal* 24 (1895): 1.

[15] Bell gives the head counts for Tilton, Mayhew, and Skiffe. See: Gordon, *Education of Deaf Children.*

[16] The inference that the hearing ancestors of a Deaf descendant were related is based on the observation that numerous genes may render a person Deaf so the odds of receiving the same gene from each parent are quite small unless the parents are related. Recent studies have shown that mutations in the gene GJB2 (connexin-26) are very common among people who were born Deaf and as many as 1 in every 40 people in the general population have at least one mutated copy of the gene. If this gene was widespread on Martha's Vineyard, marriage among relatives would not necessarily have been required for some of the offspring to be Deaf. G. E.Green, D. A. Scott, J. M. McDonald, et al., "Carrier rates in the Midwestern United States for GJB2 Mutations Causing Inherited Deafness" *Journal of the American Medical Association* 281 (1999): 193–195. W. E. Nance, X. Z. Liu, and A. Pandya "Relation Between Choice of Partner and the High Frequency of Connexin-26 Deafness," *Lancet* 356 (2000): 500–501.

[17] Groce, *Everyone Here*, see p. 123.

[18] S. Rich et al., The Lombards of Truro, Library of Cape Cod History and Genealogy #76 (Yarmouthport, Mass.: C.W. Swift, 1912).

[19] Lothrop's great-grandson, Nathaniel Brown, had a daughter, Mary, who married into the great Lovejoy Deaf clan in Maine; more on them later. (See Fig. 12, Lovejoy pedigree).

[20] Banks, *History.*

[21] Groce, *Everyone Here*, see p. 30.

[22] "Downing's family came from the Suffolk/Essex borders (he is buried in Suffolk along with his parents). His family also lived briefly in Dublin (he was born there)." Bencie Woll, personal communication, 2008. See also: J. Beresford, *The Godfather of Downing Street; Sir George Downing, 1623–1684* (London: Cobden-Sanderson, 1925); S. Jones, *In the Blood: God, Genes, and Destiny* (London: Harper Collins, 1996).

[23] B. Carty, S. Macready, and E. Sayers, "'A Grave and Gracious Woman': Deaf People and Signed Language in Colonial New England," *Sign Language Studies* 9 (2009): 287–323.

[24] J. Freeman, *Dukes County 1807*. Reprinted: *Dukes County Intelligencer* 12 (4) (1976): 1–51; D; Poole, *New Vineyard*; E. R. Mayhew, *Martha's Vineyard: A Short History and Guide*. (Edgartown, Mass.: Dukes County Historical Society, 1956).

[25] Groce, *Everyone Here.*

[26] N. Groce, "Everyone Here Spoke Sign Language," *Natural History* 89 (1980): 12–15.

[27] ibid.

[28] N.Groce, "The Island's Hereditary Deaf: A Lesson In Human Understanding." *Dukes County Intelligencer* 22 (1981): 83–95.

[29] Groce, "Hereditary Deafness," see p. 177.

[30] P. K. Valentine, "A Nineteenth Century Experiment in Education of the Handicapped: The American Asylum for the Deaf and Dumb," *New England*

Quarterly 64 (1991): 355–375. See also: B. Bahan and J. Poole-Nash, "The Formation of Signing Communities: Perspective from Martha's Vineyard," in J. Mann, ed., *Deaf Studies IV Conference Proceedings* (Washington, D.C.: Gallaudet University College of Continuing Education, 1996), 1–26; J. Woodward, "Historical Bases of American Sign Language," in P. Siple, ed., *Understanding Language Through Sign Language Research*, (New York: Academic Press, 1978), 333–348.

31 N. Groce, *Everyone Here*; B. Crouch, "Martha's Vineyard 1700–1900," *Sign Language Studies* 53 (1986): 383–391.

32 J. R. Burnet, *Tales of the Deaf and Dumb* (Newark, N.J.: Olds, 1835); Anon., "Deaf and Dumb of Squibnocket," *Deaf-Mutes' Journal* 24 (1895): 1.

33 Bahan and Poole-Nash, "Formation of Signing Communities."

34 Groce, "Everyone Here."

35 Groce, "Everyone Here."

36 W. Haygood, "The Mystery of Martha's Vineyard," *Boston Globe* (July 20, 1986): A1, A4. Quotation from p. 4.

37 Anon., "Deaf and Dumb."

38 J. Poole, "A Preliminary Description of Martha's Vineyard Sign Language." Unpublished manuscript, Boston University. (Paper delivered at the Third International Symposium on Sign Language Research, Rome, Italy. June 1983.) Summary in Bahan and Poole-Nash, "Formation of Signing Communities."

39 R. E. Johnson, "Sign Language and the Concept of Deafness in a Traditional Yucatec Mayan Village," in C. Erting, R. E. Johnson, D. L. Smith, and B. D. Snider, eds., *The Deaf Way: Perspectives from the International Conference on Deaf Culture* (Washington, D.C.: Gallaudet University Press, 1994), 103–109.

40 Johnson, "Sign language." See also: Bahan and Poole-Nash, "Formation of Signing Communities," 1–26, quotation from p. 19.

41 N. Groce, "The Island's Hereditary Deaf: A Lesson in Human Understanding," *Dukes County Intelligencer* 22 (1981): 83–95, quotation from p. 95.

42 Other assimilative and differentiating societies include: S. Kisch "Deaf Discourse: The Social Construction of Deafness in a Bedouin Community in the Negev," *Medical Anthropology* 27 (3) (2008): 283–313. Cf. Ch. 7, n. 5.

Chapter 7

1 W. M. Chamberlain, [Concerning a national convention]. *Deaf-Mutes' Friend* 1(8) (1869): 241–242. William Martin Chamberlain of So. Reading, Mass. (1832–1895), edited the monthly *Gallaudet Guide and Deaf-Mute's Companion*, official organ of the NEGA, printed in Boston 1860–1865. He also edited the *National Deaf-Mute's Gazette* and the *Deaf-Mute's Friend*. He was instructor at the Central New York Institution for the Deaf, at Rome, N.Y., and active in the Empire State Association of the Deaf.

2 J.O. David, "From New Hampshire: An Interesting Letter from Mr. David," *Michigan Deaf-Mute Mirror*, January 10 (1879): 2.

3 Brown, *In Memoriam*.

4 N. Groce, *Everyone Here*, quotation from p. 60.

5 Groce gives a list of examples of recessive deafness in small inbred communities. Groce, "Hereditary Deafness," see p. 361. See also on other assimilating

communities: A. Kusters, "Deaf Utopias? Reviewing the Sociocultural Literature on the World's Martha's Vineyard Situations," *Journal of Deaf Studies and Deaf Education* 15 (2010): 3–16; M. Fox, *Talking Hands: What Sign Language Reveals About the Mind*. (New York: Simon and Schuster, 2007); R. Senghas and L. Monaghan, "Signs of Their Time: Deaf Communities and the Culture of Language," *Annual Review of Anthropology* 31 (2002): 69–97; B. Woll and P. Ladd, "Deaf Communities," in M. Marschark and P. E. Spencer, eds, *Deaf Studies, Language and Education* (Oxford: Oxford University Press, 2003), 151–163; **Adamorobe village, Ghana**: N. Frishberg, "Sign Languages: Ghanaian," in J. Van Cleve, ed., *Gallaudet Encyclopedia of Deaf People And Deafness*, vol. 3. (New York: McGraw-Hill), 78–79; V. Nyst, "A Descriptive Analysis of Adamorobe Sign Language (Ghana)" (Ph.D. diss. University of Amsterdam, 2007). **al-Sayyid Bedouins, Negev, Israel**: S. Kisch, "Negotiating (Genetic) Deafness in a Bedouin Community," in J. V. Van Cleve, ed., *Genetics, Disability, and Deafness* (Washington, D.C.: Gallaudet University Press, 2004.); S. Kisch, "Disablement, Gender and Deafhood among the Negev Arab-Bedouin," *Disability Studies Quarterly* 27 (4) (2007): http://www.dsq-sds.org (consulted 7/23/2010); S. Kisch, "Deaf Discourse." **Amami Island, Japan**: Osugi and T. Supalla cited in B. Bahan and J. Poole-Nash (1996), "The Formation of Signing Communities: Perspective from Martha's Vineyard," in J. Mann ed., *Deaf Studies IV Conference Proceedings* (Washington, D.C.: Gallaudet University College of Continuing Education, 1996), 1–26; Y. Osugi, T. Supalla, and R. Webb "The Use of Word Elicitation to Identify Distinctive Gestural Systems on Amami Island," *Sign Language and Linguistics* 2 (1999): 87–112. **Bali Indonesia**: J. Branson, D. Miller, and I. G. Marsaja, "Sign Languages as Natural Part of the Linguistic Mosaic: The Impact of Deaf People on Discourse Forms in North Bali, Indonesia," in E. Winston, ed., *Storytelling and Conversation: Discourse in Deaf Communities. Sociolinguistics in Deaf Communities Series, Vol. 5* (Washington, D. C.: Gallaudet University Press, 1999); J. Branson and D. Miller, "The Cultural Construction of Linguistic Incompetence through Schooling: Deaf Education and the Transformation of the Linguistic Environment in Bali, Indonesia," *Sign Language Studies* 5 (1) (2004): 6–38; I. Marsaja, "Sociocultural, Sociolinguistic and Linguistic Patterns in a Deaf Community: An Ethnographic Study of a Deaf Village in North Bali" (Ph.D. Diss., La Trobe University, Melbourne, 2003); I. Marsaja, *Desa Kolok. A Deaf Village and its Sign Language in Bali, Indonesia*. (Nijmegen., Netherlands: Ishara Press, 2008). **Ban Khor, Thailand**: A. Nonaka, "The Forgotten Endangered Languages: Lessons on the Importance of Remembering From Thailand's Ban Khor Sign Language," *Language in Society* 33 (2004): 737–767. **Brazil**: L. Ferreira-Brito, "Similarities and Differences in two Brazilian Sign Languages," *Sign Language Studies*, 13 (1984): 45–56.; J. Kakumasu, "Urubu Sign Language," *International Journal of American Linguistics* 34 (1968): 275–281; **Grand Cayman, B.W.I.**: W. Washabaugh, "The Deaf of Grand Cayman, B.W.I.," *Sign Language Studies* 31 (1981) 117–134. **India**: U. Zeshan, M. Vasishta, and M. Sethna, "Implementation of Indian Sign Language in Educational Contexts," *Asia Pacific Disability Rehabilitation Journal* 16 (1) 2005: 16–40; **Jamaica**: D. Dolman, "Sign Languages in Jamaica," *Sign Language Studies* 52 (1986): 235–242; K. Cumberbatch, "Country Sign: Jamaica" (paper delivered at the Third Conference for Cross-linguistic

Research and International Cooperation in Sign Language Linguistics, in Preston, U. K., 2008). **Kosindo, Suriname**: B. Van den Bogaerde, "Everybody Signs in Kosindo Also," *Deaf-Worlds* 21 (2005): 103–107. **Nicaragua:** J. Kegl, A. Senghas, and M. Coppola, "Creation through Contact: Sign Language Emergence and Sign Language Change in Nicaragua," in M. DeGraff, ed., *Language Creation and Language Change: Creolization, Diachrony, and Development* (Cambridge, Mass.: MIT Press, 1999), 179–237. **Yucatan, Mexico:** E. Delgado, "Culture and Sign Language in a Mexican Mayan Deaf Community," *Third Conference for Cross-linguistic Research*. **Papua, New Guinea**: A. Kendon "A Description of a Deaf-Mute Sign Language From the Enga Province Of Papua New Guinea With Some Comparative Discussion," *Semiotica* 31 (1980): 1–34, 81–117, 245–313. **Providence Island, Colombia**: P. Farb, *Word Play: What Happens When People Talk* (New York: Knopf, 1973); W. Washbaugh, *Five Fingers For Survival* (Ann Arbor, Mich.: Karoma, 1986); W. Washabaugh, "Hearing and Deaf Signers on Providence Island," *Sign Language Studies* 24 (1979): 191–214. J. Woodward, "Attitudes Toward Deaf People on Providence Island, Colombia," *American Anthropologist* 63 (1978): 49–68. **Thailand**: J. Woodward, "Sign Languages and Deaf Identities in Thailand and Viet Nam," in L. Monaghan, C. Schmaling, K. Nakamura, and G. H. Turner, eds., *Many Ways to Be Deaf: International Variation in Deaf Communities* (Washington, D.C.: Gallaudet University Press, 2003). **Yucatec Mayan Village, Mexico**: R. E. Johnson, "Sign Language and the Concept of Deafness in a Traditional Yucatec Mayan Village," in C. Erting, R. E. Johnson, D. L. Smith, and B. D. Snider, eds., *The Deaf Way: Perspectives from the International Conference on Deaf Culture* (Washington, D.C.: Gallaudet University Press, 1994), 103–109; M. Shuman, "The Sounds of Silence in Noyha: A Preliminary Account of Sign Language Use by the Deaf in a Maya Community in Yucatan, Mexico," *Language Sciences* 2 (1980): 144–173; M. K. Shuman, "Culture and Deafness in a Mayan Indian Village," *Psychiatry* 43 (1980): 359–370; R. E. Johnson, Sign Language, Culture and Community in a Traditional Yucatan Maya Village. *Sign Language Studies*, 73 (1991): 461–474. Our thanks to Annelies Kusters, Centre for Deaf Studies, University of Bristol, who supplied several of these references.

6   S. Winata, I. Arhya, S. Moeljopawiro, J. Hinnant, Y. Liang, and T. Friedman, "Congenital Non-Syndromal Autosomal Recessive Deafness in Bengkala, an Isolated Balinese Village," *Journal of Medical Genetics* 32 (1995): 336–343.

7   Following Branson, Miller, and Marsaja: J. Branson, D. Miller, and G. Marsaja "Everyone Here Speaks Sign Language, Too: A Deaf Village In Bali, Indonesia," in C. Lucas, ed., *Multicultural Aspects of Sociolinguistics in Deaf Communities* (Washington, D.C.: Gallaudet University Press, 1996), 39–57.

8   J. Hinnant, "Music to their Eyes, Deaf Life And Performance in a Balinese Village" (paper delivered at the National Institutes of Health, Bethesda, Md., October 12, 1998); J. Hinnant, "Adaptation To Deafness in a Balinese Community," in C. Berlin and B. Keats, eds., *Hearing Loss and Genetics* (San Diego, Calif.: Singular Publishing Group, 2000); Branson, Miller, and Marsaja, "Everyone Here."

9   Branson, Miller, and Marsaja, "Everyone Here," quotation from p. 42.

Part III

Deaf Ancestry in Maine—Northern Cluster

Having explored the contributions of southeastern New Hampshire and Martha's Vineyard to the founding of the Deaf-World in America, our investigation turned to the state of Maine for several reasons. Many Deaf families on Martha's Vineyard migrated to Maine. Intermarriage among the Vineyard families continued there, while some of the settlers gave up and returned to the Vineyard, and still others married into unrelated Deaf families. Thus, Maine had a significant hereditary Deaf population. In the 1850 census, 266 individuals in Maine were identified as "Deaf and Dumb." (There were also 57 people identified solely as "Deaf.") Further, Maine sent a considerable number of students to the American Asylum in the nineteenth century—387—exceeded in New England only by Massachusetts and Connecticut. Thus the Maine Deaf population was substantial but of manageable size for systematic study. We refer to families with hereditarily Deaf members as "Deaf families" since, even if parents and siblings are overtly hearing, they are part of the Deaf family, for they are carriers of the Deaf trait; they pass Deaf ethnicity in its physical expression to later generations and they may pass elements of Deaf ethnic culture as well: they are likely to have developed some manual communication and to know other Deaf families, even to marry into them.[1]

On the Vineyard, Deaf families and hearing families were all bound to one another by marriage, language, and circumstances, especially those of island life. In Maine, however, marriage with hearing people was much less likely as relatively fewer hearing people were related to Deaf people or knew their language. Instead, on the mainland, Deaf people married other Deaf people most of the time and, when they married a hearing person, that person usually had Deaf parents or relatives. The result was that most Deaf households were enmeshed in a Deaf kinship network. Marriage with a person of one's own kind in an environment of otherness creates a heightened consciousness of shared identity and destiny in that group and ensures the transmission of language and culture to successive generations. We hypothesize that the links among Deaf families created by intermarriage were a key factor in founding the Deaf-World ethnic group. If this is correct, it conforms to Anthony Smith's description of the formation of ethnic groups:

> As men and women interpret and express their collective experiences, within any grouping or population thrown together by circumstance, these interpretations and expressions are crystallized over time and handed down to the next generations who modify them according to their own experiences and interaction. Thus there arise ethnic features formed out of these experiences and interpretations, which in turn limit and condition the interactions and perceptions of succeeding generations, through the temporal and spatial configuration of the collectivity and through the shared meanings which inform and guide the activities of its members. As a result, the features of an ethnic community take on a binding exterior quality for any member or generation, independent of their perceptions and will. They possess a quality of historicity that itself becomes an integral part of subsequent ethnic interpretations and expressions.[2]

We suggest that the circumstance that drew Deaf people together initially was the battle for survival in a hostile environment that required shared values and ways of communicating. This bonding was reinforced and formalized in Deaf-Deaf marriages, which had the effect of increasing numbers of the Deaf, validating the Deaf experience of each by comparison with others, and offering the Deaf child a greater opportunity for instruction in language and culture by Deaf peers and Deaf adult in-laws. The "ethnic interpretations and expressions" that take on a quality of historicity, to which Smith refers, are those of Deaf culture, expressed in Deaf language, and passed down by each generation to the next.

To examine the accuracy of this hypothesis, in Part III we focus on Deaf families and their intermarriage in the northernmost Deaf enclave—the Sandy River Valley and the surrounding region. Deaf enclaves further south are examined in Part IV. (The division between north and south, roughly at the level of Lewiston, Maine, is largely arbitrary, in part because there was extensive river travel north and south). In Parts III and IV we review some family pedigrees selected for their interconnections with other Deaf families, for the large number of Deaf people in them, or both. Pedigrees for all of these families and many more appear on the website (http://dvn.iq.harvard.edu/dvn/dv/DEA; see the Every Name Index, Appendix D). For 16 key families, pedigrees reduced to their "bare bones" for legibility are also presented in this volume; the fuller version is on the website.

In creating diffuse enduring solidarity among Deaf people, intermarriage was a very powerful institution, but it was only one of several. There were, in addition, several organizations of the Deaf that created and reinforced links among Maine Deaf individuals and families in the nineteenth century. They did this by providing the sheer joy of ethnic solidarity, as well as opportunities to use the sign language, and to accomplish good works for the Deaf-World. Among organizations that promoted the formation of the Deaf-World in Maine, the earliest and most influential was the American Asylum for the Deaf and Dumb at Hartford, founded in 1817, which offered its students language, culture, friends, education, a trade, and often a partner for life. Students spent from one to ten years at the residential school.

Four Deaf gatherings at the Asylum drew former students and their spouses from throughout the nation. The first of these was the 1850 meeting, described earlier, honoring Gallaudet and Clerc$_D$. The highlights of the 1854 meeting were the unveiling of the Gallaudet statue and the founding of the New England Gallaudet Association of Deaf-Mutes. We described the organization and development of the NEGA earlier, in conjunction with the life of Thomas Brown$_D$, its first president.[3] The 1860 meeting, the fourth NEGA convention, was notable for its large attendance and Deaf cultural events. Finally, the 1866 meeting at the Asylum, on the occasion of its fiftieth anniversary, was also the seventh convention of the NEGA. We have cited the NEGA repeatedly as it was a significant force in uniting the Deaf in Maine and reinforcing ethnic solidarity. Its fifth convention in 1862 met in Portland, Maine, and it continued to meet biennially with rare interruption until 1976.

Another influential institution was the Governor Baxter School for the Deaf at Falmouth, now Portland, founded in 1876. The fourth such institution was the Maine Deaf-Mute Mission ("the Mission"), founded by the Congregational Church in 1877.[4] Their pastor was Samuel Rowe$_D$, a Deaf missionary (on whom more later). Fifth, the meetings of the National Association of the Deaf brought Deaf people together, starting in 1880, on a national level but attendance from Maine was sparse in the nineteenth century.

The Asylum gatherings give a glimpse of the trades its graduates took up: occupation was recorded on registration. Seven returning graduates from Maine gave farmer as their occupation; there were five cabinetmakers, four factory workers, four shoemakers, three joiners, three mechanics, three equipment operators; one printer, a clerk, a teacher, a weaver, and a house worker. The Maine Deaf-Mute Mission was the institution that attracted the largest number of Maine Deaf adults. In addition to providing organized worship in sign language, the Mission afforded its members, gathered from all parts of Maine, the rare opportunity to be with others of the same ethnicity, enhancing the members' sense of Deaf identity.

8

Migration from Martha's Vineyard to Maine

In the period after the American Revolution several of the families on Martha's Vineyard—among them, Tiltons, Smiths, and Mayhews—decided to migrate to southeastern Maine. The extensive land required for sheep raising on the Vineyard was becoming scarce with the growing population. The war had crippled the whaling industry, which was increasingly centered in the south Pacific. And Massachusetts offered to any settler in Maine 150 acres on a river at a dollar an acre or 100 acres free but away from a water course, provided he would clear sixteen of those acres within four years. More lands were given away to pay Revolutionary soldiers.[1] Some Vineyard soldiers who had traveled through Maine to fight the French brought back word of its wealth of natural resources. The first settlers from the Vineyard went to the Sandy River Valley in western central Maine; abundantly forested, it contained all sorts of game and streams that teemed with fishes such as trout and salmon. Other Vineyarders soon followed, starting in 1766 but especially in the years 1789 to 1794, creating the towns of, notably, New Vineyard and New Sharon but also dozens more. These pioneers remained in contact with their families on the Vineyard; people and letters traveled in both directions, encouraging more migration.[2] There were twenty-seven Deaf pupils enrolled at the American Asylum between its opening and 1887 who gave one of the thirty towns in the region of the Sandy River as their residence.

Putting down roots in the Valley was a daunting challenge, in travel and in settlement. First there was the seagoing voyage from the Vineyard to the mouth of the Kennebec River, some two hundred miles. From there, people, food, cows, sheep, hay, firewood all traveled by river.[3] Some settlers traveled in the spring when they could haul sleds on the snow. If the season is right, the crust can be very hard and thick so large animals will not break through. The president of the NEGA and educator of the Deaf, George Wing$_D$, recounted in a letter: "I just returned from an eighteen mile drive; it's awful cold... . The cause of my thus exceeding a Sabbath's day journey was the arrival of my cousin... . I had taken him in a sleigh and put him through over the road as near [illegible] as the snow would permit."[4]

In warmer weather, boats carried early settlers. In 1791 about a dozen families from the Vineyard debarked at Hallowell, put all their belongings on oxcart, and went by foot to the Sandy River town of New Vineyard, a trudge of some forty miles as the crow flies. So poor were the roads that a horseman with a light load could make no more than ten miles a day.[5] On arrival, the settler had to cut and burn clearings, build a log cabin, and plant a crop, while braving extreme weather, wild animals, and frequent illness. Cabins built in the Sandy River Valley had roofs of hemlock or spruce bark, held with long poles. The cracks were filled with moss on the inside and plastered with clay on the outside. Chimneys were made of stones laid in a clay mortar. It wasn't like the home the settlers had left on the Vineyard, but it would have to do.[6]

Six Deaf families illustrate the migration from the Vineyard to the Sandy River Valley.

THE SMITH-PARKHURST CLAN

We saw earlier, examining Mary Smith$_D$'s paternal lineage, that her great-grandfather was Elijah Smith (1716-1802), scion of English Smiths and Parkhursts. This Elijah, a master mariner, had two sons, both farmers, Elijah and Harlock, who decided to break from island life on the Vineyard and seek their fortunes in the wilderness Maine territory, in the Sandy River Valley (see Fig. 6, Smith-Parkhurst pedigree).[7] Of the two brothers, Elijah Smith was the first to go. His wife Hannah Mayhew had died; he married her second cousin, Matilda Mayhew, and in 1791 they moved first to Farmington, Maine, later to New Sharon, nine miles away, both on the banks of the Sandy River. Many families lived in the Sandy River Plantation (Farmington) before going on to their homesteads in New Vineyard, New Sharon, or Industry. Elijah and Hannah's oldest son, Benjamin, had been living in Chilmark with his wife Ruhama Mayhew and three small children when he, too, decided to move to New Sharon; its first settler had arrived only eight years earlier. Benjamin and Ruhama were founders of the Congregational Church there. They had thirteen children in all, two of them Deaf—Hannah$_D$ and Elijah$_D$ Smith. Hannah$_D$ attended the American Asylum but left after a year to marry her cousin, Benjamin Mayhew$_D$, who was too old to have attended the Asylum. This couple had two Deaf children, Benjamin$_D$ and Jared$_D$ Mayhew, both of whom attended the American Asylum. Benjamin Mayhew$_D$ settled on the Vineyard, where he was known as "one-arm Ben" because he lost a hand in a mowing machine accident as a boy; his name-sign was a flat palm "slicing" on the other wrist. (Note that lacking a hand was a more salient characteristic than being Deaf.) Benjamin$_D$ was a fisherman but kept a cow and a horse.

He was a skilled marksman and rower (he made a harness for his stump). He married a hearing cousin, Harriet West, who had numerous Deaf nephews and nieces, and they had three hearing children.[8]

Jared_D Mayhew, Benjamin_D's brother, went to the American Asylum when he was eleven and his brother twelve. In the admission process, Jared_D laid claim to Deaf parents, a Deaf brother, five Deaf uncles, and five Deaf aunts. On entering the school in, respectively, 1864 and 1858, both boys gave Chilmark as their residence, suggesting that their parents or grandparents had moved back to the Vineyard. In maturity, Jared Mayhew_D owned several hundred acres of land on the Vineyard, a herd of dairy cattle, and a large flock of sheep. His wife was hearing as was their daughter Ethyl and her husband. Jared_D and his wife were pillars of the Methodist church, where his wife interpreted the sermons.[9]

THE DAVIS CLAN

Dolor Davis, the progenitor of this Vineyard clan, was born in Kent about 1600.[10] (Pedigree not shown, appears on the website.) He took a wife from Kent and immigrated to Concord, Massachusetts, in 1634, working as a carpenter and master builder. His son John, who plied the same trades, married a woman from Kent and the couple moved to Barnstable, Massachusetts, where they found a Kentish community, as explained earlier. John Jr., grandson of Dolor, moved the family to Falmouth, Massachusetts, on Cape Cod. His grandson Meletiah was born there but moved to Edgartown on the Vineyard to work for Thomas Butler in his tannery. We are told that Meletiah was hard-working, thrifty, a large landowner, and a colonel in the militia. His son Benjamin, also a farmer, married Mary Daggett, whose family early intermarried with Butlers, Wests, Lamberts, and others on the Vineyard. (For more on the Butlers, see Appendix A.) A little after 1805, their son Henry Davis moved to Maine, a "reverse migrant," so called because his ancestors had migrated from the mainland (Falmouth) to the Vineyard, whereas Henry moved from the Vineyard to Strong, Maine, on the mainland, located on the Sandy River, almost at its western extreme. The first white settlers to Strong came in 1784 but the first sawmill and the gristmill mill did not open until well after Henry Davis's arrival.

In Strong, Henry Davis married Betsy Athearn, a descendant of Simon Athearn of Kent, and herself a reverse migrant. This is an example of Vineyard families continuing to intermarry on the mainland. The couple also lived in two towns adjacent to Strong, Farmington and New Vineyard.[11] They had ten children of whom two were Deaf, Cordelia_D (a tailor) and Lydia_D. It appears that neither attended the American Asylum nor married.

THE NEWCOMB CLAN

Captain Andrew Newcomb, the progenitor of this clan, was one of the earliest settlers of New England, emigrating from the west of England, possibly from Devon or Wales around 1636 (see Fig. 8, Newcomb pedigree). The *Newcomb Genealogy* states that he likely came to the New World as a sea captain carrying cargo to Barbados.[12] He was later placed in Virginia where he captained one of the ships in coastal trade, probably bringing tobacco from Virginia to Boston. His son, Lieutenant Andrew Newcomb was born in Boston in 1640. Later, he lived on the Isle of Shoals, near Portsmouth, New Hampshire, and next to Kittery, Maine, where he married Sarah Young of that place and had seven children, including Peter. When Peter's mother, Sarah, died, his father, Andrew, moved the family to Edgartown, Martha's Vineyard, and remarried. In due course Peter married Mercy Smith, a daughter of the second Smith family on the Vineyard, a descendant of Reverend John Smith and Susanna Hinckley of Kent. Peter and Mercy moved to Sandwich, where they kept an inn. The inn passed into the hands of their son William, who married Bathsheba Bourne of Sandwich, and had three children with Deaf descendants, William Jr., Sarah, and Hannah.[13] William Jr.'s son Lemuel also kept the inn and had eight Deaf children, of whom three died young and five attended the American Asylum. His sister Sarah married her cousin Benjamin and their daughter would have two Deaf children and four hearing by Nathan Dillingham (see below). (For more on the Bourne family, see Appendix A).

Finally, sister Hannah married John Jennings in Sandwich in 1759. The Jennings progenitor was John Jenny, who emigrated from Norfolk, England, to Plymouth, Massachusetts, and then to Sandwich. Jennings was a prosperous Tory, imprisoned after the Revolution. On his release John took his eldest son and traveled up the Kennebec to Hallowell, then through the forest to Wayne, Maine. There Jennings, with his son's help, cleared land and built a cabin; then he sent for his wife Hannah and the other children. The pedigree shows that the couple had ten Deaf descendants in the Lovejoy and Allen families (described below).

Wayne is about twenty miles south of the Sandy River town New Sharon. The pioneers making their way from the Androscoggin River to the Sandy River Valley traveled along the Thirty Mile River, which flows directly through Wayne. The first pioneer had come about 1773, and had named the town New Sandwich after his town of origin. Wayne is bordered on the north by East Livermore, Fayette, and Readfield; on the east by Winthrop, on the west by Leeds—all these towns had Deaf families. Without ever moving, the Jennings lived in Wayne and in Winthrop because Wayne annexed land from, and set off land to, neighboring towns.[14] John Jennings' sons, John Jr. and Samuel, moved to

Leeds about 1783 in a birch bark canoe navigating the small lakes, streams, and rivers. They settled on the banks of the Androscoggin River, cleared the primeval forest, and made homes. Their sister Bathsheba and her husband Andrew Cushman joined them there. They would have two Deaf grandchildren.

THE SMITH-HINCKLEY CLAN

There was a second Smith clan on the Vineyard, as we mentioned; its progenitor was the Reverend John Smith of Sandwich (Barnstable County, Massachusetts). (See Fig. 8, Newcomb pedigree.) It seems he was born in Dorset, although some sources give Kent. Reverend Smith came to New England in 1630 and joined the church at Barnstable township a decade later. In 1643, he married Susanna Hinckley of Kent, sister of the governor of Plymouth Colony. Their son Shubael moved to Chilmark with his wife. Their daughter, Mercy, has the distinction of being the ancestor of a large number of Deaf families, namely: the Newcombs, of whom we spoke above; and the Dillinghams and Fessendens of Sandwich, the Lovejoy branch in Sebec, Maine, and the Allens of Turner, Maine—of whom we speak below.[15] This finding provides an indication of where this thread of Deaf paternity began in the United States. Since Mercy was the common ancestor of so many Deaf people, she must have been overtly Deaf herself or a carrier; it is not known which. Accordingly, at least one of her parents was a carrier of the Deaf trait; her father would have acquired the gene from one of his parents, most likely from Mercy's grandmother, Susanna Hinckley of Kent. (For more on the Dillingham and Fessenden families, see Appendix A.)

THE SEBEC LOVEJOYS

We stated earlier that there were two principal founding clans in the northeast with three or more consecutive generations of Deaf people (with the first born before 1800): these were Brown–Swett–Sanders and Lovejoy–Jellison–Berry. We have identified twenty-five Deaf descendants of Christopher Lovejoy, the progenitor. They can be sorted into three regional groups. First, Sebec, Maine, in the northern cluster, to which we now turn (see Fig. 8, lower left, Newcomb pedigree and Fig. 12, Lovejoy pedigree).—Two other groups are discussed in the next chapter: Sidney, Maine, and Concord, New Hampshire[16] The male ancestor of the Sebec branch of the Lovejoy clan is Lieutenant John Lovejoy. He was born and married in Amherst, New Hampshire, and fought in the Revolution. His wife was Mary Polly Jennings of Vineyard ancestry. At the close of the war, he bundled his wife, eleven children, and a few possessions in an oxcart and moved to Fayette, Maine.

After a time, Lieutenant Lovejoy harnessed another ox team and moved his family about six miles to Wayne-Winthrop, where the Jennings moved.

Alexander Graham Bell states that Mary Polly Jennings "traced her descent by two lines of ancestors, from persons who came from Chilmark."[17] Her ancestor, Lieutenant Andrew Newcomb, son of the progenitor, settled on the Vineyard in Edgartown in 1675. Mary Polly was also descended from Shubael Smith, son of the progenitor, who settled in Chilmark (see Fig. 8, Newcomb pedigree). Most of her ascendants, however, were born in Sandwich or Barnstable, Massachusetts (both are in Barnstable County). Mary Polly Jennings had numerous Deaf relatives, among them Newcombs, Allens, and Dillinghams. Two of her sisters had Deaf children and grandchildren: Sarah married Benjamin Allen (see next section), and Bathsheba married Andrew Cushman, a fifth-generation descendant of Thomas Cushman of Canterbury, Kent (Fig. 8).

Of Mary and John Lovejoy's eleven children two were born Deaf. Both were born at Fayette and both attended the American Asylum. Hartwell$_D$, when he was twenty-six, drowned in a pond at Winthrop; Charles$_D$ married and moved nearly eighty miles away to the town where his hearing wife was born, Sebec, Maine, on the Piscataquis River—the most northerly Deaf family in Maine to our knowledge. There they had four children of whom three were Deaf. All three attended the American Asylum and the Deaf-Mute Mission. Son Hartwell$_D$ (Jr.) and daughter Emma Jane$_D$ did not marry, while Sarah$_D$ married Major Bucknell$_D$, a Mission member who had also attended the American Asylum; they had no children. Bucknell$_D$ worked in a cotton mill. In 1887, he attended the Gallaudet Centennial, a gathering of ethnic Deaf from eleven states and three countries, celebrating the birthday of Thomas Hopkins Gallaudet.

THE SAMUEL ALLEN CLAN

Five Deaf members of the Allen family, also of Winthrop, Maine, appear in the Newcomb pedigree (Fig. 8). Their mother, Sarah Jennings, like her sisters, was descended through the Newcomb line from families that lived on the Vineyard. (Bell states that Sarah's father, John Jennings, also had Vineyard ancestors but his ancestors according to our pedigree lived on the mainland—see Jennings pedigree on the website). The Deaf Allen's father, Benjamin, was descended from Samuel Allen, the progenitor of this family (see Fig. 9, Allen pedigree). Born in Somerset, England, about 1600, Samuel died in Braintree, Massachusetts in 1669.

One of Samuel's sons, James, moved to Sandwich, where he met James Skiffe, of whom we have spoken earlier as a settler of Martha's Vineyard. The two became friends and, in the year his father died,

James Allen purchased land on the Vineyard and went there to live. His descendants intermarried on the Vineyard with Mayhews, Tiltons, Athearns, and Bournes; James Allen would prove to be an ancestor of four Deaf Mayhews and a Deaf Tilton; many of his descendants settled in Maine. James' great-grandson, Ephraim Allen, and a companion were the first settlers to spend a winter in the Sandy River Valley. While Ephraim's wife and children awaited them in Winthrop, the two hunters tended traps in which they caught an abundance of furs. In the spring they made a crude dugout and paddled down the Sandy River to the Kennebec.[18]

It is, however, James Allen's brother, Samuel at Braintree, Massachusetts, and his wife Sarah Partridge of Kentish origins, who were ancestors of the five Deaf Allen siblings of Turner, Maine: Rebekah$_D$, Sally$_D$, and Mary$_D$ Allen and their two Deaf brothers who died young: Josiah$_D$ and David$_D$. Their parents were Benjamin Allen and Sarah Jennings. Sarah's father, John, moved his family from Sandwich to Wayne-Winthrop in the spring of 1780. Benjamin Allen and his wife had their first child there eight years later.[19] All the Allen women married Deaf men.

In appealing to the state to pay for his daughters' education at the American Asylum, Benjamin Allen movingly describes his predicament: "I am a father of three deaf and dumb daughters. I have a wife much out of health and five children only two of which can hear and speak. I myself am over sixty years of age; I cannot get them to Hartford or clothe them."[20] The cumulative register of the Asylum, published in 1887, states that Rebekah Allen$_D$ had fifteen Deaf relatives: two brothers, two sisters, and eleven others, including cousins Newcomb and Dillingham (see Fig. 8, Newcomb pedigree). Rebekah$_D$ married William Blaisdell$_D$.[21] The Blaisdell progenitor, Ralph, left Lancashire in 1631, and settled in York, Maine (pedigree at the website). William$_D$ was a tailor from New Hampshire with whom she overlapped three years at the American Asylum; however, the couple waited fifteen years after graduation to marry. (About that time the Asylum admitted John Blaisdell$_D$, from New Hampshire; we have yet to discover his relation to William$_D$.) Sally Allen$_D$ married Jacob Bosworth$_D$ from Salem, Massachusetts. In appealing for his boy's tuition at the Asylum, Jacob's father wrote: "His present employer thinks him as useful as any boy his age [16]. He learned to write a pretty good hand but it is not known that he has any current idea of the use of letters. Appellant posses [sic] no property."[22]

A glimpse of the elaborate Deaf kinship network in mid-nineteenth century New England was to be had when Rebekah$_D$ and her husband attended the 1850 alumni reunion of the American Asylum. There she found numerous Deaf cousins including Abigail$_D$, John$_D$, Jane$_D$, and Josiah$_D$ Newcomb of Sandwich, Massachusetts; Charlotte Lovejoy$_D$

from the Lovejoy branch in Concord New Hampshire (a NEGA member) and Nancy$_D$ and Charles Dillingham$_D$, formerly of Pittsfield, Massachusetts.[23]

Deaf families originally from the Vineyard made up only a part of the northern cluster of Maine Deaf families. We turn next to Deaf families in this cluster who came from mainland Massachusetts (Maine was a district of Massachusetts until granted statehood in 1820), or from elsewhere in New England, or directly from Europe.

9

Other Settlers in the Northern Cluster

The Jellison–Lovejoy–Berry clan includes thirty-three Deaf members with those names and presents several major nodes in the network of kinship relations.

THE JELLISON CLAN

The first white settler in Monroe, Maine, cleared a piece of land and built a cabin. A few years later, a Revolutionary War veteran bought the property and moved his family there. He then built a carding mill (a mill for brushing wool so it can be spun into yarn for knitting or weaving into cloth) and several lumber mills. He prospered, since in that era people relied on the mills for cloth, flour, and lumber.[1]

The Jellison family had always lived in Berwick, in southern Maine, not far from Portsmouth, New Hampshire[2] (See Fig. 10, Jellison pedigree). The progenitor, Nicholas, settled there in 1671. His brother, William, was born in Kent, and came to America in 1630 in Winthrop's fleet, the first mass exodus of Puritans from England. We do not know why Nicholas's great great grandson, Samuel (1774–1862), moved relatively far north in Maine to Monroe but the family settled there and that is where Samuel's son, Moses, married his cousin, Esther Ham. She was descended from William Ham of Devonshire and distantly related to four Deaf Hams in New Hampshire.[3]

Moses and Esther had seven children, three of them Deaf, who would marry members of other Deaf families, and thereby create important links for themselves and their descendants. First was daughter Lucy$_D$ who, after graduation from the American Asylum, had three illegitimate children by a hearing man from Monroe, Howes Mayo.[4] The Mayo clan had four Deaf children in its various branches, three of whom were Howes's contemporaries; it may be that he had some knowledge of matters Deaf. Howes and Lucy$_D$ had one Deaf child, named after his father (variously spelled Howes, Harris, and Hawes); Howes$_D$ Jr. was a Mission member and, like his mother, graduated from the American Asylum.

Moses and Esther's second Deaf child, Isaac Jellison$_D$, attended the Asylum and married Lydia Lovejoy$_D$; she was from a large and important

Deaf clan discussed further below. Thus, Isaac_D became an in-law of numerous Deaf Lovejoys, but also a relative of the many Deaf families with which the Lovejoys were affiliated. Lydia_D's branch of the family lived thirty-seven miles southwest of Monroe in Sidney. There were eight Deaf Lovejoys who lived in Sidney at one time or another along with a Sawtelle_D, a Gordon_D, and a Lord_D. We do not know how Lydia_D and Isaac_D met but they did not overlap at the American Asylum and did not attend its reunions; after their marriage they attended the Mission. They had eight children, three Deaf. The first of those was John_D C., who married his cousin, Edna Hattie Johnson_D, and they had a Deaf son. Edna_D had two Deaf brothers and a Deaf sister; Edna_D and her siblings were descended from Osgoods and Blaisdells, families with Deaf members.

The second Deaf child of Isaac_D and Lydia_D, James G. Jellison_D, a mill operator, married Annie Wing; she was descended from Wing progenitor, Stephen Wing, who was a native of Kent. (Another descendant, George Wing_D, mentioned earlier in connection with travel by sleigh, invented a system for teaching English, and edited for a time the *Gallaudet Guide and Deaf-Mutes' Companion*; he had a Deaf brother.) The last of Isaac_D and Lydia_D's Deaf children was Eddie_D, who married a Deaf woman, Edna Jaron_D, and had two Deaf daughters. In the early 1900s, James_D and Eddie_D were both in Wilton, no doubt employed in the woolen mills there.

Finally, the third and last of Moses' and Esther's Deaf children was Simon_D who married Nellie Chapman_D, from an Appleton family, not far from Monroe, with several Deaf members. Nellie_D had been married to Benjamin Alden_D (both Mission members) from nearby Camden, and Alden_D had been married to Mary Hanson_D of nearby Searsport.

THE JACK CLAN

In 1878, Lucy Jellison_D married into the Jack clan, located just five miles away from Monroe in Jackson, Maine (see Fig. 13, Jack pedigree). Her husband, Alfred Jack_D, had two Deaf brothers: Ralph_D, a farmer like Alfred_D, and Dunbar_D a trapper.[5] (When enrolling in the American Asylum, members of the Jack clan variously gave Dixmont, Jackson, Monroe, and Thorndike as residence; all are quite close to one another.) Alfred's parents were hearing but he had three Deaf uncles—Levi_D, Daniel_D, and William_D Jack. In petitioning the state to pay for their education at the American Asylum, their father, Jonathan Jack, a sailor and wheelwright, stated that he had fifteen children, eleven sons and four daughters, three of the sons Deaf. Those sons apparently did not marry, but three of his hearing sons would give him Deaf grandchildren. The first of those Deaf grandchildren, Charles Augustus Jack_D (he later changed his name to Brown in honor of his step-father) lived in Belfast, twelve miles from Monroe, where he worked as a cobbler. Charles$_D$ attended the American Asylum and overlapped there with Anna Randall$_D$, from Durham, New Hampshire, who had Deaf relatives; she later became his wife. Charles Jack$_D$ was president of the Maine Deaf-Mute Mission (Ebenezer Curtis$_D$ was secretary and Rev. Samuel Rowe$_D$, state missionary). Six members of the Jack clan were Mission members. In addition, Charles$_D$ served on the board of the NEGA; he was state manager for Maine.

Another Deaf grandson, Levi Jack$_D$, was a weaver who lived in Dixmont with his sister, Sarah$_D$, and their parents. Life was not kind to Levi Jack$_D$. According to the silent press, after he graduated from the American Asylum, Levi$_D$ spent some time in the poorhouse and then went to California but returned broken in body and mind. Next he spent two years in the Insane Hospital at Augusta, at the end of which he was discharged as cured. When Levi$_D$ returned to the poorhouse, he set it on fire and it burned down. One elderly resident died in the fire. Levi$_D$ was tried and pleaded guilty; without interpreters, however, he could not have had adequate representation and a fair trial.[6] He was sentenced to be hung, but when physicians found him of unsound mind, he was recommitted to the Insane Hospital for life.[7] The last Deaf grandchild was Eta Jane Jack$_D$, who also attended the American Asylum; she had three Deaf uncles, six Deaf cousins, and a Deaf husband from Canada. She seems to have been more fortunate than her brother Levi$_D$.

THE BERRY CLAN

The ancestry of the Berry clan has four major Deaf clusters: One based in Rockingham County, New Hampshire, and three in Maine—Palmyra, Vienna, and Phillips townships. Twenty-three Deaf individuals by the name of Berry have been identified (see Fig. 11, Berry pedigree). No other clan has provided as many challenges in reconstructing its pedigree; puzzles and conflicting information remain, despite diligent inquiry with the help of eminent Maine genealogists.[8] The Berry clan is an important node in the Deaf kinship network with its several marriages to other Deaf families. The clan progenitor, William Berry, from Lancashire, England, was one of the pioneers settling an area then known as Strawberry Bank, which included all that is now Portsmouth, Rye, Newcastle, Newington, and Greenland, New Hampshire; he has descendants in all those places. William Berry received a grant of land in 1648 but died before 1654.[9]

The earliest Deaf Berrys were William's great grandchildren, Benjamin$_D$ and Elizabeth$_D$. It is noteworthy that they are the fruit of a union between a Berry and a Larrabee, for their mother comes from a family with three Deaf descendants in Maine (see Larrabee in Appendix A.,

Briefly noted lineages). In the next generation, the fifth, Ithamar Berry and wife Abigail (located toward the center of the pedigree chart) had seven children of whom four at least would have Deaf descendants. The first of these descendants in the sixth generation, Eliphalet Berry, married Lydia Morrill and had four sons, Aaron$_D$, Eliphalet, Ithamar, and Luthana, who moved to Palmyra at the same time. The town is located on the Sebasticook River which feeds into the mighty Kennebec, providing the town with waterpower for mills and rich soil. Palmyra was also on the stage road halfway between Bangor (on the Penobscot River) and Norridgewock (on the Kennebec); it would become a center of trade and business for the region.[10] Seventh generation Eliphalet and wife, Mary Polly Kimball (she had two Deaf relatives), had six children of whom four were Deaf. Moses$_D$, Sarah Ann$_D$, Thomas Harrison$_D$, and Julia Ann$_D$ Berry all attended the American Asylum, along with their cousin Aaron Webster Berry$_D$. Eliphalet's brother Aaron$_D$ married his cousin Elizabeth Berry. Bell represented that they had a Deaf son. He also claimed Aaron$_D$ was insane. However, that was not noted in the place provided in the 1850 census and Aaron$_D$ was a member of the Maine Deaf-Mute Mission.[11]

Returning to fifth-generation Ithamar and wife Abigail, the pedigree shows their children—Eliphalet Berry and wife Lydia, mentioned just above; also a son named Moses and twins, John and Ellet, who left Chester, New Hampshire, one day and moved to Vienna, Maine. Vienna, thirty-seven miles from Palmyra, is adjacent to the Sandy River town of New Sharon. Due to intermarriage with Moses's family, each of the twins acquired Deaf descendants. John's daughter, Sarah, gave him two Deaf grandchildren, according to Bell. Ellet had a Deaf daughter, Abigail$_D$, three Deaf grandchildren, and five Deaf great grandchildren.

Among the grandchildren (all of whom were members of the Mission), George Albert Berry$_D$, farmer and shoemaker, linked the Berrys and Lovejoys by marriage to Abigail Lovejoy$_D$ in 1870. Her branch of the Lovejoy family resided in Vienna. Abigail had a Deaf father, a Deaf grandfather, three Deaf siblings, five Deaf cousins, and five Deaf nephews and nieces. George$_D$ and Abigail$_D$ settled in Chesterville, adjacent to Vienna, and had four Deaf children; the family was supported by the town. They also had four hearing children, one of whom, Annie, married James F. Jellison$_D$, a noteworthy link. We would not repeat the gossip that Francis Berry$_D$ (son of George$_D$ and Abigail$_D$, lower right in the diagram) had an adulterous affair with Mrs. Isaac Jellison$_D$ (née Lydia Augusta Lovejoy$_D$) were it not for the fact that this is another indication of ties between the Berry and Lovejoy families.[12] George$_D$ and his brother, Llewellyn$_D$, attended the American Asylum, where each declared that he had a Deaf brother, four Deaf cousins, and other Deaf relatives. They were also members of the Deaf-Mute Mission.

Llewellyn$_D$ married Melintha Randall, whose pedigree has two other Deaf members (see Randall pedigree on the website).

Another branch of the Berry family begins with another son of progenitor William Berry, namely James of Portsmouth, New Hampshire. Four generations later, his descendant, Moses Berry, married Sarah Tripp; she was descended from the Tripp progenitor, John. Moses Berry and his wife Sarah had five hearing children and four Deaf: Mahala$_D$, Susan$_D$, Lydia$_D$, and Moses $_D$ Jr. The family resided in Phillips, Maine, which is twenty-seven miles from Vienna; the Sandy River runs through the center of the town. The first settler came in 1790. He was Perkins Allen, a sea captain from the Vineyard and a descendant of James Allen, of whom we spoke earlier.[13]

In addition to the marriage of George Berry$_D$ with Abigail Lovejoy$_D$ some other important linking marriages should be noted. The Berry and Randall clans were linked by Llewellyn$_D$'s marriage to Melintha. The marriage of Elizabeth Berry$_D$ in 1763 to Jonathan Osgood is noteworthy because the Osgood clan figures in the early ancestry of numerous Maine Deaf clans, including the Lovejoys, Andrews, Blaisdells, and Johnsons. The Berry-Tripp link was mentioned just above; Sarah comes from a clan with eight Deaf Tripps; she had four Deaf children. We also note in Fig. 11 a link to the Badger family, which has five Deaf children: one marriage in Phillips, and one in Palmyra in the eighth generation. (See Fig. 15, Badger pedigree.)[14]

THE LOVEJOY CLAN

The progenitor of the Lovejoys in America was John, who was born in London in 1622 and immigrated to Andover, Massachusetts, about 1633, as a young indentured servant (see Fig. 12, Lovejoy pedigree, *arrow*).[15] Andover was settled by a group of about eighteen men during the early 1640s. It was patterned after the English open field villages; each inhabitant had at least 100 acres to wrest from the wilderness for farming.[16] John Lovejoy acquired a seven-acre house lot after his settlement and eventually owned an estate of over 200 acres in the town. He married Mary Osgood in 1651. Their son and great-grandsons initiated three distinct branches of the Lovejoy clan, each of which had numerous Deaf descendants.[17] (The Osgoods are in the ancestry of many Deaf people in Maine as we mentioned, although we have identified only two Deaf descendants with that family name.)

The progenitor John was the first of many Lovejoys who fought in American wars; when he was more than fifty, he fought the Indians to protect new settlements. The Indians were allied with the French against the British in six Indian wars fought over North American territory. The Kennebec figured prominently in those wars, which lasted nearly a century. John's great grandson, Captain Hezekiah

Lovejoy, fought the British in the War of Independence, as did his son, Lieutenant John. The Captain initiated the Fayette-Sebec branch of the Lovejoy clan. Lieutenant John's son, John, married Mary Polly Jennings and moved from Amherst, New Hampshire, to Fayette; their son, Charles$_D$ moved to Sebec, as we told in the section on the Sebec Lovejoys. The two remaining Lovejoy branches to consider are based in Concord, New Hampshire, and Sidney, Maine. The progenitor John Lovejoy's son, William, initiated the Concord branch of the Lovejoy clan. Deaf Lovejoys did not appear, however, until Ebenezer Lovejoy married his first cousin, Susanna Virgin. They had four Deaf and six hearing children; one of the latter, Henry, had a Deaf daughter who married a Deaf man and moved to Illinois. The reader may recall Joel Lovejoy$_D$, Henry's Deaf brother, who worked on the Thomas Brown$_D$ farm in Henniker; Concord was only fifteen miles away. Joel's brother William$_D$ and sister Charlotte$_D$ also lived in Concord. When the New England Gallaudet Association of Deaf-Mutes held its second convention in Concord in 1856, there were thirty-four Deaf participants from that state, including the Concord Lovejoys. Further evidence suggesting there was a significant Deaf population in Concord and surrounding towns comes from a letter by the journalist William Chamberlain$_D$: "During the past month we enjoyed the pleasure of a trip to New Hampshire. We visited Manchester and Concord, where we found all our mute friends well. . . ."[18]

Captain Hezekiah Lovejoy's brother, Abiel, initiated the Sidney branch of the Lovejoy clan. He was born in Andover, Massachusetts, and served in the War of Independence as a scout under General George Washington. He married "the belle of Charlestown" (Mass.), Mary Brown, who was a descendant of the reverend John Lathrop and his Kentish wife, of whom we spoke earlier.[19]

Captain Abiel Lovejoy had a distinguished career as a soldier and ship captain. After settling in Pownalborough, a frontier village on the Kennebec River, he also became a wealthy landowner, shipbuilder, and merchant. He owned several slaves and had numerous employees. In 1775, Benedict Arnold's army passed up the Kennebec on the way to Quebec City (in the belief that once Quebec was conquered, the French colonists would join the American Revolution against the British). Legend has it that Captain Lovejoy exchanged hard currency for the army's Continental paper money, which would have been of no value to the soldiers when they reached Canada. This act of patriotism must have cost Lovejoy a small fortune as the Continental currency was never redeemed.

Captain Abiel and his wife sold their property in Pownalborough in 1776 and traveled up the Kennebec River, their possessions packed on flat boats and scows towed by row boats. They debarked at Vassalborough, part of which was later set off as Sidney, Maine. Abiel died in 1811 and his wife Mary shortly thereafter; they were buried on their property, alongside their slaves, overlooking the Kennebec. Over the years they had fifteen children; as far as we know only one was Deaf, Francis Lovejoy$_D$ (1768–). He was the ancestor of five generations of Deaf Lovejoys in the Sidney branch of the clan.[20] The Lovejoy genealogist relates the following details concerning his youth and marriage.[21] Francis$_D$'s parents at first thought he was retarded but the boy developed signs and was skilled at imitation. A certain Betsy Smith, daughter of Eliab Smith and Abigail Lewis of Waterville, Maine, was visiting Francis' sister Abigail there. She met Francis$_D$ a few times and fell in love. His rather grand parents objected to the match as the Smith family was plainly inferior socially and Francis$_D$ and Betsy might have Deaf children. In the end, however, the parents capitulated; Abiel deeded the couple a house and some land and Francis$_D$ became a successful farmer and stock raiser; his daughter Abigail served as his interpreter. Francis$_D$ was devoutly religious; a clergyman from nearby Belgrade conversed with him in sign language.

Francis$_D$ and Betsy were married in 1798 and had seven children. One daughter, Phoebe, had a Deaf son, Orrin$_D$, out of wedlock and also a Deaf daughter, Mary Jane Lord$_D$, through marriage with a Deaf family with Kentish origins (see Lord pedigree on the website). Another daughter of Francis$_D$ and Betsy, Mahala, married James Smith, son of James Smith and Mary Braley, who were related to Mahala's mother. Another of Francis$_D$ and Betsy's children, Francis$_D$, married James' sister, also named Betsy Smith, in 1829. The ancestor of these Smiths appears to be Eliab; it is tantalizing to consider that he may be a descendant of a Vineyard Smith, but so far no connection has been found. Francis$_D$ was reportedly abrasive and lazy and his wife inefficient and unreliable.[22] They had three children, all born in Sidney; one died in infancy, one was hearing, and one was Deaf– Benjamin$_D$, an Asylum alumnus and Mission member. Benjamin$_D$ was said to be "[A] quiet well-disposed person, very good [at] work. . . . has considerable mechanical ingenuity, quite intelligent."[23] Benjamin$_D$ and his wife, Susan Gordon (she was from a family with three Deaf members), had eight children, three of whom were Deaf: Roscoe$_D$, Hattie$_D$, and Lydia$_D$. Lydia$_D$ married Isaac Jellison$_D$, as we have seen (Fig. 10), thereby bridging these two large clans. Roscoe$_D$ attended the New England Industrial School for the Deaf (founded by Thomas Brown$_D$'s nephew, William Swett$_D$) and Hattie$_D$ and Lydia$_D$ attended the American Asylum. Lydia$_D$ and Isaac$_D$ had five hearing children and three Deaf sons: John$_D$, the oldest, attended the American Asylum. James$_D$ and the youngest son, Eddie$_D$, were members of "The Frat," the National Fraternal Society of the Deaf; founded in 1901, it provided advocacy and insurance.

When Betsy Smith died, Francis Lovejoy$_D$ married Matilda Copp and they had six children in Sidney, four of whom were Deaf.

Two never married—Erastus$_D$ and Phoebe Ann$_D$, both of whom graduated from the American Asylum and attended the Mission. Their daughter Abigail Lovejoy$_D$ and her husband George Berry$_D$ were also Asylum graduates and he was a Mission member and shoemaker. The couple settled in Chesterville, Maine, and were supported by the town. According to the Lovejoy genealogist, Abigail$_D$ failed to live a virtuous life and had an illegitimate hearing son. Abigail$_D$ and George$_D$ united the Berry and the Lovejoy clans; they settled in his native town, Vienna, Maine, and had four Deaf children and five hearing.

Finally, Francis$_D$ and Matilda's son Francis$_D$ married Hannah Josephine Marr$_D$ from nearby Augusta; Hannah$_D$ had a Deaf mother and three Deaf siblings.[24] Husband and wife belonged to the Deaf-Mute Mission, and had two Deaf children, Medora$_D$ and Erastus$_D$. By one report, Francis$_D$ was not inclined to steady work and in time his family became dependent on welfare provided by the town of Sidney. When the town grew weary of the burden, it moved the family to Augusta, where they were supported by charity and relatives.[25]

Concord, Fayette, Sebec, Sidney—we can now appreciate the importance of the Lovejoy node in the Maine Deaf kinship network and the founding of the Deaf-World in New England. Members of the Lovejoy clan, with some twenty-five Deaf members with that name in five generations, married into the Berry and Jellison clans, linked up with the Marr family with four Deaf members, and the Gordon family with three Deaf members. In addition to forming ties with other Deaf families through marriage, the Deaf Lovejoys created informal ties by participating in Deaf organizations such as the American Asylum and its alumni gatherings, the New England Gallaudet Association of Deaf-Mutes, and the Deaf-Mute Mission.[26]

WHERE DEAF PEOPLE LIVED

Using the 1850 federal census and other sources, we can obtain a very approximate idea of the distribution of Deaf people in Maine's early towns and cities in the first half of the nineteenth century. We identified 272 presumed hereditarily Deaf people, .5 per 1,000; they lived in nearly one hundred towns with a total population of a quarter of a million. The average town with Deaf inhabitants, then, had just fewer than three Deaf people among roughly 2,500 citizens.[27] These statistics reveal an interesting constraint that must have operated on Deaf people. Unlike hearing people, Deaf people often had to look outside their town to find neighbors and a spouse from their own ethnic group. The rivers played an important role for all Maine inhabitants, bringing in goods, supplying water for crops and livestock, bringing out farm surplus, facilitating travel, but perhaps there was a special incentive for Deaf people to locate near rivers when they could, so that they would have easier access to other Deaf people. In any event, two-thirds of the Deaf population lived adjacent to just six rivers—the Sandy River, the Penobscot, the Kennebec, the Androscoggin, the Moussam, and the Saco.

The Sandy River cluster of towns accounted for 12 percent of the Deaf population but the region was sparsely settled with only 2 percent of the total population. Consequently, the Sandy River cluster had the highest concentration of Deaf people in the state, almost three Deaf persons per thousand. Of all the river towns with Deaf inhabitants, Phillips had the highest incidence, 6.3 per thousand, in part because of the Berry clan.

Next in concentration of Deaf people come the eighteen towns gathered along the Androscoggin River. That cluster accounted for 20 percent of the Deaf population but only 6 percent of the total population; Deaf incidence was just under two per thousand in these towns. With sixty-two Deaf inhabitants, this cluster had a sizeable Deaf population, which raises the question whether some Deaf people were drawn to that region by the presence of other Deaf people. Considering just the cluster of seven towns encircling Wayne, within a radius of ten miles or less, there were, in the first half of the nineteenth century, approximately twenty Deaf people living there.[28] There were nine Deaf people in Turner alone, most of whom attended the American Asylum. Turner lies on the left bank of the Androscoggin River facing Leeds on the right bank.

There were fifteen towns along the Kennebec River accounting for 14 percent of the Deaf population and 6 percent of the total population; an average of 1.3 Deaf persons per thousand in those towns. Sidney leads the pack: four Deaf families with ten hereditarily Deaf members (six of them Lovejoys) resided in a community of just under two thousand inhabitants or five Deaf per one thousand. Sidney was well placed for contacts among Deaf families; because it is on the Kennebec River, it was within easy reach of Gardiner and, further south, Bowdoin and Bowdoinham, where nine Deaf families with sixteen members lived. Sidney was, moreover, just a day's horseback ride from the Androscoggin cluster.

There were six towns close to the Penobscot River with seventeen Deaf inhabitants in all. That includes Monroe, where the Jacks and Jellisons lived, and Bangor, home of the Larrabees and others. The two remaining river clusters are Saco and Moussam, with twenty and sixteen Deaf inhabitants, respectively, in the southernmost part of the state. There resided Deaf families like the Wakefields, Littlefields and Nasons discussed below (see Appendix A). Finally, one-third of the hereditarily Deaf population of Maine was to be found in towns and cities that do not have rivers nearby. For ethnic minorities then as now, settling in a large town or city may be the best way of ensuring that one can gather with other members of the ethnic group nearby.

Notes

Part III

1 A.G. Bell, *Memoir Upon The Formation of a Deaf Variety of the Human Race* (Washington, D.C.: Volta Bureau, 1883); see Table IV.
2 Smith, *The Ethnic Origins of Nations* (Oxford: Oxford University Press, 1986), quotation from p. 22.
3 The following were listed as members of the NEGA from Maine in the 1857 rolls: Chamberlain, Thomas J.; Cleaves, Daniel; Denny, Edward; Downing, Jacob; Emerson, John; Hunt, Hiram F.; Lemont, Wm. T.; Marsh, Jonathan R; Page, John W.; Stevens, Charles; Titcomb, Augustus. In addition, John Emerson represented Maine on the Board of Managers and Ebenezer Curtis and Samuel Rowe are listed as Boston residents
4 Congregational churches in Maine. General conference. *Maine Deaf Mute Mission, Organized Dec. 31, 1877* (Belfast, Maine: Progressive Age Press, 1881). In 1874, sixteen "Deaf-Mutes" formed an association called the Biddeford and Saco Deaf-Mute Christian Association; Chairman, R. G. Page, Treasurer, J. W. Page, Assistant, Augustus Titcomb. William Swett addressed the group. Anon. "From Maine," Silent World (1874): 5. This group may have been a precursor of the Maine Deaf-Mute Mission in 1877. The Fifteenth Biennial Convention of the New England Gallaudet Association was held at Portland, Me., August 8–10, 1886. The Boston Deaf-Mute Christian Association was organized in 1851 and incorporated in 1866.

Chapter 8

1 D. C. Poole, *A New Vineyard* (Edgartown, Mass.: Dukes County Historical Society, 1976); L. D. Rich, *The Kennebec River* (New York: Holt, Rinehart and Winston, 1967).
2 Poole, *A New Vineyard*. See also: W. Butler, "Martha's Vineyard, a Diary by William Butler," *Dukes County Intelligencer* 8 (2) (1966): 23–32.
3 B. Caldwell, *Rivers of Fortune: Where Maine Tides and Money Flowed* (Camden, Me.: Down East Books, 1983).
4 Wing correspondence, Gallaudet University Archives
5 Poole, *A New Vineyard*. See also: R. Wright, *Hawkers and Walkers of Early America* (Philadelphia, Lippincott, 1927).
6 Adapted from Poole, *A New Vineyard*, see p. 41.
7 Smith-Parkhurst: F. G. Butler, *A History Of Farmington Maine 1776-1885* (Farmington, Me.: Moulton, 1885). See also: Poole, *A New Vineyard*. We wish to thank Harriette Otteson for sharing family genealogy with us.
8 G. Huntington, "Chilmark's Deaf: Valued Citizens," *Dukes County Intelligencer* 22 (1981): 98–102. See also: B. Bahan and J. Poole-Nash, "The Formation of Signing Communities: Perspective from Martha's Vineyard," in J. Mann, ed., *Deaf Studies IV Conference Proceedings* (Washington, D.C.: Gallaudet University College of Continuing Education, 1996), 1–26; Nora Groce's thesis, p. 188, speaks of a one-arm Jedidiah and brother Nathaniel, both Deaf. N. Groce, "Hereditary Deafness on the Island of Martha's Vineyard: An Ethnohistory of a Genetic Disorder" (Ph.D. diss., Brown University, 1983).

9 Huntington refers to Jared's wife as "Lutie." The only wife of Jared we found of record in the censuses and other sources was Jerusha Reed. See also: G. Huntington, "Chilmark's Deaf: Valued Citizens," *Dukes County Intelligencer* 22 (1981): 98–102

10 H. Davis, *Dolor Davis: A Sketch of His Life With a Record of His Earlier Descendants* (Cambridge, Mass.: The Riverside Press, Houghton and Company, 1881).

11 W. C. Hatch, *A History of the Town of Industry, Franklin County, Maine. Embracing the Cessions of New Sharon, New Vineyard, Anson and Starks* (Farmington, Me: Press Of Knowledge, 1893); Poole, *A New Vineyard*. East Strong was annexed to New Vineyard in 1861. See also: Butler, *History Of Farmington Maine*; L. Brackley, *Strong, Maine Incorporated 1801: An Historical Account of a Sandy River Settlement*—(Strong, Me.: Strong Historical Society, 1992); W. Allen, "Sandy River Settlements," *Collections of the Maine Historical Society* 4 (1856) 31–40.

12 Newcomb: G. F. Hall, *Newcomb Genealogy. Library of Cape Cod History and Genealogy* #42 (Yarmouthport, Mass.: C.W. Swift, 1914); B. M. Newcomb, *Andrew Newcomb and His Descendants*, Revised ed. (Berkeley Calif., author, 1923).

13 In Bell's pedigree for the Newcomb family as published in Horne, the families of 2, 3, 5, and 7 Deaf children are shown as "deaf families," as are their great grandparents; J. C. Gordon, *Education of Deaf Children: Evidence Of Edward Gallaudet and Alexander Graham Bell Presented to the Royal Commission of the United Kingdom on the Condition of the Blind, Deaf and Dumb, etc.* (Washington, D.C.: Volta Bureau, 1892); J. Horne, "Deaf Mutism," *Treasury of Human Inheritance*. Francis Galton Laboratory for National Eugenics; Eugenics Laboratory Memoirs 27 (1909): 27–72.

14 E. S. Stackpole, *Old Kittery and Her Families* (Rockport, Me.: Picton Press, 2001); J. C. Stinchfield, *History of the Town of Leeds in Androscoggin County, Maine, from its Settlement, June 10, 1780.* (Lewiston, Me., Press of Lewiston Journal, 1901. Reprint, Bowie, Md.: Heritage Books, 1996).

15 J. Freeman, *Dukes County 1807*. Reprinted: *Dukes County Intelligencer* 12(4): 1976, 1-51.

16 C. E. Lovejoy, *The Lovejoy Genealogy* (New York: Au., 1930); Gordon, *Education of Deaf Children*; J. Richards, "The Descendants of Rev. John Lovejoy in Maine and Reminiscences of Early Maine Times," *Sprague's Journal of Maine History* 3 (3) (1915): 112–114.

17 Horne, "Deaf Mutism," quotation from p. 70.

18 Poole, *A New Vineyard*.

19 Allen sources: Poole, *A New Vineyard*; W. Allen, *History of Industry, Maine.*(Skowhegan, Me., Smith and Emery, 1869); C. E. Banks, *The History of Martha's Vineyard, Dukes County, Massachusetts in Three Volumes* (Edgartown, Mass.: Dukes County Historical Society, 1966); Hatch, *Industry*; G. Little and S. Sweetser, *Genealogical and Family History of the State of Maine*, 4 vols (New York: Lewis Historical Pub. Co., 1909).

20 Executive Council Papers, 1825–13-50 v.1 p. 347 Box 13 folder 50

21 Blaisdell Family National Association., "Blaisdell Papers: Genealogical Outline; 7th, 8th and 9th Generations From Ralph Blaisdell," *Blaisdell Papers* 11(2) (Suppl.) (1987); 10 (5) (1983).

22 Executive Council Papers, State of Massachusetts.

23 P. K. Valentine, "A Nineteenth Century Experiment in Education of the Handicapped: The American Asylum for the Deaf and Dumb," *New England Quarterly* 64 (1991): 355–375.

Chapter 9

1 Adapted from: www.townofmonroeme.net/id3.html (accessed 7/24/2010).

2 Jellison clan: We thank Eunice Ladd for sharing family genealogy with us. Gordon, *Education of Deaf Children*; M. G. Hinckley, *Nicholas Jellison of Maine [manuscript]: New Material to Supplement Material on File and Establish New Lines With Any Corrections That May Have Been Necessary* (Clearwater, Fla.: au., 1962).

3 J. R. Ham, "Ham Family in Dover N.H." *New England Historical and Genealogical Register* (26) 1872: 388–394.

4 S. Rich, *The Mayo Family of Truro, Library of Cape Cod History and Genealogy* (Yarmouthport, Mass.: C.W. Swift, 1914); E. J. Mayo Rodwick, *Rev. John Mayo and his Descendants/*(Las Cruces, N. Mex.: Blood Ties, 2001).

5 Jack clan: Bell, *Memoir*. See also: vital records for Belfast, Dixmont, Jackson, Monroe, and Thorndike.

6 Anon., "[Levi Jack]" *Deaf-Mutes' Friend*, 1 (1) (January 1869): 20. The author states there were no interpreters in the court.

7 *Deaf-Mute's Friend* 1(1) (1869): 20; 1 (2) (1869): 53; *National Deaf-Mute Gazette* 2 (19) (1868): 14.

8 We are pleased to acknowledge the invaluable help of Maine genealogists Cheryl Patten, Nancy Porter, and Flossie Dere.

9 Little and Sweetser, *Genealogical*, p. 393.

10 Anon., *Sesquicentennial Palmyra, Maine 1807—1957* (Pittsfield, Me.: Press of Pittsfield Advertiser, 1957); G. W. Ireland, *A Compilation of Data on the Early History and People of Palmyra, Maine* (Shrewsbury, Mass.:author, 1980).

11 Gordon, *Education of Deaf Children*; see Berry family insert and symbols key.

12 Source of adultery claim re: Francis Berry and Lydia Augusta Lovejoy, i.e., Mrs. Isaac Jellison.

13 A. Pease, *Phillips 150 Years* (Phillips, Me.: Phillips Historical Society, 1962).

14 Works consulted about Berry family: M. R. Andre, *Early Families of Georgetown, Maine*, (Colon, Me.: V.T. Merrill, 1945); Anon., *East Somerset County Register, 1911–1912.* (Auburn, Me.: Chatto, 1912.); Anon., *Palmyra, Maine, 200th Anniversary Bicentennial 1807–2007* (Rockland, Me.: Penbobscot Press, 2007); Gordon, *Education of Deaf Children*; C. Bell, *Facts Relating to the Early History of Chester, New Hampshire, from the Settlement in 1720 until the Formation of the State Constitution in the year 1784* (Concord, N.H., Parker Lyon, 1863); J. Berry, *Descendants of William Berry and Jane of Strawberry Bank, to and Including the Fifth Generation*, (Kearns, Utah: author, 1992); R. S. Canney, *The Early Marriages of Strafford County, N.H.* Supplement, 1630–1870 (Bowie, Md.: Heritage Books, 1997); B. Chase, *History of Old Chester [N.H.] from 1719 to 1869* (Auburn, N.H.: [np] 1869); J. C. Chase, *History of Chester, New Hampshire, including Auburn. A supplement to the History of Old Chester, published in 1869* (Derry, N.H.: Record Pub. Co., 1926); W. P. Davis, *The Berry Family of Yarmouth, Library of Cape Cod History and Genealogy* (Yarmouthport,

Mass.: C.W. Swift, 1912); J. Dow and L. Dow, *History of the Town of Hampton, New Hampshire. From its Settlement in 1638, to the Autumn of 1892* (Salem, Mass., Printed by the Salem Press Publishing and Printing. Co., 1893); Horne, "Deaf Mutism"; H. D. Kingsbury and S. L. Deyo, *Town of Vienna* (New York: H.W. Blake and Co., 1892); L. P. Lemont, *1400 Historical Dates of the Town and City of Bath, and Town of Georgetown, from 1604 to 1874* (Bath, Me.: author, 1874); Little and Sweetser, *Genealogical*; M. F. McCourt and S. Berry, *A Genealogy of the Descendants of William Drake Berry of Maine.* ([s.l.] Author, 1972); L.A. Morrison and S. P. Sharples, *History of the Kimball family in America* (Boston, Mass.: Amrell and Upham, 1897); L. B. Parsons, *History of the Town of Rye, New Hampshire, From Its Discovery and Settlement to December 31, 1903,* (Concord, N.H., Rumford Print. Co., 1905); K. Richmond, *John Hayes of Dover New Hampshire* (Tyngsboro, Mass., 1936); G. Rogers and W. Ireland, *A Compilation of Data on the Early History and People of Palmyra, Maine* (Shrewsbury, Mass.: author, 1980); M. B. Whitney, *Berry Family Genealogy* (Boston, Mass, New England Historical Genealogical Society, 1985); E. H. Young, *History of Pittsfield, New Hampshire* (Pittsfield, N.H.: Town of Pittsfield, 1953).

15 A.G. Jackson, *Genealogic Record of John Lovejoy* (Denver, Colo.: au, 1917). This latter author gives the probable birthplace of John Lovejoy to be Hants, England. See also: Lovejoy, *Lovejoy Genealogy*; J. Richards, "The Descendants of Rev. John Lovejoy in Maine and Reminiscences of Early Maine Times," *Sprague's Journal of Maine History* 3 (1915): 112–114;

16 P. J. Greven, "Family Structure in 17th Century Andover, Massachusetts," *William and Mary Quarterly* 23 (1966): 234–256.

17 I. Osgood, A Genealogy of the Descendents of John, Christopher and William Osgood (Salem, Mass.: Salem Press, 1898).

18 W. M. Chamberlain, "[Letter]" *Gallaudet Guide and Deaf Mutes Companion* 1(6) (1860): 22.

19 Lovejoy, *Lovejoy Genealogy*, see p. 80.

20 Bell made this claim in testimony p. 54 and part 2 p. 187. Gordon, *Education of Deaf Children.*

21 Lovejoy, Lovejoy Genealogy.

22 T.W. Jones, "America's First Multi-Generation Deaf Families (a Genealogical Perspective)" *Deaf American Monographs* 46 (1996): 49–54.

23 Jones, "America's First Multi-Generation," quotation from p. 53.

24 Fay states that Francis was born Deaf in one ear.

25 Jones, "America's First Multi-Generation."

26 It has not been established that Phoebe Lovejoy is the mother of Mary Jane Lord. This attribution was made by A. G. Bell but not confirmed by the Lovejoy genealogy. Lovejoy, *Lovejoy Genealogy.*

27 United States Census Office, *The Seventh Census of the United States: 1850.* (Washington, D.C.: Robert Armstrong, 1853); United States Census Office, *Report of the Superintendent of the Census for December 1, 1852, to which is appended the report for December 1, 1851* (Washington, D.C.: Robert Armstrong, 1853). A person was presumed hereditarily Deaf if their last name occurred twice in our enumeration. We identified 272 presumed hereditarily Deaf people in 97 towns with a total population of 227,373, hence an incidence of 1.2 such Deaf people per 1000 population in towns with Deaf people. The average town had 2.8 Deaf people in 2344 citizens. We arrived at 272

presumed hereditarily Deaf people as follows: We transcribed from the 1850 census all the pertinent information for individuals in Maine listed as Deaf-Mute. We added those Deaf people who on other evidence were Maine citizens in the first half of the nineteenth century, for example, students at the American Asylum and Deaf persons identified in an 1817 census of the Deaf in New England. This raised the total number of Deaf in Maine from 261 to 406. Next, we excluded those listed as Deaf or as Mute only. Finally we retained only individuals for whom there was another (presumably related) individual with the same last name; this yielded 272 presumed hereditarily Deaf. Thus, this figure is approximate as there were included in our sample unrelated Deaf with the same last name, inflating the figure, and hereditarily Deaf individuals with unique last names who were not included, deflating the figure.(See Appendix C: Pedigree methods.)

[28] Fayette, Leeds, Livermore, Monmouth, Readfield, Turner, Winthrop. The numbers are approximate only as people born in a village may leave and others may enter; censuses prior to 1850 did not identify Deaf people by name.

Part IV

Deaf Ancestry in Maine—Southern Cluster

10

Southern Cluster

THE ROGERS-HOLMES CLAN

Charles Rogers and Mary Jane Pote of Freeport, Maine, had five Deaf children and five hearing early in the nineteenth century (see Fig. 14 Rogers-Holms pedigree). Freeport is on the coast about twelve miles northeast of Portland; it is situated at the head of a fine harbor opening into Casco Bay and, in its day, it was a great shipping town, like Bath; Charles worked in the shipyard as a carpenter. The Rogers progenitor, Thomas, was born in Warwick, England, and immigrated to Duxbury, Massachusetts. We have yet to identify Charles's father but it appears that his parents were related (if Rogers is indeed his mother's maiden name). The Pote progenitor, William, came from Cornwall and settled in Marblehead, Massachusetts, before 1666. His grandson, Greenfield, a Yankee skipper, was an early settler. He had a house in Falmouth (now Portland). When a complaint was made against him for sailing on the Sabbath, he loaded his house on a flat boat and moved to Freeport. One of the hearing children in the Rogers family, William Pote Rogers, was a Civil War naval hero who captained the *Merrimac*; he travelled widely as a merchant seaman and became the Socialist Party candidate for governor.[1]

Four of the five Deaf Rogers attended the American Asylum. Robert$_D$, the youngest, overlapped there with Sarah Web Clark Holmes$_D$ of Charleston, South Carolina. About eight years after leaving school the couple married in Winnsboro and settled in Sumter, South Carolina, where Robert$_D$ took up the trade of his Deaf brother-in-law, a shoemaker. Sarah$_D$ and Robert$_D$ had five Deaf children and no hearing children, as far as we know. About 1846 the family moved to Spartanburg, South Carolina, the location of the South Carolina School for the Deaf, which all five children attended. Four of them took spouses who were also Deaf. Charles$_D$ joined his brother Robert$_D$ in South Carolina where he married a hearing woman, moved to Georgia, and was killed by a train while he was walking on the tracks.[2]

THE BADGER-BOARDWIN-BROWN-GLIDDEN CLAN

An important event in forming this complex of Deaf families (Badger, Boardwin, Brown, and Glidden) occurred when Benjamin Glidden of Somerville, Maine, married his cousin Susan Glidden (double line mid-left, Fig. 15 Badger pedigree). Their daughter, Clara_D, attended the American Asylum, where she overlapped with Oliver Badger_D from a large Deaf family of Charlestown, Massachusetts. The Glidden progenitor was Charles, from Devon, England (arrow). He immigrated with his wife to Boston about 1660. After living for a time with his in-laws, he and his wife moved to Portsmouth, New Hampshire, to an area known as Strawberry Bank.[3] Four generations later, his descendant, Clara's great-grandfather, moved to Somerville, Maine, located on the Sheepscot River about fifteen miles east of Augusta.

Oliver Badger_D had five hearing and four Deaf siblings, a Deaf mother, and a Deaf niece. Oliver_D married a fellow graduate of the American Asylum and fellow resident of Boston, Delia Boardwin_D, an African American, originally of Waterville, Maine, with two Deaf siblings, both of whom took Deaf spouses. We have not uncovered the Boardwin ancestry. The Badger progenitor, Giles, emigrated from Gloucestershire, England, to Newbury, Massachusetts, in 1635. His grandson took a wife from Charlestown, Massachusetts, and the family settled there. Oliver_D's father, William Gilman Badger, married Mary Brown_D of Charlestown in 1819; at the time she was hard of hearing but became Deaf when she was twenty-five. The Brown progenitor was Nicholas, from Worcestershire, England. Mary had three Deaf siblings; the family had moved from Lynnfield, Massachusetts, to Charlestown (and later to Maine).

Seventeen years after he married Mary Brown_D, William Gilman Badger was brought before the Boston Municipal Court on a charge of bigamy. It seems that, in addition to marrying Mary Brown_D, who was in the Charlestown Almshouse with five of their nine children, he had also married, under the name of George B. Gilman, a certain Miss Wheat. William Badger pleaded not guilty to the charge of bigamy, then retracted and pleaded guilty. He was sentenced to two years in prison. Some years after serving his sentence, he moved to California with sons George_D and Oliver_D. George_D had become Deaf at an advanced age and had married a hearing woman, Mary Rugg. They had a Deaf daughter, Hattie F. Badger_D, in 1859. George_D appears in the 1880 census in Petaluma, California. George_D's brother Oliver_D had been cohabiting with Clara Glidden_D, so she went to California, too. The two of them are listed in the 1870 census as Deaf residents of San Francisco, he as "agent for books," she as "dress maker."[4]

George_D and Oliver_D's sister, Sarah_D, who also became Deaf at an advanced age, married George Burditt, a hearing man who went to prison for robbery, and they divorced. Then she married William K. Chase_D, active in the Deaf-World, a Charlestown clockmaker. And they divorced. George_D and Oliver_D's other sister, Abigail_D, who attended the American Asylum, was scarcely more fortunate: she married former schoolmate William Nelson_D, a peddler and shoemaker, who ended up in the local "lunatic asylum." That brings us to Mary Elizabeth$_D$, who married an immigrant from Ireland, Joseph Grace$_D$; after his death, she married another Deaf man, one who, like her, had attended the American Asylum, Daniel Norwood$_D$.

All in all, we have identified twenty-three Deaf people, including Deaf spouses, in this clan; eight had a common ancestor in the progenitor Edward Gilman—yet only one bore his name. The lives of the members of the Badger-Boardwin-Brown-Glidden clan may speak to another affinity of its members in addition to ethnicity; it seems that Deaf people tended to choose partners of the same social class.

THE CAMPBELL CLAN

John Campbell and Elizabeth Adams of Bowdoin, Maine, had two Deaf boys, two Deaf girls, and four hearing children (see Fig. 16, Campbell pedigree).[5] The male progenitor of the Campbells was James Campbell, who moved from Ulster in Ireland to New Hampshire, then New York, and finally to Portland, Maine, about 1742. Elizabeth Adams's family progenitor was Samuel Adams, who arrived in Quincy, Massachusetts, in 1632, thirty years old, as an indentured servant; he went to York, Maine, in 1645 and died there eight years later. President John Adams was a distant relative of the Campbells. Their residence in Bowdoin was only eight miles west of the Kennebec River, hence rather accessible by boat from many locations. Bowdoin was part of a tract of land conveyed in 1752 to William Bowdoin, a French refugee who came to America in 1685. Fronting on the Cathance River, some two miles in width, it extended from Merrymeeting Bay to the Androscoggin River. The town was incorporated in 1788 with some one hundred families and covered nearly ninety square miles at the time.

The Deaf Campbells linked up in marriage with several other Deaf families, such as the Chandlers, Riggs, Tripps, Gibsons, Wakefields, and Littlefields (see below), and the Curtises and Rowes discussed in the next section. Dorcas Campbell married her hearing cousin, William Chandler, and they had two Deaf children, Charles$_D$ and Margaret$_D$.[6] Charles Chandler$_D$ did not marry but sister Margaret$_D$ married George Riggs$_D$, both of Turner, Maine, in the Androscoggin River settlement cluster. George Riggs$_D$ had a cousin, a sister, an uncle, and two nieces Deaf. George$_D$ and Margaret$_D$ had a Deaf son, Charles$_D$ who died at twenty-two years old when he was run over by a cart. (For more on the Riggs family, see Appendix A.)

Returning to John and Elizabeth Campbell's four Deaf children, we begin with daughter Adelia$_D$ who married Lyman Tripp$_D$, a carpenter and joiner, also of Bowdoin, Maine, who had seven Deaf relatives and a progenitor from Northumberland with a Kentish name; the couple had a Deaf son.[7] Lyman's cousins, Benjamin$_D$ and Jacob$_D$, were recalcitrant students at the American Asylum; seven Tripps in all were schooled there.[8] Adelia$_D$'s sister, Elizabeth$_D$, apparently did not marry but her brother Abner$_D$, married Olive Curtis$_D$; when she died he married her sister Ann Curtis$_D$ (both Mission members). Finally, George Campbell$_D$ married Sarah Maria Gibson$_D$.[9] All had attended the American Asylum.

Several Campbell family letters have been preserved—twenty-five that we know of. Most are from Elizabeth Adams, mother of the Deaf Campbells, addressed to her hearing daughter, Sophia, who had married a hearing man and lived for a time in East Haddam, Connecticut.[10] Sophia's brother George$_D$ wrote her a letter in 1864 that is instructive about Deaf lives.

Dear Sis Sophie, [George wrote, February 14, 1864]

Your welcome letter of two weeks ago came to hand duly and I was very glad to hear from you and of your good health and the same of your little family. We are usually well. Adelia$_D$ [their sister] is slowly getting better. She can walk but slow and weak. This morning was the first time ever she went into the kitchen and breakfasted with us since she was taken sick.

Health is the most recurrent theme in the letters. Life then was "lived next to an open grave" for hearing and Deaf alike. A few months earlier, Sophia's mother had written to her to say that her sister Adelia$_D$ was ill. Adelia$_D$ recovered, but later became gravely ill in childbirth. George's sister Elizabeth$_D$ ("Libby") lost use of her right hand. Later letters reveal Sophia not well and her mother, Elizabeth ("Betsy"), quite ill. George$_D$ himself had fainting spells and, four years after this letter to Sis Sophie, he became delirious, and died, only thirty-one years old,

[George$_D$'s letter to Sophia continues. . .]

. . . Charles Chandler$_D$ [second cousin] is here now. You spoke of pictures. I will take them for you and tell me which of your pictures you want is copied! I take better photographs than last year. I do not have much trade here this winter. Libby$_D$ is still here with us. She sends you and all [the family] her love and wants to see you very much.

The search for work is another recurrent theme—for the male Campbells. Two hearing brothers, William and Robert, had such difficulty they enlisted in the Civil War, where William died in battle. He had worked for a while in a lumber mill and his father had worked in a shipyard—these were the leading Maine industries in mid-nineteenth century. George$_D$ had found his trade as a photographer and printer. Several of the Campbell couples raised crops, and many of the women worked at carding and spinning wool and making garments.

George$_D$'s news that his cousin, Charles Chandler$_D$, is visiting announces the third theme of the letters, after health and work—contacts among the Deaf. George$_D$'s cousin, Dorcas Campbell, had married William Chandler. Their son, Charles$_D$, was visiting George$_D$ and George$_D$'s wife, Sarah Maria Gibson$_D$. In this way a clan develops that grows wider with each marriage. All the Deaf Campbells who married, married a Deaf person. And all of the hearing Campbells married hearing.

One important reason for this endogamous marriage among the Deaf was shared language. When George$_D$ was dying, his sister Elizabeth$_D$ tended to him for three months. His mother wrote to their sister Sophia: "You know, she [Elizabeth$_D$] could talk with him and they could get along with her better than with me. . . ." It appears that Sophia was fluent in sign language as well. When her sister Adelia$_D$ was sick, her mother wrote to Sophia: "I wish you was here now; perhaps you could be of some help for to talk with Adelia and inform the doctor more plainer her complaints than she can. . . ."

George Campbell$_D$'s words at the end of his letter remind us of how close many separated Maine Deaf families were thanks to river transport. George$_D$ lived in Richmond, the nearest Kennebec landing to Bowdoin. "A few days ago [George$_D$ wrote] there were a 102 sleighs on the ice, called horse trot, from here to Bath in the afternoon." That would be a fast thirteen-mile trip up the frozen Kennebec River, the Maine superhighway of that era.

Reviewing George Campbell$_D$'s entire letter, we find his writing as proficient as that of his hearing mother which, if representative, reflects very well on Deaf education in that era.

The full set of twenty-five letters leaves the reader impressed by how often the Deaf Campbells faced the same issues as hearing families did—health, work, marriage and childbirth, and religion. Within the family, hearing and Deaf Campbells were viewed pretty much in the same way and with similar expectations. True, those Deaf who went to school (George$_D$, Abner$_D$, and Adelia$_D$) went to a school for the Deaf in Hartford. And mother Campbell did express regret that she was not as fluent in sign as her Deaf daughters. But there was little or no talk of Deaf affliction. What set Deaf people apart were their language and their practice of bonding with other Deaf people.

THE CURTIS-ROWE CLAN

Nancy Rowe$_D$ hailed from a large Deaf family whose ancestors came from Devonshire in England (see Fig. 17, Curtis-Rowe pedigree). On immigrating to America in mid-seventeenth century, they settled first in Gloucester, Massachusetts. After a time, citing the poverty of husbandry on the "meager lands" of Cape Ann, they applied to the General

Court of His Majesty the King of Britain for a grant of a township in the virgin Maine interior (then a district of Massachusetts). The petition was granted in 1736, the new town, named New Gloucester, to be laid out in sixty-three equal shares, one for the minister, one for the meeting-house, one for the school, the rest for the settlers, among them Nancy's ancestors.[11] The petitioners were required to settle all the lots, to build their homes and a meeting house, and to cultivate six acres of land each. New Gloucester was located eighteen miles from the Campbells in Bowdoin and twenty miles north of Portland on the Royal River, a nat-ural route to the interior. By 1742, the nineteen original settlers had built their cabins and erected a sawmill, so they sent for their families in Gloucester, who traveled to North Yarmouth by boat and from there poled on rafts with all their possessions and supplies up the Royal River. The town also received settlers from Martha's Vineyard.[12]

With the beginning of the French and Indian War, hostile Indians threatened the settlers and it was difficult to secure more pioneers despite bounties that were offered. Soon the men were driven from their fields to defend their homes, the cabins and sawmill were burned, and the bridges carried away by freshets. The settlers fled to Gloucester or to seacoast settlements in Maine. The town was abandoned for some seven years whereupon it had a second life. Worship was conducted in the blockhouse for protection but eventually a meetinghouse was built. The areas of reserved seating are noteworthy: one area for "colored brethren," one for wardens with long poles to wake sleepers, and one area up front for those "whose hearing was impaired."[13] There were indeed about a dozen Deaf Rowes and spouses in the town.

Nancy Rowe$_D$ had five Deaf brothers and two Deaf sisters. She also had five hearing siblings, of whom three died in infancy. Nancy$_D$'s par-ents were carriers of the Deaf trait unexpressed; they were distantly related: her paternal grandparents were both Rowes, and one of her mother's ancestors married one of her father's forebears. Thus we infer that Nancy$_D$ and her seven Deaf siblings were overtly Deaf because of a recessive pattern of transmission. That both of Nancy's parents were hearing is consistent with that hypothesis but the fact that more than half of their children were overtly Deaf is not. On average, only one-fourth of the children should express a recessive trait as we have explained. It is unlikely that chance alone explains the occurrence of eight Deaf children in a family of thirteen when only a fourth of thirteen (3.25) is expected.[14]

Nancy$_D$ entered the American Asylum in 1829, age thirteen; six Deaf Rowes were to be educated there. Four years later, Nancy$_D$ graduated and Principal Lewis Weld gave her a certificate testifying that she had been "a pupil of the American Asylum, [and] made good attainments in the knowledge of written language and other branches of a common education."[15]

When she was twenty-four, Nancy Rowe$_D$ married George Curtis$_D$, from Leeds, Maine, and moved there to live with him. Leeds, of which we spoke earlier in connection with the Jennings family, is nine miles from Winthrop and twenty-five miles from New Sharon on the Sandy River.[16] Four children, all hearing, would be born to the couple over the next fifteen years. If George$_D$ and Nancy$_D$ were overtly Deaf because they both had two copies of the same recessive gene, then all of their children would have been overtly Deaf. That they were not suggests that George$_D$ and Nancy$_D$ had different recessive genes. This seems more likely as George$_D$'s ancestors came from Kent, whereas Nancy$_D$'s came from Devonshire.

Like Nancy Rowe$_D$, George Curtis$_D$ had hearing parents and several Deaf siblings. He had a Deaf brother and two Deaf sisters.[17] He also had three brothers and three sisters who were hearing; one of those was Sophia Curtis, who married Thomas Brown$_D$ of Henniker after the death of his first wife. Perhaps Thomas$_D$ met Sophia through her brother George$_D$ who overlapped with him at the American Asylum. The Brown-Curtis wedding notice in the *National Deaf-Mute Gazette* (successor to the *Guide*), reveals both Brown$_D$'s stature and the need to explain his mixed marriage: "Mr. Brown is too well known to need any notice at our hands. His wife is a hearing lady whose relationship to and constant intercourse with mutes enables her to use their language."[18] Thomas$_D$ and Sophia were married in Yarmouth, Maine, in November of 1864, and then took up residence in Henniker.

George Curtis$_D$'s paternal ancestors came from Kent, as noted, and his parents were hearing, which is consistent with recessive transmission. The fact that the Curtis family counted four overtly Deaf children out of ten is only somewhat greater than would be expected and is likely due to chance. George$_D$'s father, William, brought his family to Leeds, Maine, from Hanover, Massachusetts, in 1824.[19] William's parents were related. All three of George$_D$'s Deaf siblings overlapped Nancy Rowe$_D$ at the American Asylum; any of them could have introduced the couple, who were married in 1840. George$_D$'s sister Ann$_D$, a factory worker, married a Deaf Rowe, as did his brother Ebenezer$_D$, a joiner, so there were many Deaf ties between New Gloucester and Leeds. The towns were twenty-four miles apart, a daunting distance on foot in the Maine wilderness, but both towns are located near the Androscoggin River. River transport facilitated travel, especially in winter when sleighing was good—recall George$_D$ Campbell's attendance at "horse trot."[20] Numerous Deaf families lived rather close to Leeds, which is in the Androscoggin settlement cluster. For example, in Turner alone, six miles distant, we find the Briggs-Record clan with seven Deaf members including spouses, the Riggs clan with eleven Deaf, and the Allen family, described earlier (see Fig. 9, Allen pedigree), with eight Deaf. Seventeen miles away in Bowdoin were the Campbell clan with eleven Deaf members in all, and within a twenty-mile radius several more Deaf families came within a day's reach of Leeds.

In Leeds, George$_D$ and Nancy$_D$ farmed and raised children, but some of their Deaf siblings worked in various trades such as shoemaking and tailoring, while others went to work in the new cotton mills in Lawrence, Massachusetts. In leaving the land for factories, Deaf people were subject to the same economic forces as hearing people. With population growth (Maine's population increased more than 50 percent from 1790 to 1800) there was more competition for land, so land prices increased. With each succeeding generation, there was less land to go around. The land-poor had trouble acquiring more in New England, but the land-rich became richer as land values rose.[21] An entrepreneurial class developed as merchants pushed inland, bringing in imported goods and bringing out farmers' surplus production, as we related earlier. With the rise of factories in the nineteenth century, many women left domestic production and went to work in these facilities. Too poor to purchase the increasingly expensive land, some of the Rowes and Curtises were obliged to apprentice in a trade or work in a factory. The 1850 census found in Lawrence, Massachusetts, Lucy$_D$, Moses$_D$, Persis$_D$, and Samuel$_D$ and his wife Sophia$_D$.

An 1846 letter from Nancy Rowe$_D$'s Aunt Judith in New Gloucester to Nancy$_D$ and George$_D$ in Leeds provides some insight into Maine Deaf family life in that era. (Aunt Judith was Nancy$_D$'s father's sister.) We find in the letter that some Deaf people farmed but others entered the trades, often far from home. And health was a constant concern.

> Dear George$_D$ and Nancy$_D$ . . . I thought Benjamin$_D$ [Nancy$_D$'s brother] would come home in May, [and] he and Moses$_D$ and Persis$_D$ [two of Nancy$_D$'s siblings] would visit you. . . . We received a letter from Samuel$_D$ [one of Nancy$_D$'s five Deaf brothers]. He stated in his letter he thought B[enjamin$_D$] would hire in a Mr. Marsh's shop [a shoemaker] to work for him. [Benjamin$_D$] has not come and we think it is truly so—which is without doubt for the best—cabinet makers get small wages in N.G. [New Gloucester]. We can't any of us visit you at present. It is hurrying time for farmers. Your mother and father wish me to write it would not be profitable for Nathaniel$_D$ or Moses$_D$ [Nancy$_D$'s brothers] to go to you nor profitable for you to have them come. Best take advice of your brother Joseph [one of George Curtis$_D$'s brothers] and your parents at Leeds what is best for you and your dear little children. Persis$_D$ [Nancy$_D$'s sister] is hired to live with Mrs. Moseley this spring. . . . I was at Mary Taylor's when she was sick. . . . She died with a fever on her lungs. . . . Mrs. Reyns was taken sick the day Mary was buried. . . . I was at your uncle Charles Haskells last week, all well. Your uncle Reyns' family are now well. Your father is going to Dr. Stevens to work today. . . . We all send our love and good wishes to you and your friends at Leeds. Aunt Judith Rowe.[22]

Health and the trades also figure in this excerpted letter from Samuel Rowe$_D$, Nancy$_D$'s brother, to Ebenezer Curtis$_D$, George Curtis$_D$'s Deaf brother. We also get a glimpse of the Deaf-World at that time. Samuel$_D$ was the most accomplished of the Deaf Rowes. Active in the New England Gallaudet Association of Deaf-Mutes and general manager of the Deaf-Mute Mission, he was to be ordained in 1878 as an evangelist in the Congregational church.[23] At that time it was estimated that there were five hundred "deaf-mutes" in Maine. The brother-in-law to whom Samuel$_D$ wrote in 1849, Ebenezer$_D$, was an alumnus of the American Asylum, a joiner by trade, also a member of the NEGA and secretary of the Maine Deaf-Mute Mission.

Dear friend Ebenezer$_D$. . . This is to inform you that I am pleasantly situated in this town [Keene, N.H.] and am employed by Messrs. Hagar and Whitcomb [a tailoring firm]. . . . I left P. [Portsmouth?] for Boston and I took my opp[ortunity] in Boston at 9 o'clock and saw some former deaf-mutes, viz Homer Smith$_D$, and some old ones I did not remember well. I held good conversation with Homer$_D$ most of the time and I could find that he was a stable minded fellow and I was so attached to him that I was sorry for not conversing with him long enough for I was obliged to leave B[oston]. I was terribly afraid of walking about the streets—the reason was that the madness of the inferior people made me so and was seriously informed of a poor man who was at the bar to be examined before the judge and his crime was "murder"! And he was sentenced to be hanged next month and there was a full [?] crowd of people in the court where the murderer was at that time. I was in the Register of Deeds building and I was cordially entertained by Amos Smith$_D$ [a graduate of the American Asylum and NEGA member]. He was rather grown fast and earns well. No important news but I cannot tell you about the peoples going to California to get "Dust" [i.e., the gold rush]. I had made some attempts to find some employment [apparently in Boston] but No! I bore disappointments well. Spent four days in B[oston]. I started for this town [Keene, N.H.] from Boston on Monday afternoon and arrived at 7 o'clock in the night and the fare was $5 from my native place! Very cheap fare indeed beyond my expectation. My sister and brother were convinced. . . . I ran away or something . . . but I explained to them about being obliged to come to the "Granite State.". . . My sister Persis$_D$ is employed by Messers Hagar and Whitcomb and I also but [brother] Ben$_D$ is employed by Mr. Vandoorn [a cabinetmaker] in Brattleboro. You will laugh at me for I am every day happy to be in company with sister Persis$_D$, Lucy M. Reed$_D$ [wife of Benjamin Rowe$_D$] who works with Persis$_D$, and Lucy$_D$'s brother Adin$_D$ is in this town and works as a printer. I enjoy talking with them very well. . . . I fell in with Mr. Nelson Kelley$_D$ [an American Asylum graduate from West Rutland, Vt.] and recollect of his unfaithful offer to Ann$_D$ [Ebenezer$_D$'s sister]. Do you remember what I told you, that Mr. K[elley] is seeking a lady? Yes, he is going to see sister Lucy$_D$ [Samuel$_D$'s sister] but in my opinion he is unworthy to be married to Lucy$_D$, as I remember he once deceived your sister Ann$_D$. . . .

I heard the friends in the Asylum were sick with the influenza but now well except Mr. Turner [the principal]. He is very sick and is likely to be better . . . Last week I heard my parents and all were well, tell Nancy$_D$. Persis$_D$ gives her love to your friends. Please to tell Nancy$_D$ to write to me. You must not monopolize this letter but not [show it?] publicly. Benjamin$_D$ [Samuel$_D$'s brother] is going to be married in April. "Be silent [. . .]" Your friend, S[amuel]. Rowe$_D$.[24]

Samuel$_D$'s letter presents evidence of a Deaf-World in this early time. It is not just a matter of the bonds between two large Deaf families, which was plain in Aunt Judith's letter, as well as Samuel$_D$'s, but it is also a matter of felt and real connections among diverse Deaf people such as the Reed family from Dummerston, Vermont; Amos Smith$_D$ from Cambridgeport, Massachusetts; and Homer Smith$_D$ in Boston. Understandably, Samuel$_D$ was "every day happy" to be with Deaf friends. The school for Deaf children was an important link: Many of the people cited in the letter had attended the Asylum, and the sole hearing person mentioned in the letter is the school's director, William Turner (Weld's successor). Deaf people, like hearing people, were leaving farming at mid-century and taking up trades, many in the mills. This allowed the Deaf to spend much more time in the company of other members of their ethnic group. They were, as a result, less isolated from the hearing world. Through conversations with other Deaf people and travel, Samuel$_D$ kept informed about what was happening around him both in a primarily hearing environment and, of course, in his part of the Deaf-World. Newspapers—both the silent press and the hearing press—no doubt helped. The command of English in these letters is impressive. Indeed, Samuel Rowe$_D$'s examination for ordination was conducted in writing and found "very satisfactory." The mastery of English in these letters is consistent with the claim that the American Asylum was successful in teaching English to many of its pupils in the era when signed language was the vehicle of instruction.[25]

Four months later, on May 16, 1849, Samuel$_D$ wrote to his sister Nancy$_D$ and brother-in-law George Curtis$_D$.[26] In that letter is further evidence of Deaf society and the sheer pleasure of being with people from one's own ethnic group. In the full letter, Samuel$_D$ gave details about more than a dozen people, nearly all of them Deaf. Many worked in the mills, which drew Deaf people, as industries would in the centuries to come.

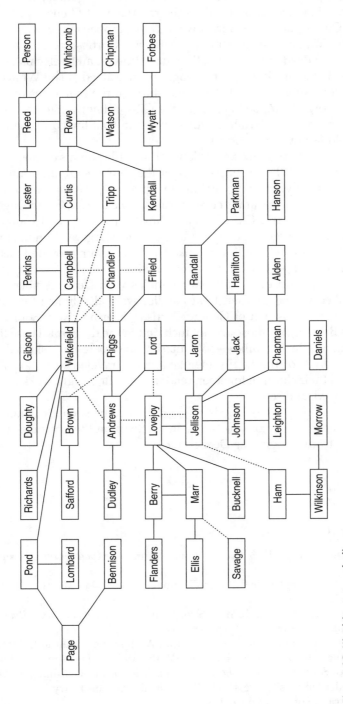

Figure 18 Kinship network diagram

Rowe$_D$ (upper right), as we have seen, and in so doing linked the Curtis and Rowe families (also linked by the marriages of Ebenezer Curtis$_D$, George Curtis$_D$, and Benjamin Rowe$_D$). The Campbell family was linked to Curtis-Rowe by Abner$_D$'s marriage to Olive Curtis$_D$ and then to Ann Curtis$_D$. The Reed family joined the Curtis-Rowe-Campbell cluster as a result of Benjamin Rowe$_D$'s marriage to Lucy Reed$_D$. The Whitcomb and Person families joined the group through the marriages of Adin Reed$_D$. George Campbell$_D$ brought the Gibson family into the group with his marriage to Sarah Gibson$_D$, which in turn linked up with the Wakefield family, and so forth.

The dashed lines show connections through the parents of those Deaf-Deaf marriages. When a couple marries, they link the groom's family to the bride's family, including linking the groom's parents to the bride's parents—and thus the family circle expands. For example, George Riggs$_D$' marriage to Margaret Chandler$_D$ also linked the Riggs and Campbell families since George$_D$'s father was a Riggs and Margaret$_D$'s mother was a Campbell. Parents' families are linked in the diagram provided there is at least one Deaf person in each of the families.

In all, Fig. 18 presents fifty-two families with Deaf members that were linked to one another. Deaf families were also linked by mixed marriages, such as that of George Curtis$_D$'s hearing sister, Sophia, to Thomas Brown$_D$ but those are not included in the diagram. These linkages among Deaf families—both marital and parental—shaped the everyday lives of the family members, who traveled to be together, socialized their children together, tended to the ill, sought work for the unemployed, and so on.

The final chapter examines the significance of such Deaf kinship networks for ethnic consciousness and reflects on the outcomes to be expected from recognizing Deaf ethnicity.

Notes

Part IV

Chapter 10

[1] F. G. Thurston and H. S. Cross, *Three Centuries of Freeport, Maine*, (Freeport, Me.: n.p., 1940).

[2] Anon., "Sad Accident in Cuthbert Georgia," *National Deaf-Mute Gazette* 2(19) (1868): 15.

[3] G. W. Chamberlain and L. M. G. Strong, *The Descendants of Charles Glidden of ortsmouth and Exeter New Hampshire* (Boston: n.p., 1925).

[4] Several other graduates of the American Asylum emigrated to California, including Albert Barnard, Edmund Booth, Almond Denison, and Elisha Osgood. See: H. G. Lang, *Edmund Booth: Deaf Pioneer* (Washington, D.C.: Gallaudet University Press, 2004.) Our thanks to Prof. Harry Lang for the identification of Almond Denison.

5 Campbell clan: S. Adams, *The History of the Town of Bowdoinham, Maine 1762–1912* (Somersworth, N.H.: New England History Press, 1985); Anon., *Window From the Past: A Mid-nineteenth Century View of the Campbells of Bowdoin Maine* (S.l.: s.n., 2000); J. E. Bickford, ed., *Early Bowdoin, Maine Families and Some of their Descendants* (Bowie, Md.: Heritage Books, 2002); Bowdoin Historical Society, *Bowdoin Bicentennial, 1788–1988: Pictorial History of Bowdoin, Maine, 1788–1988* (Bowdoin, Me.: The Society, Falcon Press, 1988); L. Campbell, *Earliest Campbell Families in Maine* (Worcester, Mass.: s.n., 1948; L. Campbell, *Early Scotch-Irish Settlers and Campbell Families in Maine* (S. Harwich, Mass.: *MSS* New England Historic Genealogical Library); R. T. Cox, E. F. Reed, and T. C. Stuart, *Vital Records of Bowdoin Maine to the Year 1892*, vol. 3 (Auburn, Me.: Maine Historical Society, 1945); C. N. Sinnett, *The Campbell Family in Maine with Ancestry [and name index]* (Fertile, Minn: n.p., 1980).

6 Chandlers: M. C. Lowell, *Chandler-Parsons . . . and Allied Families"* (Boston, Mass.: Marvin, 1911); A. M. Riley, "Chandler and Gunnison Traditions" *Old Eliot* 2 (1898): 152–154.

7 "As originally to Trip of Tripham, County Kent and London, being the only authentic emblem published to this name, and representing a family who have been seated in Kent since the days of William the Conqueror. . ." *Some of the Descendents of Sylvanus who Settled in Kittery, Maine, the Latter part of the Seventeenth Century*. Compiled by Benjamin F. Tripp www.u-aizu.ac.jp/~tripp/Tripp.Gene.txt (accessed 7/24/2010).

8 *Records of the Deaf and Dumb, Maine District, 1819.*

9 M. C. Wilson, *John Gibson of Cambridge, Mass and his Descendants 1634–1899* (Washington, D.C.: McGill and Wallace, 1900).

10 The letters are selected from: Anon, *Window from the Past.*

11 Curtis clan: Bicentennial Committee, "An Account of New Gloucester," *Collections of the Maine Historical Society* 2 (1847): 151–164; Bicentennial Committee, *New Gloucester Images* (New Gloucester, Me.: Bicentennial Committee, 1976);W. W. Clayton, *History of Cumberland County Maine* (Philadelphia, Penn.: Everts and Peck, 1880); T. H. Haskell, *The New Gloucester Centennial, September 7, 1874* (Portland, Me.: Hoyt, Fogg and Donham, 1875); Maine Deaf and Mute Mission, *How The Spirit And Letter Of The Gospel May Be Conveyed To The Deaf Mutes And The Ordination Of Samuel Rowe, A Deaf Mute as an Evangelist at the Congregational Church, West Boxford, Mass., Wednesday, February 20, 1878* (Georgetown, Me., press of Georgetown Advocate, 1878); F. H. Nelson, *The New Gloucester Book* (Auburn, Me.: Merrill and Webber, 1925.); J. W. Penney, "Records of the Proprietors of New Gloucester and Reminiscences of Some of the Early Settlers . . . Read Before the . . . Society, November 22, 1895," *Collections of the Maine Historical Society* 8 2nd series (1897): 263–288; G. L. Rossano, *A Subtle Revolution: The Urban Transformation of Rural Life, New Gloucester, Maine, 1775–1930* (Ph.D. diss., University of North Carolina at Chapel Hill, 1980).

12 D. C. Poole, *A New Vineyard* (Edgartown, Mass.: Dukes County Historical Society, 1976).

13 Nelson, *New Gloucester Book*. I. Parsons, "An Account of New Gloucester," *Collections of the Maine Historical Society* 2 (1847): 151–164.

14 Chi square = 9.3, p <.001.

15 Women in History Project. "Nancy Rowe Curtis Papers." William L. Clements Library, University of Michigan, Ann Arbor.

16 J. C. Stinchfield, *History of the Town of Leeds in Androscoggin County Maine From Its Settlement June 10, 1780* (Bowie Md., Heritage Books, 1996).

17 The father's petition gives a count of four Deaf children at the Asylum: "petition of William B. Curtis of Leeds [wife Olive] 'it has pleased the Righteous Disposer of all events to withhold from four of my dear children the capacity of hearing and of speech.' Executive Council, 1825: Resolve for the assistance of the Deaf and Dumb." However, each of the sons claimed on entry to the Asylum to have two brothers and two sisters (thus five Deaf siblings), and each of the daughters claimed three brothers and two sisters. In the Fay entry for Olive Curtis, #677, she is said to have had one sibling of unknown hearing status. E. A. Fay, *Marriages of the Deaf in America* (Washington, D.C.: Volta Bureau, 1898).

18 Anon. [T. Brown marries Sophia Sumner née Curtis]. *National Deaf-Mute Gazette* 1 (1) (1867): 16.

19 Stinchfield, *Leeds*; O.M. Wheaton. [Curtis family records], Maine State Archives.

20 J. Rowe, Letter addressed to Mr. George Curtis, East Leeds, January 24, 1842; S. E. Rowe, Letter addressed to "Dear brother and sister," written from New Gloucester, Maine, December 2, 1851. From Sarah E. [illegible; probably Hutchins].

21 K. Lockridge, "Land, Population, and the Evolution of New England Society: 1630–1790." *Past and Present* 39 (1968): 62–80.

22 J. Rowe, Letter addressed to George and Nancy Curtis from "Aunt Judith Rowe" [father Zebulon Rowe's sister], New Gloucester, Maine, May 14, 1846. The letters were obtained from Women History Project, "Nancy Rowe Curtis Papers."

23 Maine Deaf Mute Mission, *Samuel Rowe*; O. Berg, *A Missionary Chronicle: Being a History of the Ministry to the Deaf in the Episcopal Church (1850–1980)* (Hollywood, Md.: St. Mary's Press, 1984).

24 S. Rowe, Letter addressed to Ebenezer W. Curtis from Samuel Rowe in Keene, N.H., February, 1849.

25 H. Lane, *The Mask of Benevolence: Disabling the Deaf Community*. (New York: Knopf, 1992). H. Lane, "Mask of Irrelevance: A Reply to the *Annals* Review of "The Mask of Benevolence: Disabling the Deaf Community," *American Annals of the Deaf* 138 (1993): 316–319.

26 S. Rowe, Letter addressed to George Curtis from Samuel Rowe in Lawrence, Mass., May 16, 1849.

27 N. Rowe, Letter apparently addressed to Rev. S. H. Shepley, New Gloucester, Maine, April 16, 1846. Written in Leeds.

Part V

Deaf Ancestry: Summary and Reflections

SUMMARY

We observed, at the start of our investigation of Deaf ancestry in Maine (Part III), that Deaf people who married chose other Deaf people for spouses much of the time, with the result that many Deaf households were enmeshed in a Deaf kinship network. We reasoned, based on the lives of Deaf families like the Browns of Henniker, New Hampshire, that marriage with a person of one's own kind in an environment of otherness creates a heightened consciousness of shared identity and destiny. We suggested that Deaf ethnicity is an upward projection of family, of language, and of cultural rules and values. Now we can go further and propose that an intermediate stage between Deaf family and Deaf ethnicity is intermarriage across Deaf families, forming larger Deaf clans. We have thus had the opportunity to observe some features of the founding of an ethnic group, specifically the formation of clans and kinship networks, features that in the case of many other ethnic groups have been obscured by the passage of time.

Members of kinship networks need not know one another and that is true for the kinship network diagrammed in Fig. 18. The more degrees of separation the less likely the acquaintance.[1] Not all of the Deaf people in this kinship network were contemporaries and some of the descendants of these linkages may not have been aware of their ancestry.

The kinship network schematized in Fig. 18 is larger than it appears in the diagram. Hearing spouses in mixed marriages can certainly link Deaf families, although we did not include them in Fig. 18. For example, Sophia Curtis's marriage to Thomas Brown$_D$ would have brought the Brown and Swett families into the network shown in Fig. 18. Finally, links were created between Deaf families by the marriages of two hearing people but these are also not shown. Including such bonds among the families would increase the size and complexity of the kinship mapping.

At the same time in early America that Deaf people sought out one another and intermarried, so too did members of the dominant ethnicity, Anglo-Saxons. The two ethnicities were developing side by side but with several important differences. First, the marriage options of the Deaf ethnic minority were much more restricted. Second, Deaf partners in marriage were more often related to one another. Third, early Deaf Americans were creating Deaf ethnicity, shaping its language, culture, and values, while the descendants of the Puritans and other immigrants from England imported their ethnicity, as it were, from the Old World, although it would be shaped by conditions in the New. All three factors contributed mightily to Deaf solidarity: marriage between Deaf people, marriage between relatives, and *de novo* creation of Deaf ethnicity.

Abetted by institutions such as the American Asylum, the New England Gallaudet Association and the Deaf-Mute Mission, the Deaf of southern New Hampshire and Maine came to see themselves as a class apart from the hearing world, a group with its own distinctive language, culture, and physical makeup. The members of this ethnic group took pleasure in their shared identity. As Deaf inhabitants of Martha's Vineyard increasingly attended the American Asylum, married Deaf in much greater numbers, and joined Deaf institutions, their ethnic consciousness would have increased as well. The movement to replace signed languages, formally inaugurated in the Congress of Milan, had stifled that consciousness but could not extinguish it. Finally, that consciousness blazed anew as a result of the American Civil Rights Movement and continues to grow today with the flourishing of Deaf activism, Deaf arts and Deaf Studies. Deaf people are entering the professions in large numbers, especially professions that serve Deaf people. This expanding Deaf middle class reflects the growth of Deaf enrollments in college programs, many of which are Deaf culture affirming.

Developments in the larger society present both challenges and opportunities for all ethnic groups. Although there are forces that promote Deaf separatism, most Deaf people have hearing parents; moreover, hearing society both restricts and facilitates what Deaf people can achieve, so the Deaf-World, it seems to us, seeks engagement and a degree of bilingualism. We mentioned earlier that the Deaf clubs have been dwindling while other venues for Deaf association have developed. Perhaps vlogs on the internet, email, texting, pagers, and video-telephony reduce the need to some extent for physical presence. Most American Deaf children today are in local schools, depriving many of their ethnic heritage and of all the Deaf-World has to offer. Increasing numbers of students receive cochlear implant surgery. Many such children require a command of ASL in order to communicate with their teacher or interpreter and to converse with other Deaf people, but programs of implant surgery often discourage the use of ASL—thus the historic struggle between minority and majority language continues.

We have presented evidence and reasoning with regard to language, culture, and boundary maintenance that encourages a reconceptualization of Deaf ASL signers as an ethnic group. In response to those scholars who insist that ethnicity also requires shared ancestry, either real or mythical, we replied that a majority of the members of the Deaf-World inherited their ethnicity, which they owe to a small number of shared ancestors.

We have made a start at identifying those ancestors for the island of Martha's Vineyard and the illustrative case of Maine. Tracing those ancestors back to their American progenitors and beyond revealed that nearly forty clan progenitors in the Vineyard and Maine had ancestors in the county of Kent in England.[2] Kent apparently had Deaf people and a sign language, quite early on. That sign language likely was brought to the Vineyard by settlers and likely played a role in the shaping of ASL. This remains to be shown definitively by further research.

In some Deaf families, every generation has had Deaf members and the ethnic physical difference is always expressed. In other cases, the trait is carried forward unexpressed, and then appears or reappears overtly. This dual pattern of ethnic transmission may be peculiar to Deaf ethnicity but there can be no doubt that Deaf heritage—language and culture, including strategies for boundary maintenance and the reliance on vision—are transmitted from generation to generation both through families and through social institutions. *The People of the Eye* thus contributes to two fields—ethnohistory and comparative ethnography—applied to Deaf Studies.

REFLECTIONS

The consequences of an ethnic conceptualization of the Deaf-World go well beyond academic studies; the quality of Deaf lives (and the lives of those who relate to them) is in large part determined by how Deaf people are conceptualized. Are ASL signers simply hearing people manquées, most of them beset by a genetic mutation passed on through intermarriage, or are they members of an ethnic group whose common descent, language, and culture can be traced across generations? The conceptualization of any ethnic group is a powerful force in self-acceptance and acceptance by others, and a lens through which relations are perceived and managed between majority and minority. Recognizing Deaf American ethnicity, what obligations does that impose on the majority in its dealings with the Deaf? Contemporary ethical standards with regard to the treatment of ethnic minorities are captured in part in the *United Nations Declaration of the Rights of Persons Belonging to National or Ethnic, Religious and Linguistic Minorities*.[3] The treaty calls on governments to protect and foster the existence and identity of linguistic minorities; it affirms the right of such minorities to enjoy their culture and use their language; it asks that governments take measures to ensure that persons belonging to minorities have adequate opportunities to learn the minority language. Most fundamentally, members of the Deaf-World ethnic group have a right "to participate in decisions on the national level affecting their minority."[4]

None of these provisions has been honored broadly in the experience of ethnic Deaf Americans. The failure to conceptualize sign language speakers as an ethnic group is, we believe, an important reason for the failure to apply to them the ethical standards that concern ethnic groups. Here follow some examples of the potential rewards of adopting an ethnic perspective on Deaf ethnicity. However, the accuracy of viewing ASL signers as an ethnic group is independent of the gains and losses associated with embracing that identity.

Recognized Authorities

Changing the conceptualization of ASL signers opens the way to apply the accumulated wisdom of the Deaf-World to Deaf children and adults. There would be many more service providers from the minority: Deaf teachers, foster parents, information officers, social workers, advocates. Non-Deaf service providers would be expected to know the language, history, and culture of the Deaf-World.[5]

Legal Status

Most members of the Deaf-World would no longer claim disability benefits or services under the present legislation for disabled people. The services to which the Deaf ethnic group has a right in order to obtain equal treatment under the law would be provided by other legislation and bureaucracies. Civil rights laws and rulings applied to ethnic groups protect their rights in arenas such as education, employment and language use. There is a body of law in the United States that predicates language rights on ethnicity. As minorities come to occupy a larger part of the population, the need to accommodate ethnic groups and especially their languages will become increasingly apparent. Interpreters are not normally a right of handicapped persons; rather they are a right of ethnic groups based on the principle of equal access.

Cochlear Implants

Changing the conceptualization changes the nature of interventions. In 1990, the U.S. Food and Drug Administration approved surgical implantation in children of a cochlear prosthesis, a device that converts sound waves into electrical currents that are delivered to a wire implanted in the child's inner ear. Deaf organizations worldwide have deplored the surgery,[6] contending that Deaf babies are healthy babies with no need of surgery; that the surgery has medical and psychosocial risks and highly variable results; that children are too young to give consent and their parents are often uninformed about the Deaf-World; and that it is in principle injurious to the Deaf-World.[7]

The program of childhood cochlear implantation in America and elsewhere has as a primary goal to enable Deaf children to acquire the majority spoken language. In their efforts to achieve this goal, surgeons, audiologists, and special educators commonly instruct parents not to use sign language with their children nor allow others to do so. This practice violates the child's right to language and the ethnic group's right to flourish.[8] If the goal of replacing ASL with English could be achieved on a wide scale, the consequence, however unintended, would be ethnocide, the systematic extinction of an ethnic minority's freedom to pursue its way of life. An implant scientist quoted in the *Atlantic Monthly* claimed that ethnocide will indeed be the likely consequence of programs of cochlear implantation: "The cochlear prosthesis on which I have worked for years with many other scientists, engineers and clinicians, will lead inevitably to the extinction of the alternative culture of the Deaf, probably within a decade."[9] The author likens Deaf culture to Yiddish culture and concludes, "Both are unsustainable." Is it self-indulgent nostalgia to want to protect Deaf culture and Yiddish culture? Ethnic diversity enriches life; it is a fundamental good. When ethnic diversity is sustained, so is society's adaptive potential.[10] Moreover, most of us recoil at the idea of undermining an ethnic group because it is morally wrong, because it has led to crimes against humanity, and because we want our own ethnicity protected from powerful others. If our society generally has failed to recoil at the prospect of Deaf ethnocide, it is because most fail to recognize Deaf ethnicity.

Furthermore, if Deaf ethnicity were more widely recognized, parents could have a more positive understanding of their Deaf child, they could see more clearly why interacting with Deaf adults and promoting ASL use is so important, and they could weigh more carefully and wisely the risks and benefits of cochlear implantation.

Deaf Education

The recognition of Deaf ethnicity also orients us differently to Deaf education. The *Framework Convention on the Protection of National Minorities* of the Council of Europe calls on educational systems to ensure that "persons belonging to those minorities have adequate opportunities for being taught in the minority language."[11] The use of the ethnic minority language is a human right as well as wise educational practice.[12] If teachers could communicate with their Deaf students in the language of their ethnic group, a language the students can readily understand, many more Deaf students would be prepared for important roles in our postindustrial society. Moreover, it is the law: schools with large numbers of pupils whose primary language is not English are eligible for funds under the Bilingual Education Act and must conform to court rulings that require, transitionally at least, employment of the minority language, of minority role models, and of a curriculum that reflects minority heritage.[13] No ethnic group has a stronger claim on an education that draws on their minority language than does the Deaf-World, for no ethnic group encounters greater obstacles to mastering the dominant language. Because parents who carry the Deaf trait unexpressed can pass on the physical element of Deaf ethnicity but frequently cannot pass on language and culture, it becomes essential for the children in this ethnic minority to interact early on with Deaf peers and with adult Deaf role models. If the opportunity to learn an accessible natural language is withheld, those children will spend years languageless, reduced to using primitive home sign. An ethnic conception of the Deaf child, however, could foster early recognition of the need for Deaf language models; it could lead parents and parent-infant programs to ensure early language learning; and it could lead schools to exploit that sign language mastery for effective instruction in the dominant language and all else.

Deaf Reproduction

The ethnic conceptualization of the Deaf-World casts a new light, further, on efforts to control Deaf reproduction, efforts like genetic screening and prenatal testing to avoid Deaf births.[14] Is it ethical to undertake a program of medical intervention aimed at reducing the membership of an ethnic group, a program contrary to the wishes of that group? Most Deaf people are opposed to genetic testing for restricting Deaf births and are equally pleased to have a Deaf or a hearing child.[15] The tendency to see pathology and not ethnicity in the Deaf-World fosters demeaning and outmoded forms of speech such as citing the *risk* of having a child belonging to that ethnic group or the need for *therapy* to avoid or *remediate* ethnic identity. If the Deaf were widely understood to be an ethnic group, eugenic measures to restrict the birth of Deaf ethnics would be seen as conflicting with our fundamental values.

There are many more issues in ethnic relations between the mainstream and the Deaf that would be altered to mutual advantage by the ethnic perspective. The comprehensive promise of such a paradigm change has been well described by Tom Humphries$_D$: "Acceptance of Deaf ethnicity removes one more obstacle to a clear understanding of who Deaf people are (and are not). This alters the relationship between Deaf and hearing people and creates opportunities for Deaf people to bring about change."[16]

Notes

Part V

[1] A. J. Boyce et al., "Neighborhood Knowledge and the Distribution of Marriage Distances," *Annals of Human Genetics* 30 (1967): 335–338.

2   Simon Athearn, Joyce Baker, Patience Bigge, Nicholas Butler, Joanna
    Clements, William Curtis, Andrew Cushman, Thomas Cushman, Dolor
    Davis, John Davis, Samuel Eddy, Ralph Farnum, Ralph (2nd) Farnum,
    Thomas Farnum, Nicholas Fessenden, Richard Foster, Margaret Gowen,
    Susanna Hinckley, Hannah House, William Jellison, Edward Kennard,
    Thomas Lambert, Benjamin Lathrop, John Libby, Edmund Littlefield,
    Abraham Lord, James Lord, Nathan Lord, Hannah Lynnell, Sarah Partridge,
    Elizabeth Savery, James Skiffe, Rev. John Smith, Isabel Tempest, John
    Wakefield, Joyce Wallen, Hannah Whitney, Margery Willard, Stephen Wing.

3   United Nations, *Declaration on the Rights of Persons Belonging to National or
    Ethnic, Religious and Linguistic Minorities*, 1992, Resolution 47/135. www.
    un-documents.net/a47r135.htm (accessed 7/25/2010).

4   United Nations, Article 2, # 3.

5   S. Gregory and G. M. Hartley. *Constructing Deafness*. (London: Pinter, 1991).

6   H. Lane, "The Cochlear Implant Controversy," *World Federation of the Deaf
    News* 2–3 (1994): 22–28.

7   P. Hyde, R. Punch, and L. Komesaroff, "Coming to a Decision about Cochlear
    Implantation: Parents Making Choices for Their Deaf Children." *Journal of
    Deaf Studies and Deaf Education* 15 (2010): 162–178; D. Moores, "Cochlear
    Implants: A Perspective [not very successful]," *American Annals of the Deaf*
    154 (2010): 415-416.

8   A. M. Muhlke, "The Right to Language and Linguistic Development:
    Deafness from a Human Rights Perspective," *Virginia Journal of International
    Law* 40 (2000):, 707–766; L. M. Siegel, *The Human Right to Language:
    Communication Access for Deaf Children* (Washington, D.C.: Gallaudet
    University Press, 2008).

9   G. Loeb, Letters to the editor; "Doomed Ghetto Culture." In E. Dolnick,
    "Deafness as Culture," *Atlantic Monthly* 272 (1993): 37–54. Reprinted *Deaf
    Life* 6 (1993): 33.

10 Robert Johnson, personal communication, 2009.

11 conventions.coe.int/treaty/en/Treaties/Html/157.htm   Quotation   from
    Article 14. (accessed 2/15/09). See also: *Consultation Sur Les Différentes
    Approches de l'Education Des Sourds*. ED-84/ws/102. Paris: UNESCO, 1985.

12 R. E. Johnson, S. K. Liddell, and C. J. Erting, "Unlocking the Curriculum:
    Principles for Achieving Access in Deaf Education," *Gallaudet Research
    Institute Working Papers* (1989); R. C. Johnson, ed., "Access: Language in Deaf
    Education. Proceedings of a Seminar Sponsored by the Gallaudet Research
    Institute Concerning 'Unlocking the Curriculum.'" *Gallaudet Research
    Institute Occasional Papers* (1990); R. C. Johnson, "The Publication and Early
    Aftermath of 'Unlocking the Curriculum,'" *Sign Language Studies* 69 (1990):
    295–325.

13 H. Lane, *The Mask of Benevolence: Disabling the Deaf Community*. (New York:
    Knopf, 1992); J. Haft, "Assuring Equal Educational Opportunity For
    Language-Minority Students: Bilingual Education and the Equal Educational
    Opportunity Act of 1974." *Columbia Journal of Law and Social Problems*
    18 (1983): 209–293.

14 K. W. Anstey, "Are Attempts to Have Impaired Children Justifiable? Couples
    Should Not Be Allowed to Select Either for or Against Deafness. (Current
    Controversy)," *Journal of Medical Ethics* 28 (2008): 286; M. Spriggs, "Lesbian

Couple Create a Child Who Is Deaf Like Them: A Deaf Lesbian Couple Who Chose to Have a Deaf Child Receive a Lot of Criticism," *Journal of Medical Ethics* 28 (2008): 283.

15 S. J. Stern et al., "The Attitudes of Deaf and Hard of Hearing Individuals Toward Genetic Testing of Hearing Loss," *American Journal of Human Genetics* 67 (4) suppl. 2 (2000): 32.

16 Tom Humphries, personal communication, 2009.

Appendix A

Briefly Noted Lineages

The pedigrees cited in this section are a selection from a larger set posted on the web at: http://dvn.iq.harvard.edu/dvn/dv/DEA Families addressed in Appendix A: Bourne, Butler, Daggett, Deering, Dillingham, Edwards, Fessenden, Frank, Larrabee, Libby, Littlefield, Luce, Ludwig, Nason, Norton, Perkins, Riggs, Skillin, Small, Titcomb, Wakefield.

OTHER VINEYARD LINEAGES

In addition to the Vineyard lineages with progenitors from Kent, described in Chapter 6, several other Vineyard families had Deaf descendants. The Norton progenitor, Nicholas, immigrated to Edgartown on the Vineyard from Somerset in England. His daughter married John Butler of Kentish ancestry in Edgartown in 1673 and that is the last time we see the Norton name in the Deaf pedigree. Five generations later in this pedigree, Deaf children start to appear named Mayhew, West, and others. The progenitor of the Look family immigrated to Lynn, Massachusetts, from Scotland; he was a collier at the iron works. His son Thomas moved to Tisbury and operated a grist mill. In the late 1600s, Thomas's daughters initiated three lines of descent (one was married twice) that yielded Deaf descendants—with names like Mayhew, Tilton, and West—when remote and not-so-remote cousins married.

In the Bourne pedigree, the progenitor Richard Bourne, who emigrated from Devon to Sandwich, Massachusetts, had numerous Deaf descendants. His son married a Skiffe of Kentish ancestry, and they initiated three lines of descent with Deaf members: Their daughter married a Mayhew, moved to Chilmark, and had four Deaf descendants; another daughter married an Allen and had a Deaf great grandson; finally, a granddaughter married into the Newcomb family and had twenty-two Deaf descendants.

John Doggett (or Daggett) emigrated from Suffolk, England, to Plymouth, Massachusetts, in 1630 in Winthrop's fleet. He moved to the Vineyard not long after his townsman in Watertown, Thomas Mayhew. Daggett had two sons who initiated two branches but extensive marriage between the branches (that is, consanguinity) followed in later generations. After the progenitor's grandchildren, no further Daggetts appear in the Deaf pedigree.[1]

The progenitor Henry Luce traveled from Gloucestershire, England, to Scituate and then in 1670 to Tisbury, Massachusetts. Early in the nineteenth century, there were forty Luce families on the Vineyard with five Deaf members, including Charles, a NEGA member. Eleven of those Luce families migrated to Maine; half of those to the Sandy River Valley (see Chapter 8).

THE DILLINGHAM-FESSENDEN CLAN

Abigail$_D$ and Nancy$_D$ Dillingham of Lee, Massachusetts, both attended the American Asylum (see Fig. 8, Newcomb pedigree).[2] In the school rolls, they were credited with fifteen Deaf relatives. Both women were said to be "remarkably intelligent."[3] Brother Charles, a Coda, and teacher at the Pennsylvania School for the Deaf, married Martha Heaton$_D$ from that place; she had three Deaf siblings. The Dillingham sisters trace their lineage back to the Reverend Henry Dillingham (not shown), who left Leicestershire, England, to settle in Sandwich on Cape Cod. There his descendants remained until the parents of the two Deaf sisters moved to Lee and then Pittsfield, Massachusetts. The Dillingham sisters' maternal grandfather, Benjamin Fessenden of Sandwich, was descended on his mother's side from the progenitor Reverend John Smith. The woman he married, Sarah Newcomb, was the granddaughter of Chilmark resident Mercy Smith and a descendant, like Benjamin, of the Reverend John Smith. This Benjamin's grandfather, Nicholas Fessenden, was born in Canterbury, Kent, and died in Cambridge, Massachusetts. Nicholas was a glove and harness maker.[4]

THE RIGGS CLAN

The Riggs$_D$ of Turner, Maine, of whom we spoke earlier in connection with Margaret Chandler$_D$'s marriage with George Riggs$_D$, intermarried with four other Deaf families that lived in the Androscoggin cluster of nearby towns. It all began when Sarah Wakefield$_D$ and Alfred Riggs$_D$ of Jay, Maine, married in 1818. Or perhaps it would be more accurate to say it all began when the Wakefield progenitor, John, immigrated to Wells, Maine, from Kent, as mentioned earlier. The Riggs progenitor, Edward, came from Essex, England. Sarah$_D$ and Alfred$_D$ Riggs had two Deaf children and seven hearing. Their son George$_D$, who had a sister, a cousin, an uncle, and a niece Deaf, married Margaret Chandler$_D$ and they had a son, Charles$_D$, in Leeds. Charles$_D$ married Mahala Fifield$_D$ from Deer Isle, Maine; (they overlapped at the American Asylum). Mahala$_D$ had a Deaf brother and a Deaf uncle and was a member of the Mission. George Riggs$_D$' sister, Mary Ann$_D$, married a hearing man, Moses Brown, who would die at sea, but they had two Deaf daughters,

Elizabeth$_D$ and Helen$_D$ (whose uncle, cousin, and great uncle were Deaf). Both attended the Asylum and Helen$_D$ was a member of the Mission, along with her husband, Mellen Safford$_D$. After Moses Brown died, Mary Ann$_D$ married John Andrews$_D$, a shoemaker in Turner, Maine (he had divorced Mary Jane Lord$_D$; his parents were cousins).[5]

THE LARRABEE CLAN

The Larrabee family with three Deaf children lived in Bangor, Maine. Bangor is 140 miles from Portland and located on the Penobscot River, about sixty miles from the sea. In the era of the Deaf Larrabees, at mid-nineteenth century, vast amounts of lumber were floated down the river to waiting ships in the deep harbor, and lumber-related trades flourished. From the mills and farms in the region goods and food traveled to Bangor and in turn Bangor supplied the region with manufactured and other goods from coastal and trans-Atlantic trade. The three children—Phoebe$_D$, John$_D$, and Charles$_D$–attended the American Asylum. Their parents were cousins. The Larrabee progenitor was Stephen, who emigrated from Pau, France, to Jewell's Island, Maine.[6] Phoebe$_D$ married a schoolmate from the Asylum, Gustavus Converse$_D$. Charles$_D$ did not marry; John$_D$ married Rachel Ann Scoles$_D$, a classmate from the Asylum, whose parents were from Canada and lived in Augusta. Rachel Ann$_D$ had an unmarried Deaf brother, and a hearing sister who married a Deaf man, Howard Mayberry$_D$, from Otisfield. Howard$_D$ had two Deaf sisters who married Deaf men.

THE LUDWIG CLAN

The Ludwig clan, like the Larrabee, reminds us that although progenitors of Deaf families were very often from England it was not always the case. Three families from Germany lived in the town of Waldoboro, Maine, in the mid-eighteenth century. The land, quite close to the sea in eastern Maine, had been bought around 1720 by Samuel Waldo. After an initial settlement, Indian attacks caused the settlers to flee. When peace returned, Waldo's son recruited about 1500 immigrants to the village from Germany. No doubt the Ludwigs, Seiders, and Winchenbachs were drawn to intermarry once in the New World by their shared language and traditions. Joseph Ludwig and Margaret Winchenbach married in 1791; they had a Deaf son, Jacob$_D$, and a great grandson, Elmer$_D$. They also had a hearing son, Simon, and a hearing daughter, Jane. Simon Ludwig married his cousin, Jane Winchenbach and they had a son, Simon$_D$, who married a Mary Spillman$_D$. Jane Ludwig married her cousin John Seiders and they had three Deaf children, Luella$_D$, Emma$_D$, and David$_D$, all of whom attended the American Asylum.[7]

THE BUTLER-EDWARDS CLAN

In the seaport of Thomaston, adjacent to Waldoboro, lived the family of John Butler and Mary Stone and their five children of whom three were Deaf. Thomaston was established on the eastern bank of the St. George River, then considered the boundary between New England and New France. In the Butlers' day it had numerous mills, kilns, shipyards, and quarries. The progenitor of this family was Steven Butler, who immigrated with his wife, Sarah Edwards, from Braintree in England to Hartford, Connecticut, in the early 1600s. (Thus there appears to be no connection to the Nicholas Butler family of Martha's Vineyard whose progenitor was from Kent.) In Hartford, Steven Butler and his wife had two sons, Richard and William, who established two Maine branches of the family that would have Deaf descendants: the one in Berwick that included Mary Butler$_D$ (1790), the other ultimately in Thomaston that included the three Deaf children of John and Mary. The oldest, Hannah$_D$, a tailor, married Oliver Deering$_D$, a carpenter (see next family); they attended the American Asylum but at different times and both were active after graduation in the Mission. The two Deaf sons, John$_D$ and James$_D$, a stonecutter and a trucker, married Deaf women. A hearing son married a hearing member of the Ludwig clan.[8]

THE DEERING CLAN

The progenitor of the Deering family was Roger, who emigrated in the mid-seventeenth century from Devon, England, to Kittery, Maine; he was a mariner and shipwright. One of his sons initiated a branch that would culminate in William Deering$_D$, a farmer in Richmond, Maine. (Richmond, the nearest Kennebec landing to Bowdoin, was where George$_D$ Campbell lived.) William Deering$_D$ married Katy Fletcher$_D$ of Massachusetts in 1885. Both had attended the American Asylum, as well as its reunions. This line of descent included marriages with the Boothby family, which had two Deaf scions in Waterboro, and with the Sawyer family (see Titcomb clan) with at least four Deaf members.

Roger Deering's second son, Thomas, initiated a branch that descended to Oliver Deering$_D$, who lived in Saco, Maine. Saco is situated beside Saco Bay on the Gulf of Maine, about fifteen miles south of Portland. Settlers first arrived in 1631. The village grew steadily throughout the eighteenth century as farming, lumbering, and shipbuilding prospered. By the time of the Revolution, the growth of international commerce in the town required a customs house. Shipbuilding brought to the area a steady flow of carpenters (among them Oliver Deering$_D$), riggers, and the like, as well as blacksmiths and, of course, mariners. These in turn caused an influx of doctors, lawyers, traders, joiners, masons, shoemakers, tailors, and cabinetmakers.[9] In the nineteenth century, numerous cotton mills were opened on the western falls of the Saco River.

Oliver$_D$ first married his schoolmate Hannah S. Butler$_D$, as mentioned above, and after she died in 1858, he married another schoolmate, Hannah Sweet Richardson$_D$, a tailor from Newburyport, Massachusetts. Hannah$_D$ had a Deaf brother and two Deaf sisters; their parents, Moses Richardson and Sophia Foster, were cousins. Sophia's pedigree included six Deaf members as far as we have ascertained.[10] The Richardson progenitor was Samuel, who emigrated from Hertfordshire, England, to Woburn, Massachusetts. Hannah Richardson$_D$'s siblings were Ellen$_D$, Moses$_D$, and Nancy$_D$. The first two apparently did not marry; Nancy$_D$ married a hearing man.

THE FRANK-SMALL-SKILLIN CLAN

This clan, based in Gray, Maine, some sixteen miles north of Portland, has fifteen Deaf members. There were five in the family of Josiah Frank and Mary Small. There were three in the family of Thomas Frank and Lucy Small. William Frank and Susanna Frank (who were cousins) had two children, Joseph$_D$ and Sarah$_D$, who attended the American Asylum as did their second cousin, Francis$_D$. Their hearing sibling, Sewell, married Sarah Skillin$_D$ (who had three Deaf relatives). The Frank progenitor was Thomas, born 1665, who emigrated from Bedfordshire in England to Gray, Maine. The Skillin progenitor was Thomas Skillings (or Skilling or Skillin) born 1614 in Suffolk, England, who immigrated to Portland, Maine. Turning to the Small family, Susan Small and Andrew Libby, also of Gray like the Franks, had a Deaf daughter Matilda$_D$. Joseph and Cynthia Small, cousins, had two Deaf children, Albert$_D$ and Frances$_D$ in Danville, Maine. Both attended the American Asylum as did Albert's wife, Clara Seaverns$_D$. Marshall$_D$ and Ashley$_D$ Small of Bowdoin bring the count to fifteen. (In Bowdoin or right adjacent to it lived Lyman Tripp$_D$, George Campbell$_D$, and William Deering$_D$.) The Small progenitor was Francis, born 1625 in Devon, who immigrated to Cape Cod; one branch of the family settled in southern Maine, ultimately in Gray. Susan Higgins$_D$, who had five Deaf relatives, lived in Gray, as did Hiram Hunt$_D$ (treasurer of the Mission) and his wife Harriett$_D$, and Matilda Libby$_D$. Further, Gray is adjacent to New Gloucester where the Rowe family with eight Deaf members dwelled.[11]

THE PERKINS CLAN

Ephraim Lord Perkins and his wife, Elizabeth Furbish, of Sanford, Maine, were related and had five hearing children and three Deaf daughters, two of whom—Phoebe$_D$ and Sally$_D$—attended the American Asylum.

Sanford is located on the Mousam River about thirty-two miles south of Portland. Phoebe_D married Moses Curtis_D, a Deaf ship carpenter, descended from the Curtis progenitor, William of Kent. The Perkins progenitor emigrated from Warwick in England and these Perkins descended from one of his sons, Jacob. Another son, Thomas, established a second branch, and a prosperous branch it proved to be. In 1797, the eminent portraitist, John Brewster_D Jr. was commissioned to paint ten portraits of the Perkins extended family. The third branch of the family had Deaf issue in the person of Freeland Perkins_D of Woodstock, Maine, who married Joanna Glines_D in 1866; both had attended the American Asylum and both were members of the Mission.[12]

THE TITCOMB CLAN

The pedigree of the Deaf Titcombs connects with those of the Deaf Tripps, Pattersons, Sawyers, and Pikes. Samuel Bitfield, born in Somerset, England, in 1592, and his wife Elizabeth Parker settled in Essex County, Massachusetts. Two of their daughters would found two distinct branches of the family that would intermarry generations later. Elizabeth Bitfield married William Titcomb. Their sixth generation descendant, George Titcomb, was the father of five Deaf children with Jane Patterson, who had two Deaf relatives and a progenitor from Ireland. The couple lived in Cumberland, Maine, adjacent to Gray, six miles north of Portland and twenty from Saco. The oldest of their children, George Titcomb_D Jr., married Cordelia Sawyer_D of Saco. Cordelia_D, had several Deaf relatives; she was a descendant of the other Bitfield daughter, Ruth, and her husband William Sawyer. George had three Deaf sisters: Nancy_D, who married John Poore_D; Sophronia_D, who married David_D Porter; and a third sister yet to be identified. George_D also had a brother, Augustus Titcomb_D, who was a well-known figure in the Maine Deaf-World, a member of the NEGA and the Mission, an Asylum alumnus who went to its reunions and who attended the Gallaudet Centennial in Boston. Augustus_D married a schoolmate and fellow Mission member, Elizabeth Pike_D, who lived close to Saco. Elizabeth's cousin Horace Pike_D was married to Elizabeth Tripp_D, from the large Deaf Tripp family of whom we spoke earlier. The Titcomb genealogist states:

> Augustus Titcomb was a sea captain and he resided at Saco, Maine, until his wife's death when he apparently moved to Concord New Hampshire (N.H. vital records). A grandson states that he was deaf and dumb from birth. (Mr. Clifford E. Titcomb, Keene, N.H. to Mr. C. Philip Titcomb, Medford, Mass., 14 Mar. 1933). If this is true it is difficult to understand how he could have led the active life of a sea captain as he undoubtedly did.[13]

THE NASON CLAN

Richard Nason and his wife, Sarah Baker, emigrated prior to 1639 from Stratford-Upon-Avon in England to Kittery, Maine, at the New Hampshire border. Four of their sons established lineages that culminate in Deaf members. In the first branch, fifth generation, Elizabeth$_D$ (1743–) was the daughter of Azariah Nason and Abigail Staples who had at least two Deaf relatives. Elizabeth had a hearing brother, James, who married Lydia Kennard and they had six hearing and two Deaf children, David$_D$ and John$_D$. The progenitor of the Kennard family was Edward, who was born in Kent and emigrated from Portsmouth, England, to Portsmouth, New Hampshire. The second branch of the Nason family leads to Mary Nason$_D$; her parents were William Nason and Keziah Lord. We have ascertained three Deaf Lords, whose progenitor is Nathan, born in Kent and died in Berwick, not far from Kittery. The third Nason branch includes four Deaf Nasons: the earliest is Elizabeth$_D$ (1776–). Three generations later, Florence$_D$, Viola$_D$, and Leila$_D$ Nason lived in Waterboro, not far from Sanford. The three women did not attend the American Asylum. All three married hearing men; Leila$_D$ had a Deaf son. Finally, a fourth branch of the Nason pedigree includes the three Deaf children of Hannah and Amos Nason, who were cousins. Nabby$_D$, Richard$_D$, and Mary$_D$ all lived in Berwick, home town of the Jellisons. Hannah and Amos's parents were Richard Nason and Mercy Ham, who were cousins. The Ham family of Strafford, New Hampshire, counts four Deaf members.[14]

THE WAKEFIELD-LITTLEFIELD CLAN

Some years after George Campbell$_D$ died, his wife, Sarah Gibson$_D$, married George Wakefield$_D$, of Brownfield, Maine, who had nine Deaf relatives. (Both were Mission members; see Fig. 16, Campbell pedigree). George$_D$ would later be affiliated with the National Deaf-Mute College (today, Gallaudet University). George Wakefield$_D$ also married Martha Pond$_D$, who had had two other Deaf husbands, each with Deaf relatives, Lothario Lombard$_D$ from Oxford, Maine, and John Page$_D$. Page$_D$, a carpenter from Saco, Maine, married Mary Bennison$_D$ from a Deaf family in Massachusetts; both joined the Mission. The Wakefield family progenitor, John, was born in Kent in 1615 and emigrated with the Littlefields, of whom Elizabeth would become his wife.[15] The Littlefield progenitor, Edmund, was born in Titchfield but the family name has Kentish origins. The two families settled initially in the seacoast town of Wells, the third town to be incorporated in Maine. Littlefield established a sawmill and a gristmill on one of the many nearby rivers, as early as 1640. Indian Wars took a devastating toll on the settlers but after the Revolution, Wells prospered from shipping and trade with the

West Indies and Europe. In Wells, John Wakefield and his brother-in-law received a grant of one hundred acres and a license to sell liquor to the Indians. Wakefield and Littlefield descendants occasionally intermarried. Frederick Littlefield$_D$ and his sister, Elizabeth$_D$, and George Wakefield$_D$ and his wife, Sarah Gibson$_D$, were all graduates of the American Asylum and members of the Maine Deaf-Mute Mission. Three other Wakefields attended the school, Daniel$_D$, Esther$_D$, and Helen$_D$, all of Gardiner, Maine, on the Kennebec.[16]

THE LIBBY CLAN

The progenitor, John Libby, emigrated from Kent and was one of the first settlers of Scarborough, Maine. Libby's Neck and Libby's River are so named in tribute. The town is adjacent to Saco and Portland. Libby had eleven Deaf descendants in all by his first and second wives. One branch begins with son John; four generations later, Charles Libby married his cousin, Mary Libby, and they had two Deaf children, William$_D$ and Lettice$_D$ in Scarborough. A second branch begins with son David, who had a Deaf granddaughter, Martha$_D$, and great great granddaughters Eunice$_D$ and Shirley$_D$. Finally, descended from a third son, Matthew, born in Kittery of John's second wife, we have, Deborah$_D$, whose parents were cousins, and Matilda$_D$, of whom we spoke earlier in connection with her mother's family, the Smalls. Matilda$_D$ had a Deaf nephew and niece, Henry$_D$ and Martha$_D$ Hicks. Through marriage between the Libby and Hunter families, Harriet$_D$, Lottie$_D$, Estella$_D$, and William$_D$ Hunter were born; the three women took Deaf husbands. The Libby family intermarried as well with other Deaf families such as the Larrabees, Skillings, and Dyers.[17]

Appendix B

What the Pedigrees Reveal about Genetic Transmission

DOMINANT TRANSMISSION

As the Brown pedigree shows (Fig. 2), the marriage of William B. Swett$_D$ and Margaret Harrington$_D$ produced two Deaf and three hearing children. Thomas B. Swett$_D$ and Ruth Stearns$_D$ produced three Deaf children and one hearing child. We hypothesize that the Swetts received a single dominant gene arising from grandfather Nahum Brown$_D$; therefore, we expect that half of their offspring would also receive the dominant gene and hence be Deaf themselves. Taking the two families together, five of their children were Deaf and four hearing, compatible with the hypothesis that they received a dominant gene. Their wives' ancestry and genetic status are unknown. If Margaret Harrington$_D$ and her husband both had a dominant gene, three-fourths of their children would be Deaf. If on the other hand Margaret$_D$ was Deaf due to a recessive gene or to illness, that would not affect whether her children were Deaf or not. Since only two of her five children were Deaf, they were likely Deaf due to the dominant gene of their father. Turning to William Swett's$_D$ brother, Thomas$_D$, who married Ruth Stearns$_D$, three of the four children of this couple were Deaf. Ruth Stearns$_D$ was apparently recessively Deaf as she had a Deaf brother and her parents were both hearing; accordingly, her genetic endowment did not affect her children. Similarly, Thomas Brown$_D$ who married Mary Smith$_D$ inherited a dominant gene from his farther and the couple had one hearing and one Deaf child. Mary Smith$_D$ (Fig. 6) was apparently recessively Deaf since she had consanguineous hearing parents, she had Deaf relatives, and she was descended from James Skiffe of Kent; accordingly the fact that she was recessively Deaf did not affect her children.

Since we know of no Deaf relatives of Sarah Maria Gibson and she declared the cause of her being Deaf as "brain fever," we assume that she was Deaf for adventitious reasons and has no bearing on the Brown pedigree.

Francis Lovejoy$_D$ (1768-1841), the first Deaf member of the Lovejoy clan (Fig. 12, Lovejoy pedigree) had Kent ancestry (Hannah House) and could therefore have a recessive gene like many hearing and Deaf people on the Vineyard. But he is succeeded by four generations of

Lovejoys with Deaf members none of whom appears to be consanguineously married. All of Francis's Deaf descendents who have children have Deaf children and none of his hearing descendents do (see note)[18]. This result is consistent with the hypothesis of dominant transmission. If Francis was indeed Deaf due to dominant transmission, we expect approximately half of his children to be Deaf and half of the children of his Deaf descendents to be Deaf as well. We count eighteen Deaf and thirty hearing descendents which is not inconsistent with the dominant gene hypothesis.[19] Other branches of the Lovejoy family give evidence of recessive transmission (see below).

RECESSIVE TRANSMISSION

Hearing parents

In the pedigrees of Figures 2 through 17, we examined the children of thirty-seven hearing couples who had at least one Deaf child and found 110 Deaf and 172 hearing yielding a total of 282 children. With recessive transmission, we would expect by chance at most 25 percent of the total number of children to be Deaf, that is, 71 children. However, 39 were. This discrepancy is statistically reliable. We may have underestimated the number of hearing children in the following ways. We went to great pains to identify all Deaf children and endeavored to accurately ascertain the numbers in their sibships. By beginning with the Deaf members of sibships, however, we risked overlooking consanguineously related hearing parents who had the necessary recessive genes but, by chance, had no Deaf children and whose hearing children, then, are not included in our figures. Furthermore, it is much easier to overlook a hearing child than Deaf children because several sources concur in identifying Deaf children (school registers, Fay's census of Deaf marriages, etc.) Such sources of bias are known as ascertainment bias.

Deaf parents

In the pedigrees of Figures 2 through 17, we examined the children of thirty-seven couples with both members Deaf. We found forty Deaf and eighty hearing yielding a total of 120 children. With recessive transmission, we would expect a Deaf couple to have all Deaf children (provided that the parents are both Deaf by virtue of the same genes.) Three couples among the thirty-seven are known to be consanguineous. Two of them had only Deaf children, as expected and the third had some hearing children. An additional two Deaf couples, with one member dominant and one recessive, were examples of dominant transmission; they had six Deaf and five hearing children, as expected.

The marriages of Freeman Smith$_D$ and Deidama West$_D$ (Fig. 7, Lambert pedigree), and of Benjamin Mayhew$_D$ and Hannah Smith$_D$

(Fig. 4, Mayhew pedigree) were consanguineous. Therefore, the members of each couple most likely had the same pair of recessive genes and all of their children are expected to be Deaf, which was the case. (The Deaf-Deaf marriage of Thomas Brown$_D$ and Mary Smith$_D$ is different because, as we have maintained, Thomas Brown$_D$ inherited a dominant gene from his father, Nahum$_D$.) Nevertheless, contrary to expectations, some of the Deaf-Deaf marriages also had hearing children. Franklin Tilton$_D$ and Sarah Foster$_D$ (Fig. 3, Tilton pedigree) had some hearing children as did Rebecca West$_D$ and Eugene Trask$_D$ (Fig. 7, Lambert pedigree), Jacob Bosworth$_D$ and Sally Allen$_D$ (Fig. 9, Allen pedigree); and George West$_D$ and Sabrina Rogers$_D$ (Fig. 9, Allen pedigree). Unlike the consanguineous Deaf couples discussed above, husband and wife were not known to be related in any of these couples. When it comes to such Deaf-Deaf couples whose members are unrelated, we can make no prediction about the numbers of Deaf and hearing children they will have.

In some cases Deaf couples had only hearing children. The Curtis-Rowe pedigree (Fig. 17) shows three marriages between Deaf partners with all told six hearing and no Deaf children. If the parents shared the same genes, we would expect all the children to be Deaf. Setting aside the marriage of Benjamin Rowe$_D$ and Ann Curtis$_D$ who had no children, it is likely that the parents of the six hearing children were Deaf because of different gene pairs. Looking at the marriage of Ebenezer Curtis$_D$ and Lucy Rowe$_D$, we see that Ebenezer's$_D$ father, William B. Curtis, is descended from the Kentish progenitor by the same name. Hence Ebenezer$_D$ may be Deaf owing to Kentish genes. His wife, Lucy Rowe$_D$, has no known ancestry in Kent which may explain why their two children are hearing, since a pair of Deaf parents with different genes will not have Deaf children. The situation for George Curtis$_D$ and Nancy Rowe$_D$ is the same and their four children were all hearing.

Appendix C

Pedigree Methods

PEDIGREE SOURCES

We began our inquiry into the early Deaf families of Henniker, New Hampshire, Martha's Vineyard, Massachusetts, and southern Maine by identifying Deaf individuals in those locales, using the 1850 census, which listed 266 "Deaf and Dumb" persons living in Maine. We retained only those individuals whose family names occurred twice or more.[20] This principle includes in the set of hereditarily Deaf a few people whose surnames happen to coincide but are not related—such as different Brown families. We have endeavored to ferret those out. The principle excludes some singletons who are in fact hereditarily Deaf. Next we searched for ascendants, descendants, and siblings of those Deaf men and women who had been retained, using numerous general sources and Deaf-related sources. Among the general sources we include other censuses; beginning in 1830, the federal census reserved a column for "Deaf and Dumb" but only a count was given next to the household—individuals were not identified until the 1850 and later censuses. We also used town histories, vital records, biography, and genealogy accessed in hard copy or through the internet. Our primary internet services were FamilySearch.org and Ancestry.com.

Specific source references are given in the notes associated with the corresponding family and town. We also made extensive use over the years of the New England Historic Genealogical Society, which has superb resources, both human and documentary, including many pertinent manuscripts. Likewise, the staff and collections of the Maine Historical Society in Portland and the Maine State Archives in Augusta were very helpful.

Among Deaf-related sources we found particularly valuable the rolls of the American School for the Deaf from its opening to May 1, 1887, published in the school's 71st Annual Report, and a copy of school registry entries for students from Maine, provided by the school archivist, Gary Wait.[21] In 1817, Massachusetts conducted a census of Massachusetts and Maine school-age Deaf children associated with paying their tuition at the American Asylum.[22] We also made use of state finance records of payments made to the American School, and of attendance lists from the four reunions of the American School in 1850, 1854, 1860, and 1866. The Gallaudet University Archives provides a free online facility to search some forty Deaf publications as well as Gallaudet alumni association obituaries and records of the National Fraternal Society of the Deaf.

The membership rolls of the New England Gallaudet Association of Deaf-Mutes and of the Maine Deaf-Mute Mission were also valuable. The notebooks of Alexander Graham Bell, kindly photocopied in part at our request by the Volta Bureau, provided a rich lode of Deaf names. It is not surprising that a century after those notes were written, and with the tools now available to us, we find errors in identifying Deaf people and their ancestry. Nevertheless, the voluminous notebooks bear witness to Bell's deep and abiding interest in Deaf ancestry. Bell also provided information on Deaf families to a Royal Commission and to a journal concerned with inheritance.[23]

Finally, among Deaf-related sources, and of great importance, we cite the survey of Deaf marriages conducted by Edward Allen Fay.[24] In 1898, Fay, a professor at Gallaudet College (now Gallaudet University), published a nationwide sample of pedigrees on 30,000 individuals in 4,471 marriages between 1803 and 1894 in which one or both partners were Deaf. Marriages between two Deaf people accounted for 76 percent of the marriages.[25] The information in the Fay book was obtained from Deaf marriage partners and, occasionally, from Deaf educators or others who knew them. The data included the birth dates of the marriage partners, the number of Deaf and hearing siblings that each possessed, age at becoming Deaf and assigned cause, marriage date, schools attended, numbers of children Deaf and hearing, cross-references to Deaf relatives, and helpful remarks (such as identifying a spouse as hearing).

Family names have been replaced by reference numbers in the Fay book, so two files supplied by the Gallaudet University Archives are indispensable: Fay Index Husbands and Fay Index Wives. The Fay book is actually a condensation of data on survey forms, which can be found at the Gallaudet University Archives, the Volta Bureau, and (with a subscription) on the internet at Ancestry.com. These forms contain a wealth of additional material, such as the names of the husband and wife's parents.

CAUTIONS ON SOURCES

We could not have pursued this research without access to genealogic information through the internet. Genealogies are usually constructed for one family. The task of creating pedigrees for a large group of families was out of reach for most genealogists until the recent advent of internet services. Using the internet comes at a price—loss of accuracy. It is not uncommon for two equally good sources to give conflicting information about dates, locales, and even ancestors. Fortunately, there are many constraints on descendants and their dates. For example, an individual's birth date must fall within a given range to conform to those of his or her parents and children. Furthermore, we complemented research on the internet with the resources of two excellent genealogical libraries: the New England Historic Genealogical Society and the Maine Historical Society.

In the nineteenth century, the chances of an infant surviving to age five were one in three, so many Deaf and hearing children could be missed in the decennial censuses. The wives' maiden names were not given. The census sheets were sometimes inconsistent, identifying persons as Deaf in one census and failing to identify them so in the next. The spelling of names was at times faulty and inconsistent. Most censuses report the age, not the date of birth, of persons enumerated. We subtract the age that was reported from the date of the census to obtain the invariant year of birth; however, that is accurate only plus or minus one year.

In early vital records people are occasionally said to be "of X" whereas in fact they moved to X. For example, a Mayflower passenger is said to be of London, when his or her birthplace was Kent. Conflicting information is occasionally found when comparing sources, so pedigree assignments are made on the weight of the evidence, knowing that some will prove erroneous. The numbers of hearing and Deaf offspring may be inaccurate because of the high perinatal mortality of the time. It is a commonplace with genealogic information on the internet that parents are listed with only a subset of their children; thus the number of hearing siblings must be used with great caution when deciding whether trait transmissions were dominant or recessive. The form of the gene associated with the Deaf trait may be variably expressed—that is, some individuals may be hard of hearing and underreported as Deaf in some censuses; our pedigrees for hereditarily Deaf persons, do not distinguish between hard of hearing and Deaf. The hearing status of early ancestors is difficult to ascertain accurately. In some cases paternity is also in doubt.

FORMING PEDIGREES

Our focus has been on people who were direct ancestors of Deaf people. Therefore, analyses that require a complete enumeration of the families of the ancestors cannot be accomplished with our data. We did not include in our quantitative analyses families for which we were not confident of the sibship, the numbers of Deaf and hearing children. We generally did not extend the search for Deaf descendants beyond 1900 as our focus was on early Deaf families. Further, we wished to respect the privacy of living individuals. However, all our information came from public sources or from family members. Once we undertook to discover the genealogy of a Deaf family, our search for Deaf members sometimes extended over state boundaries or into the twentieth century. We included out-of-state Deaf individuals when it seemed helpful but many of the pedigrees would contain more Deaf members if a regional search were conducted.

The pedigrees presented in this book also appear on the web along with many others: http://dvn.iq.harvard.edu/dvn/dv/DEA. For legibility in this book, pedigrees have been reduced by pruning members unrelated to the Deaf and by purging all information except first and last name and dates of birth and death. These same pedigrees appear at the website in emf and pdf format, also pruned but with full information on each individual restored. Finally, numerous pedigrees are presented, pruned and with full information, that could not be accommodated in this book. "Pruning" involves two stages. In the first, the pedigree includes all the candidates for ancestor, child, or sibling of a Deaf person; this first stage is as inclusive as possible. Then, in the second stage, the inclusive group was pruned retaining only the Deaf people, their ancestors, their descendants, and their siblings—no one else. (We thank Jason Freitas for his masterful programming of data collection, analysis and reduction.) Diagramming of lineages was achieved with Cyrillic software.

Each pedigree gives the descendants of the named progenitor who are in the line of descent to a Deaf person, as well as that Deaf person's siblings and descendants. Readers looking into genealogy should check each of the multiple entries for a given individual in the Every Name Index for the pedigrees on the website (Appendix D). The website "workbook" contains many partial pedigrees, where diligent effort did not yield solutions. Despite its incompleteness, we have put our workbook on the web because it contains pedigree information for many more families than this book can accommodate and because we wish to assist those who are interested in studying the genealogies and family histories. In that regard, we welcome corrections and additions whose sources are substantiated.

Genealogies usually trace ascendants only as far as the first male of the given family name who immigrated to America; that person is called the "progenitor." The pedigrees are organized around the male ancestor in part because children and their mothers take on the male ancestor's name. However, the hereditarily Deaf child may have received this trait from the paternal lineage, the maternal lineage, or both; we did not encounter sex-linked transmission of the Deaf trait. We stress that both lineages are equally important for genetic transmission but, in many families, maternal lineages were impossible to trace because the maiden name of the mother was not given or the documents to which we had access were organized to present only the male lines. We may, therefore, have overlooked some consanguineous relationships.

Shared ancestry is shown in the pedigrees by a bar (double line) joining marriage partners. When the common ancestor is known, a consanguinity index (CI) appears above the bar. It is the proportion of genes that two descendants share from a common ancestor. If they share parents, the value of CI is 0.5 (for example, brothers share half of each others' genes); grandparents, it is 0.25; great grandparents 0.125 and so on. The more remote the ancestor shared, the smaller the fraction of shared genes and thus the smaller the CI. When two people have more than one common ancestor, the proportion of genes they receive from each ancestor is summed. The numeric value of the consanguinity index appears only in the pedigrees posted on the web. That posting includes the figures in this book, which appear there without abridgment.

When parents are said to have been related—for example, in Fay's survey of Deaf marriages—but the common ancestor has not been identified, the bar appears without the index value. Conversely, if it is evident from the pedigree that in all likelihood the parents were related but we did not know that to be the case, we did not show the bar. Each individual may appear in one or more pedigrees. For example, Thomas Brown$_D$ appears in the Brown pedigree and in his wife's pedigree, Smith-Parkhurst. Readers looking into genealogy should check each of the multiple entries for a given individual in the Every Name Index (Appendix D.)

Abbreviations used in the plots:

.0065 consanguinity index
AA attended the American Asylum
AAr attended 1st, 2nd, 3rd, or 4th reunion
a. residence on Asylum admission
b. born
c. census
d. died
DMM Maine Deaf Mute Mission
Ec Executive Council Archives
l. living (place)
m. married
MV Martha's Vineyard
NEGA New Engl. Gallaudet Assn.
THGC T. H. Gallaudet Centennial
diamonds indicate persons without specifying gender; circles, females; squares, males; filled symbols, Deaf; half-filled, hard of hearing; double bar between spouses, consanguineous marriage; superscript circle, restored individual for reference after purging.

Appendix D

Every Name Index to Pedigrees at Our Website

Most of the families cited in this book have pedigrees in our workbook, which is posted on the web at: http://dvn.iq.harvard.edu/dvn/dv/ DEA The website also provides fuller pedigree information for the pedigrees in Figures 2-17 in this book (see 200 series at website) and additional pedigrees not cited in the text. This Every Name Index shows if a given individual appears in one or more of the pedigrees there. The numbers following the names refer to pedigree numbers on our website. (Note: Two persons with the same name are disambiguated by date of birth or, if that is not available, by spouse. In the latter case, individuals are distinguished by number in parentheses.)

Abbott, Elizabeth (1676-) 64
Abbott, Elizabeth (1715-) 70
Abbott, Patience 70
Adams, Elizabeth 216
Adams, Evelyn 52, 210
Adams, John (1576-) 216
Adams, John (1756-) 216
Adams, Mary 100
Adams, Mary A. 40
Adams, Nancy 100
Adams, Nathan 216
Adams, Phillip 216
Adams, Priscilla 102
Adams, Samuel 216
Adams, Thomas 216
Agnes, Anne 40
Alden, Almira E. 102
Alden, Benjamin H. B. 52, 102, 210
Alden, Claude 102
Alden, David 102
Alden, Ebenezer 102
Alden, Elihu (1775-) 102

Alden, Elihu (1802-) 102
Alden, Elizabeth (1591-) 14
Alden, Elizabeth (1) 14
Alden, Horatio 52, 102, 210
Alden, Jabob 102
Alden, John (1599-) 102
Alden, John (1674-) 102
Alden, John (1718-) 102
Alden, Joseph 102
Alexander, David 49
Alexander, Hannah 49
Alexander, Hugh 49
Alexander, Margaret 49
Alexander, William 49
Allen, Abigail 70
Allen, Anna 88
Allen, Benjamin (1764-) 23, 25, 28, 57, 60, 84, 97, 205, 208, 209, 212
Allen, Benjamin (1801-) 192
Allen, Benjamin (1721-) 23, 57, 209
Allen, Benjamin (2) 28

Notes

Appendices

1 Daggett: R. A. Pierce, "Joseph Daggett of Martha's Vineyard, His Native American Wife and Their Descendants," *New England Historical and Genealogic Register* 161, no. 641 (2007): 5–21; Poole, New Vineyard.

2 Dillingham clan: W. Alexander, *A Genealogy of the Dillingham Family of New England* (East Lynn, Mass.: [n.p.],1943); D. Dudley, "Dillingham Family," *Library of Cape Cod History and Genealogy* #95 (Yarmouthport, Mass.: C.W. Swift, 1912); K. A. Field, Dillingham-Bartlett: *A Genealogy and History With Allied Families* (W. Melbourne, Fla.: Kenneth A. Field, 1994).

3 E. A. Fessenden, *The Fessenden Family in America* (Vestal N.Y.: Baker and Taylor, 1971), quotation from p. 697.

4 Ibid.; J. C. Gordon, *Education of Deaf Children: Evidence of Edward Gallaudet and Alexander Graham Bell Presented to the Royal Commission of The United Kingdom on the Condition of the Blind, Deaf and Dumb, Etc.* (Washington, D.C.: Volta Bureau, 1892).

5 W. R. French, *A History of Turner, Maine from its Settlement to 1886.* (Portland, Me: Hoyt, Fogg and Donham, 1886); M. Z. Garrett et al. Index - *History of Turner, Maine*, by W.R. French (Unpublished document, Maine Historical Society, 1976); M. Z. Garrett et al., *Marriages from History of Turner, Maine, by W.R. French* (Unpublished document, Maine Historical Society, 1976).

6 W. R. Buckminster, *The Larrabees* [manuscript]. (Boston: New England Historic Genealogical Society, n.d.).

7 M. R. Ludwig, Ludwig Genealogy. *Sketch of Joseph Ludwig, who was Born in Germany in 1699, and his Wife and Family, who Settled at "Broad Bay, Waldoboro in 1753* (Augusta, Me.: Kennebec Journal, 1886).

8 Anon., "Butler, James Davie; the Butler Family," *The New England Historical and Genealogical Record* (1847): 167–170; C. Eaton, *History of Thomaston, Rockland, and South Thomaston Maine: From Their First Exploration, A.D. 1605; With Family Genealogies* (Thomaston, Me.: Thomaston Historical Society, 1972); M. A. Groves, *Vital Records of Thomaston, Maine* (Rockport, Me.: Picton Press, 2002); S. E. Sullivan, *Vital Records from the Thomaston Recorder of Thomaston, Maine, 1837–1846* (Camden, Me.: Picton Press, 1995).

9 L. Sprague, *Agreeable Situations: Society, Commerce and Art in Southern Maine 1780–1830* (Boston, Mass.: Brick Store Museum, 1987).

[10] S. D. Jones, *The Deering Family of Southern Maine* (Portland, Me.: author, 1979).

[11] Small clan: S. Adams, *The History of the Town of Bowdoinham, Maine 1762-1912* (Somersworth, N.H.: New England History Press, 1985); J. E. Bickford, ed., *Early Bowdoin, Maine Families and Some of Their Descendants.* (Bowie, Md.: Heritage Books, 2002); R. T. Cox, E. F. Reed, and T. C. Stuart, *Vital records of Bowdoin Maine to the year 1892* (Auburn, Me.: Maine Historical Society, 1945); Gray Historical Society, *Gray, Maine, Past and Present, 1778-1978* (Gray, Me.: Gray Historical Society, 1978); L. M. Knapp and Gray Historical Society, *Gray Maine, Images of America* (Charleston, S.C.: Arcadia Publishing., 1999);

[12] T. A. Perkins, *Jacob Perkins of Wells, Maine and his Descendants, 1583-1936* (Haverhill, Mass.: Record Publishing Co., 1947).

[13] G. M. Titcomb, *Descendants of William Titcomb of Newbury, Massachusetts, 1635* (Ann Arbor, Mich.: Edwards Brothers, 1969), quotation from page 182. See also: Pike Family Association, *Records of the Pike Family Association of America* (n/a, 1901); G. T. Ridlon, *Saco Valley Settlements and Families* (Rockport, Me.: Picton Press, 2003).

[14] E. H. Everett, *Hawley and Nason Ancestry, Including the Following Contributory Lines: Welles, Hollister, Treat, Boothe, Thompson, Caldwell, Staples, Tetherly, Coffin, Greenleaf, Brocklebank, Bartlett, Heard, McLellan, Patterson* (Chicago, Ill.: R.F. Seymour, 1929); T. F. Jordan, *Leighton Genealogy: An Account of the Descendants of Col. William Leighton of Kittery Maine.*(Albany, N.Y.: Munsell, 1885).

[15] On Littlefield-Wakefield, see: G. T. Little and H. Sweetser, *Genealogical and Family History of the State of Maine* (New York: Lewis Historical Publishing Co., 1909); H. Wakefield, *Wakefield Memorial, Comprising an Historical, Genealogical and Biographical Register of the Name and Family of Wakefield* (Bloomington, Ill.: au, 1897).

[16] W. H. Smith, "Area Marriages 1780–1833, Gardiner," Downeast Ancestry 13 (1) 2, 10-13, 1989); W. H. Smith, "Gardiner Deaths 1805–1837," Downeast Ancestry 13(2) 43-74 (1989); W. H. Smith, "Gardiner in the 1830s, an 1880s View," Downeast Ancestry 14 (5) 158, 182–186 (1991).

[17] C. T. Libby, *The Libby Family in America 1602–1881* (Portland, Me.: Thurston, 1882).

[18] However, there is Francis's hearing daughter Phoebe who had two Deaf children despite hearing partners. Phoebe had a Kentish ancestor and one of her partners, James Lord, did as well. The other partner's ancestry is unknown and their children took Phoebe's name.

[19] Chi-Square = 1.82, p > .10

[20] Superintendent of the Census, *Seventh Census, Report of the Superintendent* (Washington, D.C.: House of Representatives, 1853)

[21] American Asylum for the Instruction of the Deaf and Dumb, *Seventy-first Annual Report* (Hartford, Conn.: Case, Lockwood and Brainerd, 1888).

[22] Massachusetts. Office of the Secretary of State. *Returns of the Deaf in towns, 1817–1827.* (Boston: Massachusetts State Archives.)

[23] Gordon, *Education of Deaf Children.*; J. Horne, "Deaf Mutism," *Treasury of Human Inheritance. Francis Galton Laboratory for National Eugenics; Eugenics Laboratory Memoirs* 27 (1909): 27–72.

[24] U.S. Special Census on Deaf Family Marriages and Hearing Relatives.

[25] E. A. Fay and Volta Bureau, *Marriages of the Deaf in America. An Inquiry Concerning the Results of Marriages of the Deaf in America* (Washington, D. C., Gibson Brothers, 1898). See also: K.S. Arnos et al., "A Comparative Analysis of the Genetic Epidemiology of Deafness in the United States in Two Sets of Pedigrees Collected More Than a Century Apart.," *American Journal Of Human Genetics* 83 (2008): 200–207; J. Murray, "'One Touch of Nature Makes the Whole World Kin': The Transnational lives of Deaf Americans, 1870-1924" (Ph.D. diss., University of Iowa, 2007).

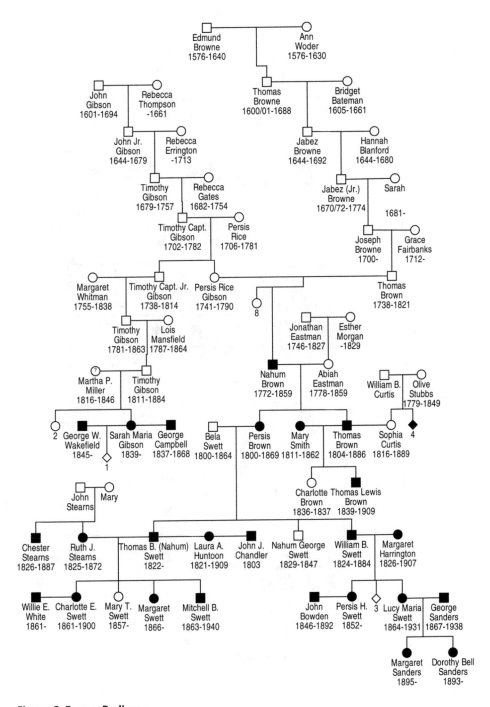

Figure 2 Brown Pedigree

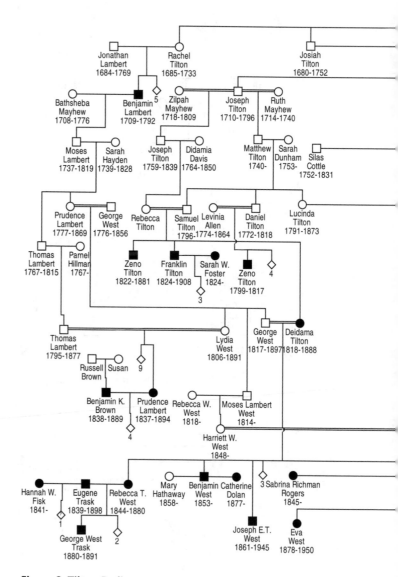

Figure 3 Tilton Pedigree

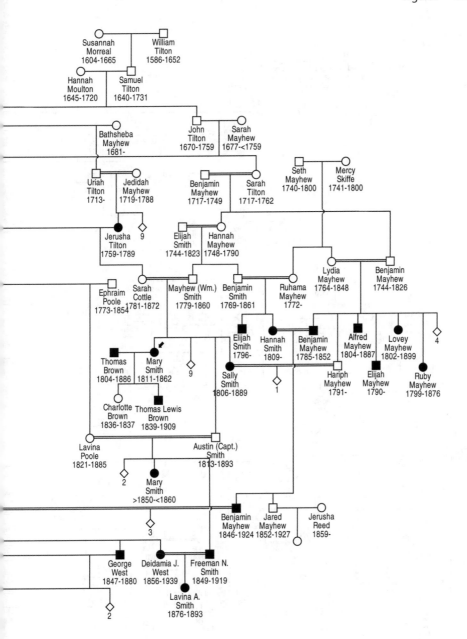

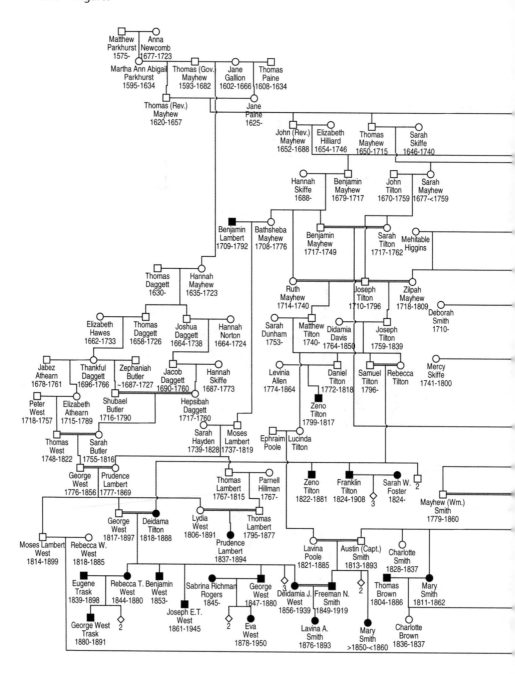

Figure 4 Mayhew Pedigree

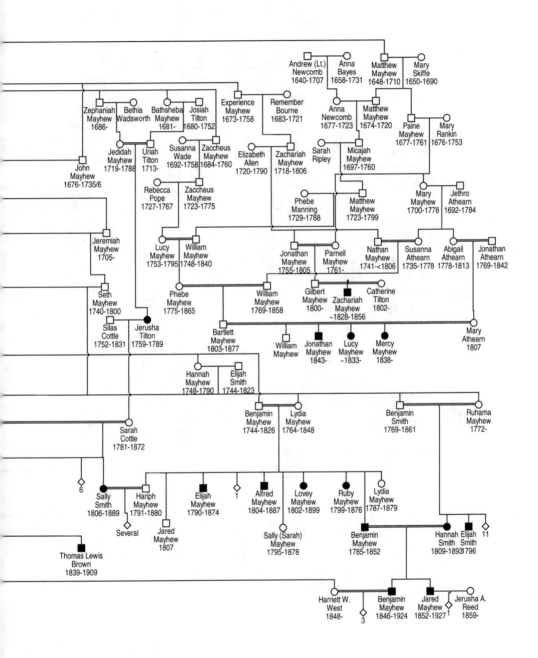

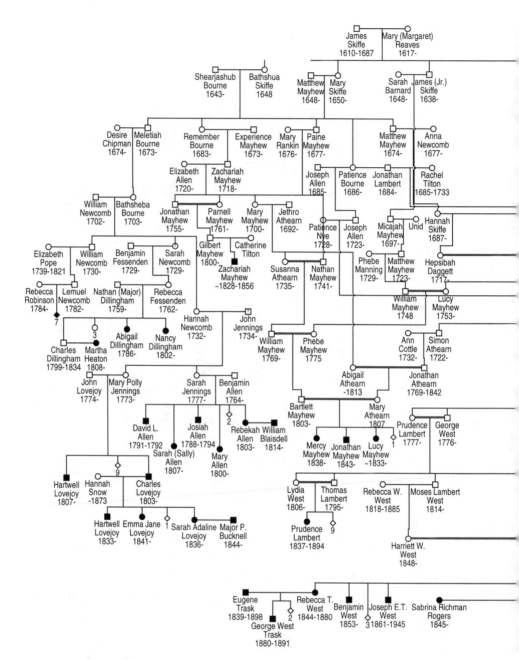

Figure 5 Skiffe Pedigree

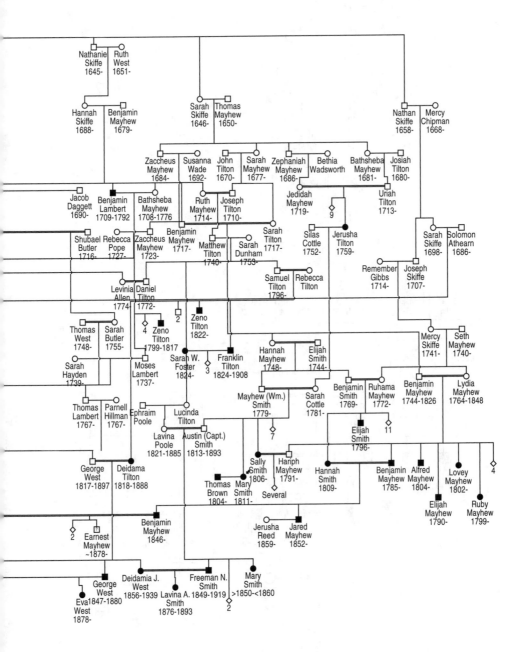

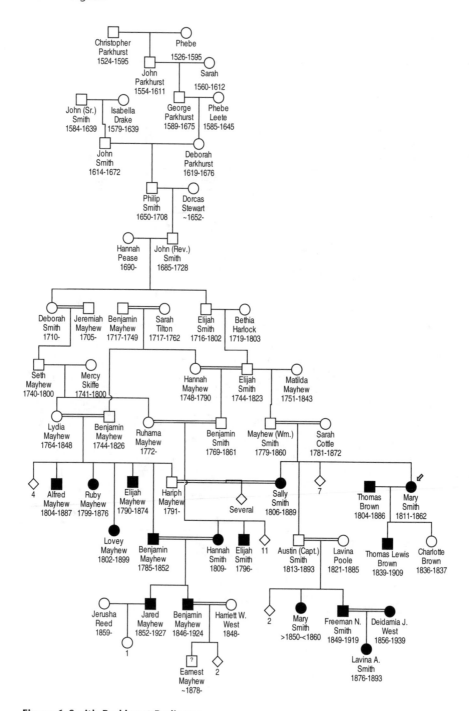

Figure 6 Smith-Parkhurst Pedigree

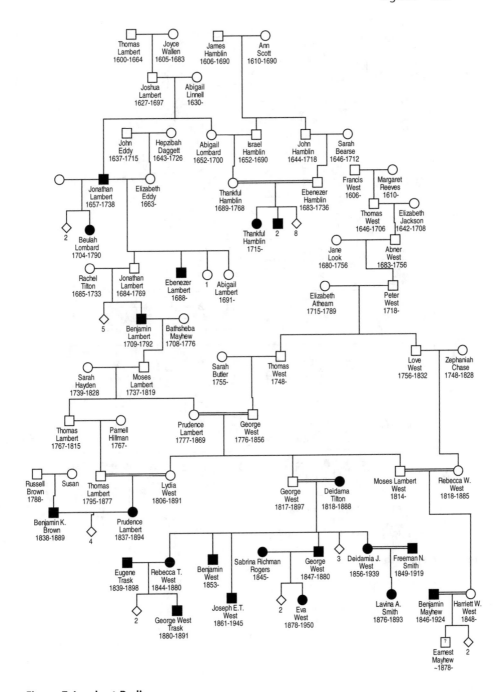

Figure 7 Lambert Pedigree

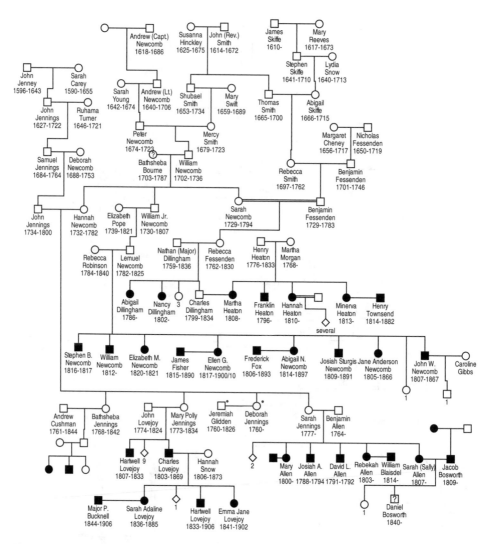

Figure 8 Newcomb Pedigree

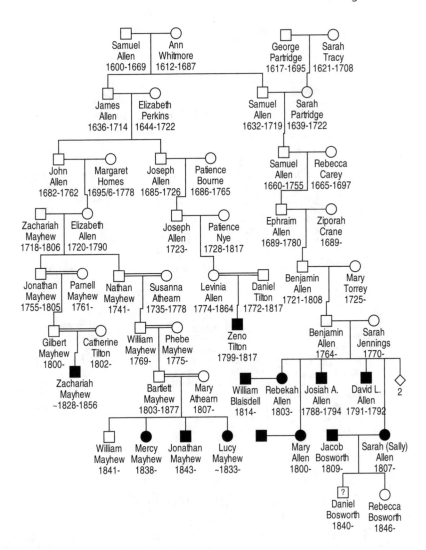

Figure 9 Allen Pedigree

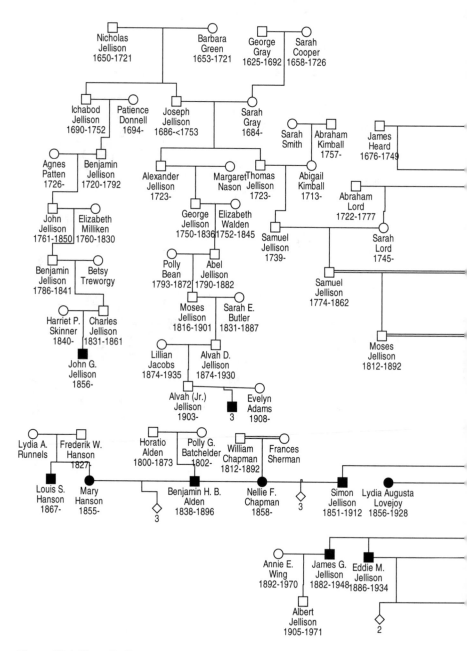

Figure 10 Jellison Pedigree

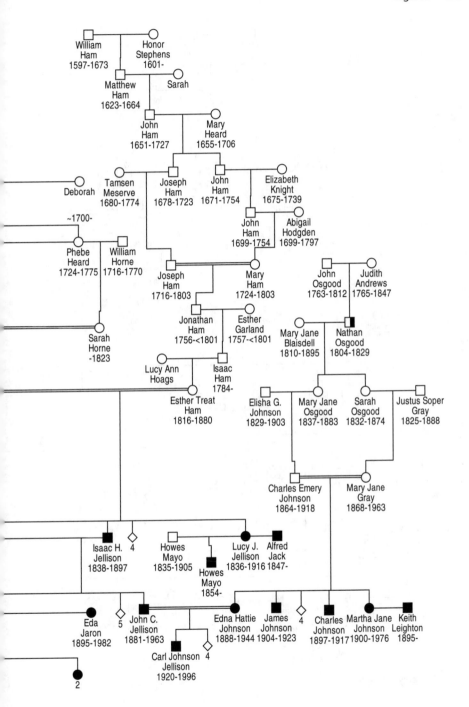

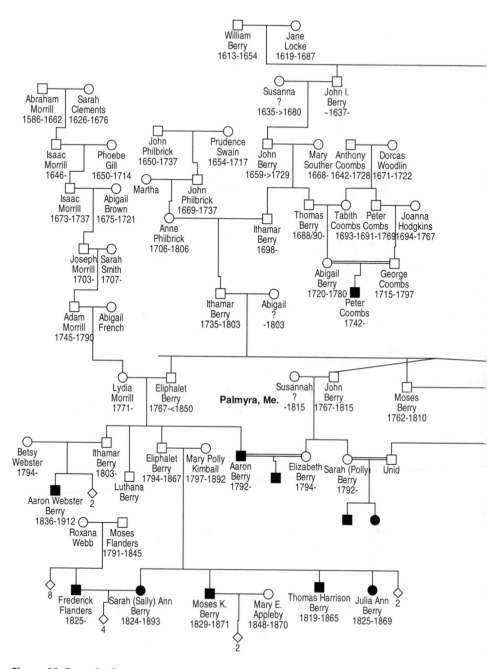

Figure 11 Berry Pedigree

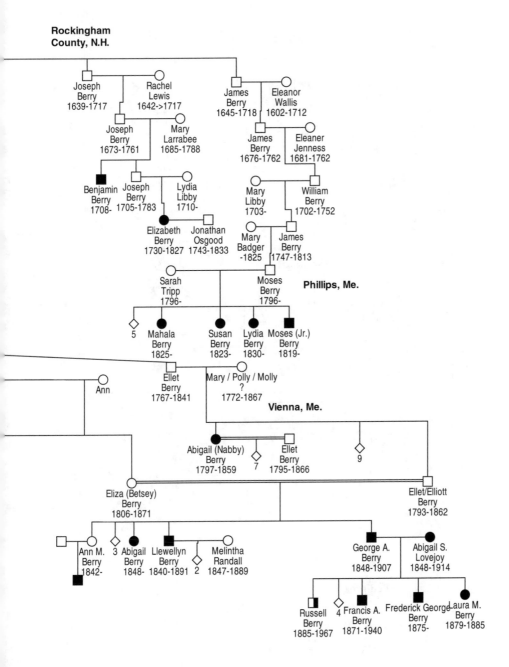

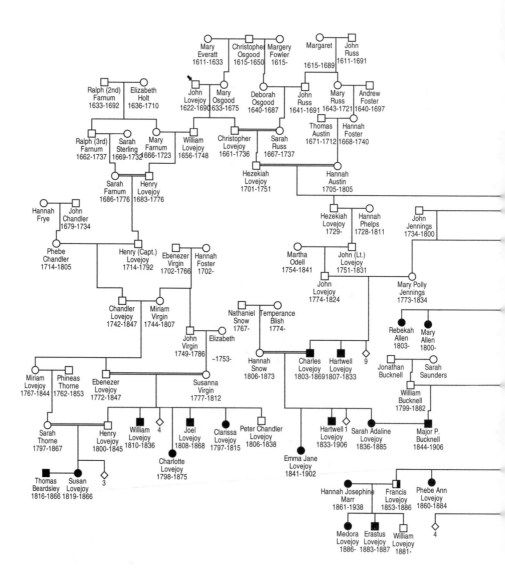

Figure 12 Lovejoy Pedigree

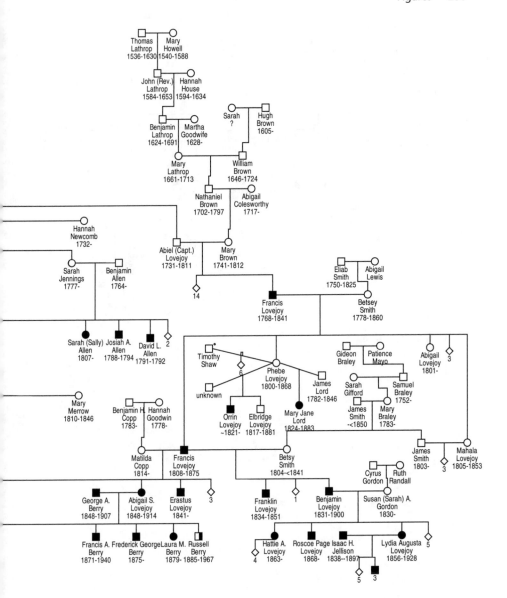

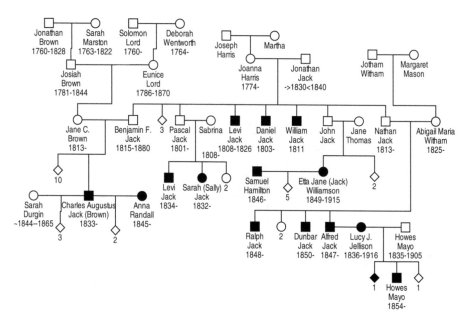

Figure 13 Jack Pedigree

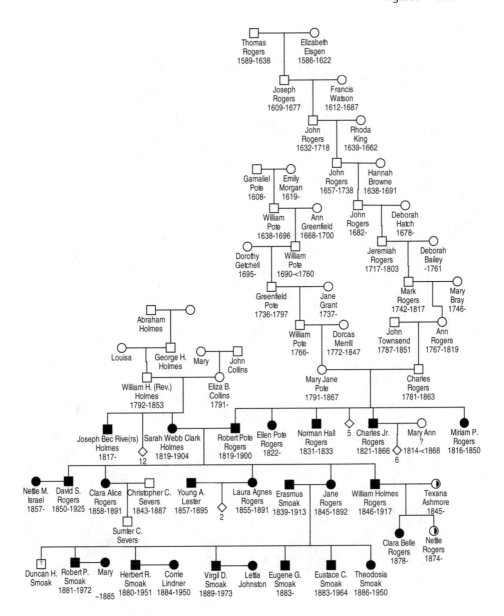

Figure 14 Rogers Pedigree

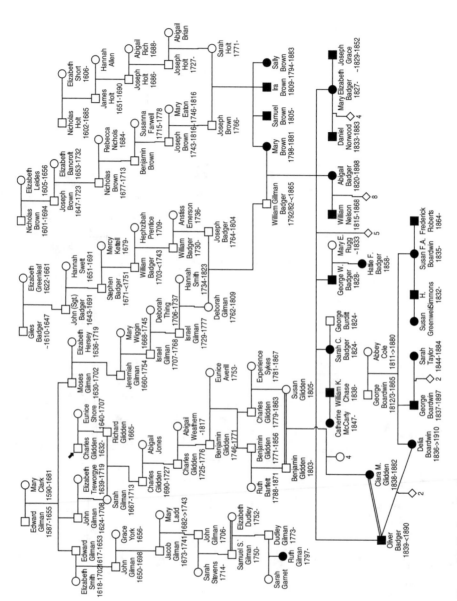

Figure 15 Badger Pedigree

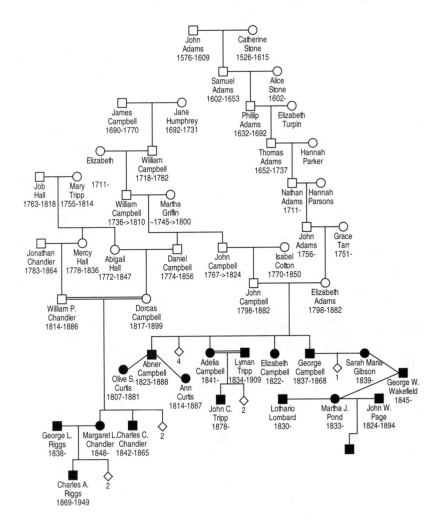

Figure 16 Campbell Pedigree

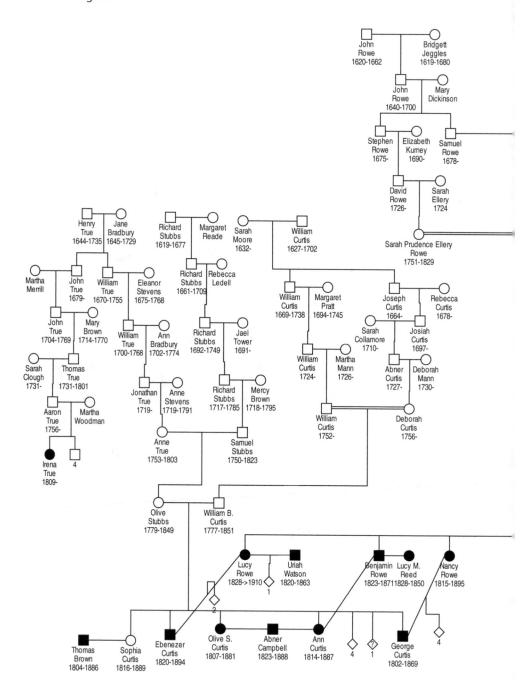

Figure 17 Curtis-Rowe Pedigree

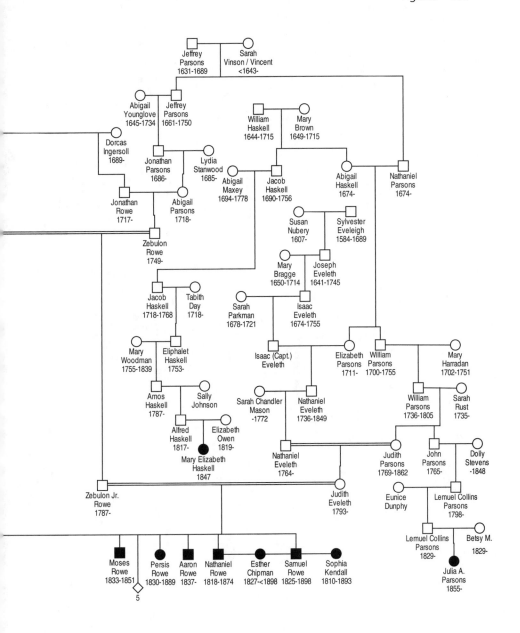

Index

Note: Page numbers followed by "*f*", "*t*" and "*n*" denote figures, tables, and endnotes respectively.